People and Computers
The Impacts of Computing on End Users in Organizations

CORPS (Computing, Organizations, Policy, and Society) Series
Rob Kling and Kenneth L. Kraemer, General Editors

People and Computers

The Impacts of Computing on End Users in Organizations

James N. Danziger and
Kenneth L. Kraemer

COLUMBIA UNIVERSITY PRESS
NEW YORK 1986

Library of Congress Cataloging-in-Publication Data

Danziger, James N.
  People and computers.

  (CORPS (computing, organizations, policy, and
society) series)
  Bibliography: p.
  Includes index.
  1. Computers—Social aspects. I. Kraemer, Kenneth L.
II. Title. III. Series.
QA76.9.C66D36   1986   004'.01'9   85-29989
ISBN 0-231-06178-1

Columbia University Press
New York   Guildford, Surrey
Copyright © 1986 Columbia University Press

Printed in the United States of America

This book is Smyth-sewn.

Book design by Ken Venezio

To Nicholas, Kurt, and Kim:
the next generation of people
who must shape the next generation of computers.

Contents

Data Collection Approaches; Analytic Methods; Dependent
Variables in the Study: Impacts of Computing; Independent
Variables in the Study: The Context of Computing Use

Preface

The roots of *People and Computers* are in the URBIS (Urban Information Systems) Project that has been carried out by the URBIS Research Group of the Public Policy Research Organization at the University of California, Irvine. Since 1973, a multidisciplinary team of researchers at Irvine and elsewhere has been addressing an array of important questions, all of which can be subsumed broadly under the subject of "the social impacts of computing." The work began with the most extensive and intensive research ever undertaken on the use and impacts of computing in American local governments. Over time, our interests have extended to include a broadened set of high technologies, and the analysis of these technologies in various public and private sector social systems ranging from the home to national governments in a variety of nation-states.

The particular focus of *People and Computers* is, as the title suggests, people. Much of the earlier research by our group examined the impact of the technology on organizations. However we recognized that some of the most important and most tractable questions address the effects of computing on individuals. Does computing seem to affect the manner in which individuals think and behave? How extensive are such effects? Do these impacts of computing vary from person to person? If there is variance, can a reasonable explanation for the between-person differences be provided? In short, what accounts for the relative success or failure of computing for the people in organizations?

It is these questions that we attempt to address in *People and Computers,* using the individuals who work in public organizations as our units of analysis. We term these individuals "end users" to indicate that these are people who are the ultimate users of computers and computer-based information. To facilitate our capacity to develop generalizations, the 2,537 end users in our study are grouped into four role-types of information workers: managers, staff professionals, street-level bureaucrats, and desk-top bureaucrats. And the impacts of computing that are examined are those most relevant to information workers in the service sector: the level of utilization of computing, the benefits of computing for job performance, the problems experienced with computing, and the effects of computing on the individual's work environment. To explain differences between role-types and between individuals, three elements of the context of computing use are employed: the organizational environment, the computer package, and the characteristics of the user.

Distilling our complex of findings to their essence, we find that there are very considerable differences in the impacts of computing across end users and that these differences are related to a person's organizational role. On balance, the effects of computing on the end users we study are positive, in the sense that benefits are experienced by many end users and these benefits seem to surpass the negative effects that end users report. It is possible to account for some of the between-individual differences in the impacts of computing by specifying role-type, although the patterns of effects defy simple characterization.

However, within roles, there is a relatively clear pattern of structural relationships between the impacts of computing and the context of computing use. The basic generalization that emerges from our study is that the characteristics of the individual end user, and particularly his/her computing competence and the quality of his/her interactions with computer specialists, are substantially associated with the level and nature of the impacts he/she attributes to computing. And in many cases, the features of the available computer package, especially its routinization, extensiveness and decentralization, are also linked to the impacts of computing on the end user.

We also find that, in contrast to more conventional notions of DSS (Decision Support Systems) and MIS (Management Information Systems), the predominant type of computerized system-in-use are ones which we term "data-based systems." Such systems are characterized by interactive use, by routine rather than selective utilization, and by an array of data-bases and software that enable the end user to undertake "prospecting," a style of information-searching that is ad hoc and is guided by the end user's personal experience in doing his/her work. In the final chapter of the book, our findings are the basis of recommendations for how end users, computer specialists and managers can enhance the benefits of computing for the people who use this technology in their work.

This book builds on a valuable body of empirical and theoretical work that has emerged in the last decade. And it is fundamentally grounded in the research that has been done by members of the URBIS Group. Many people, including those in the core URBIS Group, were involved in a multi-year effort to conceptualize, design, implement and analyze the extensive study of computing in local government. Some of these people have been acknowledged in our earlier work, and especially in the prefaces to *The Management of Information Systems* by Kenneth Kraemer, William Dutton, and Alana Northrop (Columbia University Press, 1981), *Computers and Politics* by James N. Danziger, William Dutton, Rob Kling, and Kenneth Kraemer (Columbia University Press, 1982), and *The Dynamics of Computing* by John Leslie King and Kenneth L. Kraemer (Columbia University Press, 1985.)

For years of exciting and sometimes frustrating intellectual interaction, we are deeply indebted to those with whom we shared the central analytical and field research efforts of the original URBIS Project. This group includes William Dutton from the University of Southern California, Rob Kling, John King, and Alexander Mood, all from the University of California, Irvine, and Alana Northrop from California State University, Fullerton. After years of joint discussion, field work, and collaborative writing, their ideas are inextricably meshed with our own. We thank them for all their contributions, including the many of which we are aware and the others which we cannot separate from our own. Others who contributed to this work through their active role in the project include Joseph Matthews and David Schetter.

People and Computers has been supported in a most direct and crucial fashion by Dr. Fred Weingarten, Dr. W. Richards Adrion and Dr. Larry Oliver, who supervised the grant from the Division of Mathematical and Computer Science at the National Science Foundation that made this book possible.

The professional staff of the Public Policy Research Organization rendered essential support throughout the project. We are grateful for the continuing assistance of Marti Dennis, Shirley Hoberman, and Julie Takahashi, who facilitated the administration of the project. And we received first-class secretarial support from Sherry Merryman, Helen Sandoz, and Kathy Bracy, who typed and surreptitiously refined our prose. We also thank Dr. Susan Koscielniak and Elizabeth Sutton who provided thoughtful guidance from Columbia University Press.

Finally, the most direct and substantial contribution to *People and Computers* has been provided by Dr. Debora Dunkle, the Senior Data Analyst at PPRO. Those who have attempted to reconstruct a massive data base to answer different questions at a different level of analysis will understand one aspect of the exceptional service that Debbie provided directly and in her supervision of Mark Dunlap and Susie Jones. But even more crucial were her continuing efforts to offer critical and analytic insights as we engaged in a very long process of developing, refining and applying the appropriate methodological approaches for interpreting the data. We did not realize how difficult and challenging this secondary analysis would be when we began the project, and Debbie's assistance was invaluable, in the truest sense of the word. While Debbie and our other colleagues mentioned above provided us with substantial help, we recognize our clear responsibility for the errors and omissions that remain.

In our effort to understand the social impacts of computing, our underlying concern is to determine what is, rather than what could be or should be. We are also quite aware of the extremely complex dynamics within which these impacts occur and evolve. For these reasons, we expect that every reader will find issues on which they disagree with us. But we believe that grounded theory, the derivation of tentative generalizations from various kinds of empirical data, is the sine qua non for enhancing our understanding of the role of computer technology in society. It is in the quest for such understanding, emerging from the cumulative work of many scholars with many viewpoints, that we offer the data and findings in *People and Computers.*

The research has been supported by a grant from the National Science Foundation (MCS-7905521). Any opinions, findings, and conclusions or recommendations expressed in this report are those of the authors and do not necessarily reflect the views of the National Science Foundation.

People and Computers
The Impacts of Computing on End Users in Organizations

1. Assessing the Impacts of Computing on People in Organizations

Two powerful and contrary images are widely linked with the use of computer technology in organizations. In one view, this technology is the great problem solver, producing important gains in the efficiency and effectiveness of people in their work. In the contrasting view, computing is a problem generator—an expensive and disruptive technology that has often failed to match its promise in many of the actual tasks to which it has been applied, has generated many negative effects for people who use it, and sometimes seems uncontrollable by these "end users." Since computing is often identified as the key device in the third great "revolution" of humankind (after the plow during the agricultural revolution and the machine during the industrial revolution), it is essential that the impacts of computing be clarified. In the context of organizations, the crucial issues concern the nature and level of the impacts of computing and the conditions that seem to account for its "successes" and "failures."

In this book, we provide a thorough, empirical assessment of these issues, analyzing the impacts of computing on people who are end users of computing in organizations. An "end user" is, in the broadest sense, any person who uses a computer or its products in the performance of his/her functional activities. In particular, the impacts we examine are the level of utilization of computing, the benefits of computing for job performance, the problems experienced with computing, and the effects of computing on the employee's work environment. We attempt to establish the *actual* nature and levels of computing impacts in organizations and to determine whether differences in the impacts of computing between people can be accounted for by variations in the contexts of computing use.

SUCCESS AND FAILURE OF INFORMATION SYSTEMS

Despite the computer's presence in business and government organizations for over two decades, the success of computerized information systems seems to vary greatly. There are many accounts of the failure of information systems projects:

- Large-scale computerized models and simulations used briefly and then abandoned (Brewer 1973; Dutton 1981; Dutton and Kraemer 1985; Lee 1973; Pack and Pack 1977; Kraemer 1985; Kraemer, Dickhoven, Fallows, and King 1986);
- Complex data-based systems used because there was no alternative, but resisted by users, fed incorrect information, and even sabotaged (Dery 1981; Dickson, Simmons, and Anderson 1969; Malvey 1981; Markus 1984; Mumford and Banks 1967; Mumford et al. 1972);
- Management information systems producing such excessive volumes of data that they overloaded middle managers with data-reduction and analysis tasks, leaving them little time for their regular task responsibilities and placing them in a double bind over these competing tasks (Ackoff 1967; Dearden 1966; Guthrie 1974; Immel 1985).

Keen and Gerson suggest that such failures can occur "even when the project is completed on time, the documentation is clear and accurate, and the program code reads like poetry" (1977:1). And Markus concludes that some failures are due to changes which "occur in areas of the organization that were never even considered when the system was designed" (1984:viii).

Moreover, these failures sometimes go considerably beyond a single project. In a report to Congress, the Comptroller General concluded that "generally the Departments of Agriculture, HEW, Labor and Transportation do not have effective programs to help development and transfer of well designed information systems supporting federal assistance programs which they financed. Therefore, neither the Federal Government nor the State governments are receiving full benefit from these expenditures" (GAO 1981).

In a recent report on the use of computers in the Social Security System, the Comptroller General reviews both the problems encountered in the Agency's computer systems over a period of nine years and also the recommendations to resolve the problems (GAO 1983). Few of the recommendations were ever implemented. In its report the GAO again tries to makes recommendations to resolve some of the problems found in Social Security's computer systems. But, given the agency's past record, there is considerable question about whether these recommendations can be implemented successfully.

Yet there are also numerous accounts of successful computerized systems—finished on time and within budget, well used, and perceived as generally satisfactory by both their system designers and end users (Dee and Liebman 1976; Edwards 1978; Gifford and Spector 1984; Kling, Scacchi, and Crabtree 1978; King 1984; Kraemer 1985; Kraemer, Dickhoven, Fallows, and King 1986; Leduc 1979; Limaye and Blumberg 1976; Long 1984; Spector and Gifford 1984). Indeed, the quite phenomenal expansion in the use of computer technology would not continue if most computerized systems were not evaluated as having produced net benefits. In general, though, they produce mixed results—there is substantial variation in the relative "success" of information systems in organizations. Yet our understanding of this variation—its nature, its causes, its dynamics—is limited and clearly inadequate. The fundamental objective of this book is to add to our understanding of these important concerns.

The stake in the performance of information systems is large because these systems permeate modern organizations.[1] And the consequences of information systems "failure" spread throughout the organization. For the public sector organization, inadequate information systems can result in the waste of hundreds of thousands of dollars in development investment and the loss of actual or potential productivity. For top managers and department heads, such failures increase computer-related problems which require their attention rather than enhance their effectiveness. For line and staff personnel, unsatisfactory computerized systems might result in the decline of both personal performance and quality of working life. For information-systems departments and computing specialists (programmers, analysts, designers), failures mean systems that are not utilized, opportunities lost and, ultimately, a loss of credibility. And for the citizens, all of these consequences reduce the capacity of their government to serve them with efficiency and effectiveness.

It is clear that computing within an organization can have powerful impacts on many different actors. Our primary focus will be on the end users of computing, since it is their activities, as individuals and groups, that are most directly and pervasively affected by the organization's information systems. And second, our concerns will be with "systems designers"— those who can significantly influence the design, implementation, and effects of computerized systems. This group might include managers and other end users, as well as computer specialists.

If, as Keen and Gerson (1977) suggest, things can go wrong even when information systems are technically "successful," then a key question is: what are the conditions under which end users and system designers can avoid problems and failures associated with the use of computing and can most fully enhance the positive effects of computing on work performance? Our analytic task is to determine whether there are key factors in the context of computing use—in the organizational environment, in technological arrangements, and/ or in the linkages between the end users and the technology—that systematically affect the impacts of computing. Is there some path(s) the managers, systems designers, and end users can follow to avoid the pitfalls and exploit the opportunities manifest in the application of computer technology within an organization?

THE IMPACTS OF COMPUTING

When we talk about the successes and failures of computing, we are referring to an array of phenomena produced by computer technology as a causal agent. We shall employ the general concept of "computing impacts" to designate this array. Two features of our use of this concept are important to note. First, our view of "computing" is a broad one, incorporating not only the computer hardware and software, but also the skilled technical personnel and the organizational arrangements by which computing services are provided and the information processing tasks performed by computer systems. And second, our concept of "impact" is not the conventional connotation of a direct, relatively sudden and visible coming together of phenomena. Rather, computing has effects on individuals, as on groups and institutions, that typically emerge in a varied, subtle, and evolutionary manner and it therefore is most accurate to understand that these "impacts" become manifest over time (Danziger 1985).

Because computing impacts are so pervasive in postindustrial society, it is useful to define the domain of computing impacts that is the focus of this study. There are impacts of computing on collectivities, such as the work group, the department, the organization, or even the society, and impacts on individuals, such as a person's personality, sense of self, and life outside of work. Here we examine the impacts of computing on information workers in service-sector organizations. To a large extent, these people use computing to assist them in their information processing tasks as they make decisions and take actions. Such use of computing has been referred to by such labels as "automated information systems," "computer-based data systems," "management information systems," and "decision support systems." In general, two images of these systems are now prevalent: model-based systems and operations-based systems. These two conceptions are characterized briefly in Table 1.1.

The *model-based system* is the more traditional notion, largely tied to the theoretical and professional literature of operations research, management science, and decision science, and it now typically appears under the DSS (Decision Support Systems) label (see, for example, Alter 1980; Ackoff 1967; Benett 1983; Gorry and Morton 1971; House 1983; Keen and Morton 1978; and Simon 1960). This concept stems from theories which posit "problem-solving" as the essence of professional work and prescribe model building as a means of solving problems. Information for decision and action is the output of formal analytical models and simulations (e.g., models for police manpower allocation, or for projecting revenues and expenditures). Use of information in such models is highly selective, relying mainly on data generated specifically for the analysis, and the analysis is usually done by computer specialists.

Table 1.1.   Key Characteristics of Computerized Systems

	Type of System	
	Model-based	*Operations-based*
Activity served	Problem solving	Problem finding
Basic data	Data generated specifically to measure model parameters	Data are a product of routine operations
Examples	Traditional DSS: Revenue/expenditure forecasting model; manpower allocation model	Traditional MIS: Integrated financial system: personnel payroll system: utility billing system: real property records system

The *operations-based system* has its heritage in the intellectual and practitioner literature of computer science, information systems, and data processing, and it appears commonly under the MIS (Management Information Systems) label (see, for example, Blumenthal 1969; Pendleton 1971; Pounds 1969).[2] In this conception, "problem finding" is the key activity to which professionals apply computing. These systems employ extremely simple, nonanalytical models, mainly involving data comparisons—such as those over time, across organizational boundaries, or between planned and actual. The relevant data for such uses are mainly captured from the day-to-day operations of the organization and computer specialists usually produce the information.

One of our objectives in this study is to determine whether the empirical evidence indicates that the systems-in-use among information workers correspond to these conceptions of computerized systems. It will be suggested in the chapters that follow that there is a third conception which best fits the kinds of computerized systems that are most commonly employed by end users. We term this the *data-based system,* and it is characterized by "prospecting" through data files in the search for specific facts, for linkages among facts, or for meaningful patterns among facts. Much of the relevant data are drawn from operational records, but other data must be gathered explicitly for these uses. The end user is more likely to make direct, personal use of the system, rather than relying on an intermediary. This third type of computerized system will be discussed in chapter 6 and further elaborated in subsequent chapters.

It is important to note that these three types of systems might be implemented on a variety of computer equipment: mainframe, minicomputer, or microcomputer. In the past, the computer technology underlying these systems tended to be a mainframe or minicomputer with the user connection via terminals. Today, these systems are also being implemented on the microcomputer in a stand-alone mode. Increasingly, however, these three types of systems are being implemented on microcomputers connected to a mainframe or minicomputer that serves as a central data store and provides communications capability with other users. In a sense, the microcomputer replaces the terminal as the means of end user connection to a larger computerized system of an organization. What is significant about the microcomputer is that it can provide the users with direct (hands-on) control over their data and programs. Mainframe and minicomputer equipment with timesharing and interactive software that interfaces with the users via terminals (or microcomputers) provides the same capability.

While some readers might be concerned that these changes in computer technology make a critical difference, our analysis will make a case that the key relationships between end users, computer technology, and the organizational environment are relatively unchanged by the introduction of microcomputers. Two key elements buttress the continuing relevance of our findings. The first is our continuing fieldwork in organizations. As we suggest in the previous paragraph, we find the same dynamics at work for direct end users, regardless of the newer technologies. The second is the empirical studies that have recently emerged on end-user computing and microcomputers in business organizations. Although most of these studies involve relatively small samples across disparate organizations, their findings are consistent with the findings of our more extensive study of 2,500 end users in public organizations. We suggest that when the reader has examined our complete analysis, and considered our continuing fieldwork as well as the interstudy consistency on findings (see chapter 11), he/she will be persuaded that our conclusions are powerful and compelling.

In this analysis, we shall focus on four areas where the impacts of the three types of computerized systems-in-use are likely to be especially important for individuals in service sector organizations: (a) the utilization of computing; (b) the impacts of computing on job performance; (c) the problems generated by computing; and (d) the effects of computing on the individual's work environment.

At a fundamental level, the impacts of computer technology are a function of *utilization*—the extent to which automated applications and computer-generated products are actually employed (Lucas 1975). Therefore, we are first and foremost interested in explaining the levels of computer use across different modes of use and different types of computer users. Second, one of the great promises attached to computer technology has been its capacity to produce improvements in efficiency and effectiveness for individuals and organizations. Thus a fuller understanding of the conditions associated with *job performance benefits* from computing is an essential feature of our assessment of the implications of the technology for individual and organizational behavior. Third, our focus on *problems* with computing stems from the widespread disagreement about the extent to which users do experience problems with computers, and from our interest in the nature of those problems. We aim to determine whether there are factors that seem to account for higher and lower levels of computing problems, and whether problems are linked with other aspects of computer performance. Fourth, consideration of the computer's *effects on the work environment* is intriguing, given the conflicting representations of computer technology as the great liberator that frees the individual from dreary work, and as the great alienator that merges laborer and machine into a less-than-human instrument.

In exploring these four kinds of consequences from computer technology, we use American local governments as our setting for empirical research. We believe local governments are an interesting setting, since they are service sector organizations that touch all of our lives directly and frequently, since computers have been widely adopted in their operations, and since they seem excellent organizations for comparative analysis. We do not insist that this research site is perfectly representative of all organizations. But our extensive field research and our reading persuade us that computer impacts on end users in local government are similar to those evident in other public organizations and, to a lesser extent, even to those in many private organizations (Bensen 1983; Carlson, Grace and Sutton 1977; Culnan 1983; Gasser 1983; Markus 1984; Kling and Scacchi 1979; Rockart and Flannery 1984).

OUTLINE OF THIS BOOK

Chapter 2 restates as research questions the crucial issues examined in this book, it summarizes the relevant theoretical and empirical research, and it details our own analytic strategy for developing empirical answers to these questions. The first set of questions concerns the nature, level, and differences in the impacts of computing on individual end users; and the second set of questions explores the conditions that seem to account for the relative success or failure of computing for end users. We distinguish four role-types among organizational end users of computing and four arrays of computing impacts on worklife. We explicate our conceptual framework, which hypothesizes that "the context of computing use" might have a significant effect on the differential impacts of computing on end users. This context of computing use is defined in terms of three general elements: (a) the organizational environment; (b) the computer package; and (c) the characteristics of the user. This chapter operationalizes our key explanatory variables, and it describes the methodological strategies we shall employ as we assess whether there are between-user differences in computer impacts and whether these differences are associated with end users' roles and/or context of computing use.

Chapter 3 begins our substantive discussion by describing the extent of "direct," "indirect," and "passive" use of computers among the four types of organizational end users: managers, staff professionals, street-level bureaucrats, and desk-top bureaucrats. This discussion emphasizes the fact that the frequency of computer use increases among all these types of actors as the mode of use becomes more passive. That is, end users in public organizations are more likely to receive and examine routine reports or other information that have been generated by others from computerized files than to generate such information themselves or to request others to generate the information. Yet there is substantial variation among actors, based upon their roles within the government. Generally, bureaucrats report higher levels of computer use than managers or staff professionals, and the street-level bureaucrats report the highest level of computer use. Interestingly, managers report the most limited use of computers in all modes of utilization. The characteristics of the users, particularly their sociotechnical interface (STI), most influence the level of computer use among all public employees. The organizational environment and the computer package also are influential factors, but the technology is not as generally significant as expected and the personal traits of the user have little systematic effect on level of use of computers.

The actual use of computers by staff professionals is very modest, despite images in the literature of extensive involvement by professionals with computers and computer-based information. Consequently, chapter 4 examines staff professionals' computer use more closely. The frequencies with which staff professionals use computing in the direct, indirect and passive modes of use are combined to create a taxonomy of user types among professionals, who are classified as total users, instrumental users, or reactive users. Both user characteristics and the computer package seem to substantially affect whether a staff professional is one or another type of computer user. Generally, computing use is more active and extensive as a staff professional works with responsive computer specialists and feels more competent with computing. Interestingly, the emergence of different types of computer users is also significantly shaped by features of the technology itself. Although the pattern of effects is less straightforward, those professionals who are total users (about one in four staff professionals in our sample) have available a computer package that is more routinized and extensive.

Chapter 5 shifts to an examination of a set of more explicit impacts from computing—its benefits for job performance. Measures are developed that tap the extent to which computing has increased the quality of information available to the individual, and has increased the department's capacity to serve the public efficiently and effectively. In general, end users in all four roles tend to report positive job performance benefits from computing. Effectiveness benefits and information benefits are most widely enjoyed, and efficiency benefits from computing are the least frequently reported. In relative terms, we were somewhat surprised to discover that it is the street-level bureaucrats who enjoy the greatest information benefits and efficiency benefits generated by computing, since this was contrary to our expectations that information benefits would be strongest among those roles with the most pervasive data handling and that efficiency benefits would be most prevalent for the role which has least organizational discretion (and hence is most subject to the "rationalizing" effects of computing innovations). In most cases, the end user's characteristics are most clearly associated with differential benefits across individuals, with the quality of the user's relations to computing staff being a powerful explanator in virtually every instance.

Chapter 6 provides a detailed study of how computing has affected the investigative work of police detectives, a subset of the street-level bureaucrats who report the greatest job performance benefits from computing. It is very clear that the computer package has had a major impact on the work and productivity of detectives. These people operate in an information-intensive environment and the vast record-keeping and multifaceted record-searching capabilities of computing substantially increase the detectives' productivity, measured in terms of workable cases, arrests, and clearances. In general, these performance benefits occur for those detectives who have access to a computer package that is more sophisticated, extensive and decentralized.

Chapter 7 focuses on the "negative" side of computing impacts—the problems that people experience in using the technology in their work. We distinguish between problems people have with the information contained in computerized systems and the problems that they face in their day-to-day interactions with computers and computer services. For the end users in our study, computing is certainly not "problem-free," since about three-fourths of those in all roles experience operational problems with computing at least occasionally. But few report high levels of either operational or information problems, and problems with the information in computerized systems are infrequent for fully half of the people. The user's experiences with computing staff is the feature of the context of computing use that is most directly related to the level of problems reported. Indeed, unsatisfactory responsiveness from computing staff can be considered a problem in itself, and our data make clear that this problem is substantially associated with, although far from identical to, other computing problems. The level of computing problems that an end user experiences seems to be a very personal matter, since there is little systematic relationship between computing problems and any aspects of the computer package or organizational environment and since there are few clear between-role differences.

Chapter 8 reveals how desk-top bureaucrats are a role whose job space and information processing tasks have been substantially penetrated by computing. The chapter explores more fully the pattern of problems as well as benefits experienced by end users in this role. In particular, we analyze the computing problems and benefits reported by the clerks in the traffic ticket processing role. About one in ten of these people report information problems and operational problems at a high level and one in six reports high operational problems. The "average" person experiences operational problems occasionally and information problems infrequently. Two groups are distinguished—the relatively high problem clerks and the relatively low problem clerks. The "high problem" clerks use a computer package that is more extensive, centralized, and supported by resources, work in a more professionalized government, and have negative relations with computing staff and a negative sense of their own competency with computing. While most clerks report consistent patterns of relative benefits from computing, the findings reveal an interesting pattern, where a substantial proportion of the clerks who experience higher problems also credit computing with generating higher performance benefits. Thus it seems that a more developed computer package is a double-edged sword, often being the source of both benefits and problems. But it is improvements in the sociotechnical interface that seem to hold the greatest promise for mitigating higher levels of computing problems.

In chapter 9, we examine the impacts of computing on the work environment of the people in local government. The analysis begins with data that indicate how computing alters the end user's control over the work environment, including such issues as influence over others and time pressures on the job. The major focus of the chapter is the relative effects of computing across the different roles in our study. Overall, we find that the effects of computing on the work environment have generally been either benign or very slight. However, when we compare across roles, staff professionals enjoy relatively higher positive effects from computing, since computing increases their influence over others and their sense of accomplishment with their work and results in relatively low increases in supervision by others. Among the surprising findings is the fact that managers have the least favorable appraisal of the impacts of computing on control in the work environment. The managers report relatively higher increases in supervision of their work and less capacity for increased influence than those in other roles.

These impacts of computing on the work environment of managers are at some variance with the conventional notion that computing has very positive effects on managerial control. Chapter 10 explores in depth the actual impacts of computing on managers as they attempt to control the resources and personnel under their supervision. We find that computing is most useful in managerial control of the financial resources of the organizational unit and is least helpful in enhancing the capacity of the manager to control the behavior and job performance of personnel. Managers who derive more control benefits from computing tend to experience more favorable interactions with computing staff and also to have a stronger sense of their own competency with computing. It is also clear that a more sophisticated, extensive and centralized computing environment is associated with greater managerial control of organizational resources.

Chapter 11 considers the overall patterns of findings from our study of the effects of computers on people in organizations. Despite imagery of computing as a homogenizing technology, there are many areas where the effects of computing vary substantially across people in organizations, and even among people in the same organizational role. The only place where computing does have a relatively homogeneous impact is on isuses of control in the work environment, and even here, there are notable differences. There are quite considerable variations among people in their levels of utilization of computing, in the benefits that people enjoy from that use of computing in their work and in the problems that computing generates for them. In general, our findings make it clear that *the context of computing use can significantly influence the kinds of impacts that computing has on a given person.*

While aspects of *the organizational environment* are sometimes important, when employed as part of a general explanation of differences, this element of the context of computing use is rarely decisive and often has virtually no significant effect. This conclusion is contrary to what might be expected on the basis of many existing theoretical and empirical analyses, which tend to stress the importance of the organizational environment, especially variables reflecting size. Our conclusions are probably at variance with that literature because we focus on the individual end user of computing as our primary unit of analysis. While the organizational environment might account for much of the variance between organizations, individuals are more powerfully influenced by the computer package available to them and, most frequently, by the aspects of the context of computing use that are unique to them. In fact, the variables with the most consistent explanatory appeal have been those which tap aspects of the sociotechnical interface—people's assessment of the responsiveness and service of those providing computing and their own level of competency in the use of computing.

While variables measuring aspects of *the computer package* are not consistently associated with the impacts of computing, there is a general trend for certain characteristics of that package to be linked to differential impacts. Broadly, greater utilization and higher benefits from computing occur for those people who have access to computing that is more extensive, less centralized, and more routinized. Both greater benefits and greater problems are also more prevalent for those people whose computing environment is relatively developed. As part of an alternative explanation, the computer package is significant for many impacts of computing, but it is rarely the dominant factor. Thus, our research does not support the observation in some studies that the crucial element determining the impacts of computing is the technical features of the technology.

While the computer package explains part of the variation across people in the impacts of computing, it is *user characteristics* which add the largest part of the explained variance for most impact variables. While personal traits such as age and education are occasionally significant, the crucial explanatory variables are usually those reflecting the nature of the sociotechnical interface. As the end user has greater competence with computing and as there are more constructive and favorable interactions between the end user and the technical computing staff, both utilization of the technology and the positive effects of the technology tend to increase. It is interesting that these are also the end users who experience more problems with computing, suggesting that greater benefits from computing are not enjoyed without some additional costs.

Overall, this pattern of findings has great policy relevance, since both the user element and the technological element can be altered by decisive policy interventions to enhance success and reduce the failings associated with computing use. Our study leads to the suggestions in chapter 12 that *it is possible to alter the context of computing use in order to enhance the impacts of computing on people*, whether they use the technology in their capacity as private individuals or in their roles within organizations. From this perspective, people need not view computing as an "autonomous technology" over which they have virtually no control. But the fact that people can exercise some control over computing, at least over its direct, short-run effects, does not guarantee that this will happen. Whether people have the insight and the will to implement strategies that do increase the positive effects and mitigate the negative effects of computing remains an open question and a challenge for everyone who must deal with the technology. The title of our book places people before computers, because people can and should dominate this relationship.

2. Studying End-User Computing

Chapter 1 outlined the crucial questions we intend to address in this book. This chapter explains our analytic strategy for answering these questions. Specifically, it presents our conceptual framework, methodological techniques and key concepts, as these are informed by theory and existing research. Readers who are not interested in these technical issues can skip to the beginning of our substantive discussion in chapter 3.

CONCEPTUAL FRAMEWORK

Two central research issues are at the core of this book. First, we examine whether the nature and level of computer impacts match conventional images and expectations in the literature. That is, we gather and analyze empirical data that establish the levels of computer utilization, computer-based performance benefits, problems with computing, and effects of computing on the work environment. Our concern is with understanding similarities and differences in the impacts of computing on the individual people who work in public organizations rather than simply testing conventional expectations. The second central research issue is to determine whether between-person variation in the level of computer impacts can be explained.

That is, we analyze whether there are factors in end users' context of computing use that seem to account for higher or lower levels of utilization, performance benefits, problems, and work environment effects. Our concern is to discover factors that might be systematically related to the success and failure of information systems-in-use.

Our anlysis of the variation in computer impacts is based on the fundamental assumption that the context of a person's computing use might have a significant effect on those impacts. This assumption is embedded in much of the theoretical and empirical literature on the impacts of computer technology, although the conceptualizations and the analyses of this context of use have often been less precise and rigorous than one might desire (Ein-Dor and Segev 1982). Whether the interest is in the impacts of computing on collectivities or on individuals, the same types of explanatory variables tend to appear in researchers' attempts to account for variation in the level of those impacts. We have attempted to capture these aspects of the context of computing in a conceptual framework that has analytic elegance and simplicity while also allowing for the inclusion of a wide array of the variables that might systematically affect the impacts of computing on people. We have conceptualized the context of computing in terms of three general elements: (a) the organizational environment; (b) the computer package; and (c) the characteristics of the user. Since our central research interest is the impacts of computing on individuals (who are the object units of analysis), these elements of the computing context will be transformed into variables at the individual level of analysis (see Eulau 1967). One might also analyze these impacts of computing at such other levels as the work group, the department, the organization, or even the society.

In our analysis, the *organizational environment* is the broadest context within which the individual's computing use is embedded. It includes both the organization itself and also aspects of the broader environment that are relevant to the use of computing within the organization. Some examples might illustrate the kinds of linkages that could exist between the organizational environment, the individual, and the impacts of computing. It is widely assumed, for example, that the scale and complexity of demands, opportunities and constraints in the wider environment will influence the information processing activities of people in organizations. Thus, as the population and the land area served by a government become larger, one might predict that government staff will experience increased use and utility from computer systems that handle the growing amounts of operational information that they must manage, search and manipulate. Similarly, one might predict that government policymakers will experience increased use and utility from data systems and models that increase their ability to symbolically represent both the community and government environment by precise quantitative measures and to simulate the likely effects of proposed actions before commitment to implementation. However, one might also predict that people working in governments with more extensive information environments will experience a higher level of problems with computers and computer-based systems (than people in less extensive information environments) because their information handling tasks have become so complex that problems occur more frequently.

In another example, the level of partisan controversy over issues might influence the propensity of government employees to use computer-based information to inform or to justify decisions and actions. It is also possible that a government which attaches greater importance to the use of professional management practices and celebrates efficient, businesslike operations will create an environment in which people feel more comfortable with the use and impacts of computers (relative to people in governments less committed to such a "reform government" orientation).

Within the organizational environment, although sometimes extending beyond it (Kling 1983), is the second element of the context of computing use—the *computer package* itself. We use the term computer "package" to denote a set of characteristics of the technology that include not only the hardware and software, but also the personnel and the organizational arrangements for the delivery of computing services (see Danziger, Dutton, Kling, and Kraemer, 1982: ch. 2). It seems obvious that the impacts of computing on a person will be affected by the computer technology available to the person. Some assume that, *ceteris paribus,* more sophisticated computer hardware and software will increase the likelihood of successful job performance on nearly any organizational task (Simon 1970; Inbar 1981). Others disagree, suggesting that high technical sophistication might be valuable for some of the information processing tasks that people in the organization perform, but not for others. For example, Lucas observes that "the complexity of the decision and the technology of the underlying computer system might be inversely related" (1975:10). One might also hypothesize, for example, that more sophisticated technology will increase not only a person's performance benefits from computing but also the problems experienced in its use. Similar kinds of hypotheses about the impacts of computing can be generated for such other features of the computer package as its decentralization, its extensiveness, its routinization, and the organizational arrangements for its provision.

The most direct aspect of the context of computing use, given our focus on the individual end user as the object unit of analysis, is the *characteristics of the user*. One of the questions of our analysis is whether computing has relatively homogeneous impacts on all the people in a specific government, given its common organizational environment and computer package. Our working hypotheses assume that there will be considerable interpersonal variation in the impacts of computing, and that this variation might be best accounted for by the personal traits of the individual end user. Broadly, we hypothesize that all four impacts of computing will depend in part on the type of organizational role that a person fills, and we shall develop a classificatory scheme based on four generic role-types within our sample. Moreover, it is reasonable to assume that the impacts of computing, such as the level of computer utilization, for example, will be related to the person's education, age, length of service in the same job, and professional orientation.

In addition, the literature has stressed the end user's dynamic interaction with the computer package, referring to this relation as the "sociotechnical interface" (Bostrom and Heinen 1977; Danziger 1979b; Mumford and Banks 1967). Thus, the characteristics of the user also consist of his/her experience with the computer package,[1] such as the completion of courses, years of computer use, and involvement in applications design activities, and also his/her cognitive, affective and evaluative orientations toward the computer package, such as the user's attitudes toward computers and the user's perceptions of the quality of the interactions with the computing staff. We assume these user characteristics could also have substantial influence on a person's use of, performance benefits from, problems with, and work environment effects from, computing.

Chapter 1 identified four characteristic areas of the impacts of computing on people in organizations: utilization, job performance benefits, problems, and work environment effects. These are the dependent variables. And we have now specified three aspects of the context of computing use that might account for between-individual differences in the level of these impacts: the organizational environment, the computer package, and the characteristics of the user. These are the independent variables.

In later chapters, specific measures are developed for each impact of computing on people in organizations. For example, we distinguish between direct, indirect, and passive use of computing, between such job performance impacts as efficiency benefits, information benefits, and effectiveness benefits, between information problems and operational problems with computing, and between the work environment effects of computing on closeness of supervision, influence over others, and time pressure. In this chapter, we begin the process of operationalizing our concepts. We discuss some of the relevant empirical research that has examined aspects of the context of computing use, we specify four broad role-types that will be employed in our analyses, and we present the set of indicators that will be used to characterize the key aspects of the context of computing use.

To assess our first major research question: Do people vary in the level of their utilization, job performance benefits, problems, and work environment effects from computing?, we use relatively straightforward analyses of our data-base, primarily frequency distributions and descriptive statistics. Our second major research question: Do any of the three contextual elements account for any between-individual differences in the impacts of computing, requires a more complex approach. The philosopher Gilbert Ryle distinguishes "competing explanations," which are contradictory and mutually exclusive, from "alternative explanations," which are complementary and reinforcing. Our conceptual framework will allow us to examine both of these possibilities. From the perspective of competing explanations, we can assess whether the set of variables for any of the three elements of the context of computing use provides a superior level of explanatory appeal with respect to the between-individual variation in computing impacts. Thus we shall examine the explanatory power of the organizational environment versus the computer package versus the characteristics of the user. From the perspective of alternative explanations, we must consider whether all three elements combine to provide a more powerful explanation for between-individual variation in computing impacts. Our empirical analysis of this second question requires the use of more sophisticated quantitative techniques, including regression analysis and discriminant analysis.

Our conceptual framework for this second research question is derived from a long tradition in organization theory which assumes that both environment and structure might influence organizational performance (see Blau and Schoenherr 1971; Pugh et al. 1969; Lawrence and Lorsch 1967). Recently, much of the research in this tradition has been labeled "contingency theory" because a central concern has been to specify the extent to which organizational structure is contingent upon varied configurations of environmental factors which, in effect, represent different environmental "contexts" (see Jenkins 1978). In general, our conceptualization shares with these approaches the strong interest in contingent effects and the assumption that there might be characteristic "contexts" producing particular variations in performance outcomes.

Figure 2.1 suggests the hypothesized linkages among the three key contextual aspects in our analysis of the impacts of computing on people in government. As we have noted above, features of either the computer package or the individual user might directly influence the impact of computing on a person. We also allow that there might be interactive effects between these two aspects.[2] For example, the sophistication of the technology might interact with the user's sense of competency regarding the technology. The figure also indicates that both these elements are embedded in a broader context—the organizational environment. This environment might have a direct effect on the level of a computing impact, or it might have an indirect effect due to its effect on either the nature of the computer package or the user.

Thus, figure 2.1 identifies the major patterns of relationships which must be assessed in our attempt to determine whether there are systematic associations between the context of computing use and the level of computing impacts on individuals in organizations. The analytic methods we shall employ are fully described in the appendix. It is important to point out that our approach uses multivariate statistical methods and cross-sectional data to derive conclusions that are couched in causal language. Such methods and data cannot conclusively demonstrate causality, particularly regarding the end users' longitudinal assessments of the impacts of computing on their job performance.

However, we believe that our causal inference structure is sound and that the linkages we describe do reflect patterns from which cause and effect can be reasonably inferred. Our end users are especially capable of reporting on their involvement with the computer package over time and most measures are well-grounded in their direct work experiences. Our interpretations of the data are based not only on careful use of statistical methods but also on our dozen years of extensive fieldwork in these and similar organizational environments. We use causal language because we feel it best communicates the kinds of relationships that we infer from our data analyses and our field experience.

PRIOR RESEARCH

The existing empirical research in both public and private organizations on the impacts of computing offers some guidance for the development of variables and hypotheses for parts of our analysis. In general, this research tends to emphasize one or another of the kinds of computing impacts we consider, and one or another of the contextual elements in our conceptual framework. Moreover, even when all three elements have been measured in a single study, they usually have been treated as competing explanations rather than also being assessed as alternative explanations, in the sense defined above. Clearly, our conceptual framework enables us to examine both possibilities.

Table 2.1 summarizes the key explanatory factors in representative empirical analyses of the impacts of computing in public and private organizations. The main body of prior research has concentrated on behavioral factors, stressing the characteristics of users that influence their reactions to the implementation of computerized information

Figure 2.1. Computing Impacts and Context of Use

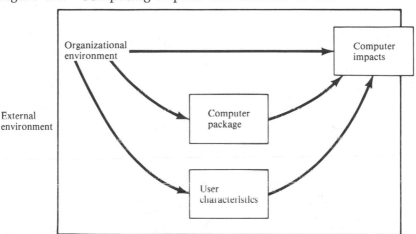

systems (Dickson and Simmons 1970; Dickson, Simmons, and Anderson 1969; Eason et al. 1975; Guthrie 1972, 1974; Mumford and Banks 1967) or the sociotechnical interface as a special feature of user characteristics (Hedberg and Mumford 1975; Hedberg, Mumford, and Anderson 1977; Mumford 1972; Pettigrew 1975; Pettigrew and Mumford 1975). A smaller proportion of the empirical research has emphasized the organizational environment (Delehanty 1966, 1967; Keen and Scott Morton 1978; King and Kraemer 1985; Laudon 1974; Sellenberger 1968; Tomeski 1972; Whisler 1967, 1970). Most of the studies reflect a mainframe computing environment, with earlier studies reflecting a batch computing environment and later studies reflecting on-line or interactive environments. Only a few empirical studies deal with microcomputer technology (Rockart and Flannery 1984; Rivard and Huff 1984), and the most significant of the microcomputer studies is still in progress (Child 1984; Child et al. 1985).

While some of our own earlier work does have empirical measures derived from all three contextual elements, it has primarily treated the organization or the department as the object unit of analysis, and the findings can be viewed only as suggestive of the kinds of factors that might account for differences in the impacts of computing at the individual level of analysis. One study (Kraemer, Dutton and Northrop 1981) assesses issues of utilization, productivity gains and

Table 2.1. Summary Comparison of Explanatory Factors Included in Representative Empirical Studies of Computer Impacts in Organizations

	Sector		Contextual Elements			Computing Impacts			
	Public	Private	Organizational environment	Technology	Traits of users	Utilization	Performance impacts	Problems	Work environment
Child 1984; Child et al. 1984		X	X	X	X	X	X	X	X
Danziger et al. 1982	X		X	X	X		X	X	
Delehanty 1966, 1967		X	X	X	X				X
Dery 1981									
Dickson, Simmons & Anderson 1969; Dickson & Simmons 1970	X	X	X		X	X		X	
Eason et al. 1975		X			X	X		X	
Frantzich 1982	X		X			X			
Guthrie 1974, 1972	X	X	X		X	X		X	X
Hedberg & Mumford 1975; Hedberg, Mumford & Anderson 1977		X			X				X
King & Kraemer 1985	X		X	X		X	X	X	
Kraemer, Dutton & Northrop 1981	X		X	X	X	X	X		X
Laudon 1974	X		X			X			
Lucas 1975		X		X		X			
Malvey 1981		X	X				X	X	
Mumford 1972		X	X						X
Mumford & Banks 1967		X			X				X
Pettigrew 1975; Pettigrew & Mumford 1975		X	X	X	X	X		X	
Rivard & Huff 1984		X		X		X	X		
Rockart & Flannery 1983		X		X		X	X		
Sollenberger 1968		X	X	X		X		X	
Tomeski 1972	X		X	X		X	X	X	
Whisler 1970, 1967		X	X	X		X	X	X	

work impacts for a number of quite specific information-processing tasks. It primarily relies upon quantitative analyses using city-level or department-level measures for 42 cities, and concludes generally that the nature of the computer package, particularly the extensiveness and sophistication of automation, accounts for variance in performance quality substantially more than does the organizational environment. But a second study (Danziger, Dutton, Kling and Kraemer, 1982), based on a comparative case study approach using data from the same 42 cities and a larger data base from more than 700 local governments, also emphasizes the importance of the organizational environment. In particular, the distribution of overall power and authority within the organization and the political dynamics of bureaucracy are important in determining the shape and nature of the political impacts from the use of computers.

The major completed study that does attempt to incorporate alternative explanations for information systems performance at the individual level into a single analysis is Lucas' (1975) *Why Information Systems Fail*. Lucas systematically examines the traits of the user and also aspects of the computer package, including the quality of the technical aspects of the system, and such dataprocessing arrangements as management support, user involvement, design, and operation policies. Table 2.2 indicates the nature of the relationships predicted by Lucas between these explanations and his impact variables—user attitudes about the information system, level of utilization, and a general impact measure he terms "performance." On the basis of empirical data from more than 2,000 information systems users in 16 business organizations, Lucas concludes that all the posited relationships are supported to some extent. While he begins with the premise that behavioral factors are more important determinants of information systems failures than are technical factors, he ultimately concludes that an adequate explanation of information systems performance must include both behavioral and technical factors, and also organizational factors (Lucas 1975:106).

The shared conceptualization of the general research question between Lucas' research in business organizations and our own research in public organizations should be clear. While the Lucas study is a valuable contribution to fuller understanding of information systems performance, it has several shortcomings. One problem is

Table 2.2.   Predicted Relationships Among Independent and Dependent Variables in Lucas' Study

| | Dependent Variables | | |
Independent Variables	User Attitudes	Use of System	Performance
Structure of the EDP Unit (Computer Package)			
Systems design and operations policies	+	0	0
Adverse contact involvement by users	−	0	0
User involvement	+	0	0
Management support	+	0	0
Technical system quality	+	+	0
Traits of Users			
User attitudes	0	+	0
Decision styles	0	+	+
Personal traits	0	+	+
Analysis action	0	+	+

that the causal linkages posited among the major sets of variables in the study are not analyzed in a systematic, empirical manner. Rather, the linkages are inferred from the discrete analyses. Second, the data base is better characterized as a series of separate studies rather than as single and integrated. Lucas notes that "in several cases only one study furnished data on a proposition and, in some of the studies, only one data source was available" (Lucas 1975:110). Third, the study has no major set of structural variables tapping the organizational environment. And finally, the impact variables are limited and differ across cases.

A major longitudinal study which is currently being conducted by John Child and Ray Loveridge also attempts to incorporate alternative explanations for information systems performance into a single analysis (Child 1984; Child et al. 1983; Loveridge et al. 1981). Their study focuses on the introduction of microcomputer technology in the hospital, banking, and retailing sectors. Observations are being made to permit analyses of specific decisions, of decision processes within an organization, and of policies and decision processes cross-nationally.

Child and Loveridge are examining how various "evolved" managerial strategies toward the introduction of new technology actually impact organizations. The "impacts" being studies are similar to our own and include changes in the work environment, tasks to be performed, power structures, hierarchies, and skill requirements in organizations. Also similar to our study, Child and Loveridge suggest that the use of new technology to advance particular managerial strategies is usefully understood in terms of contextual factors. Their study identifies market, task, and organizational factors as important within a particular country, and governmental, institutional, and cultural factors as salient in cross-national comparisons (Child 1983).

From the perspective of key research concerns in our work, the Child and Loveridge study promises to be significant and complementary. It focuses on microcomputer technology whereas our study has focused on mainframe and minicomputer technology. Therefore, this new study has the potential to assess our conclusion that the key contextual factors for end-user computing relate to the fact that end users' use is direct (hands-on) and involves a computer package over which they have some control. If this is correct, we expect to see similar patterns of utilization and similar impacts from the technology among comparable types of end users in both studies.

On balance, the major studies of information systems performance that have been completed present some promising empirical grounding, but are difficult to merge into a coherent set of findings. As might be expected, the studies vary in terms of the number of cases, the comparability of organizations, the operational measures employed, and the object unit of analysis (e.g., organization, role, individual). But the more serious problem is that these studies do not in general examine explanations of information systems impacts in an integrated framework that facilitates both the comparison between competing explanations and the simultaneous assessment of alternative explanations. These studies do not enable us to derive conclusive statements about the relative importance of the organizational environment, the computer package, and characteristics of the user in explaining information systems success and failure. Thus, we have designed our conceptual framework, data base, and analytic methods with an eye to producing a more integrated analysis of the impacts of computing on people in organizations.

COMPUTER IMPACTS AND ROLE TYPES

In studying the impacts of computing on the people who are end users, it is possible to treat all personnel as a single aggregate or to partition them into distinct role-types. For several reasons our analyses are based on the separate analysis of each role-type. First, it is obvious that the functional responsibilities and the level of discretion exercised by individuals at different levels in the organizational hierarchy are significantly different. Second, the dominant modes of information-handling and the manner in which various kinds of information and data are used to support the decisions and actions of people in different roles are quite dissimilar.[3]

For example, some local government personnel have clerical jobs in which their primary tasks involve the highly routinized processing of traffic tickets, utility bills, or tax bills recorded in a computerized system. They do all or most of the record keeping, record searching, and record updating on the automated system because that is the medium in which most of the data are available and because their use of the system is dictated by the standard operating procedures of their jobs. At the other extreme, most top managers have a diverse array of relatively unstructured tasks upon which they have discretion over decision and action and which they support by their own selection and use of information from multiple sources.

At both a theoretical level and also on the basis of our extensive research in both public and private organizations, there are reasonable grounds to predict that the different roles will be involved with computing in different ways and that the impacts of computing will vary considerably as a function of these distinctive roles. Ultimately, of course, it is an empirical question whether there are different computing impacts on these different role-types. Our analyses below will indicate that there are sound empirical reasons for distinguishing among the roles.

Our role taxonomy is based on the two dimensions suggested above: the employee's autonomy and discretion within the organizational hierarchy; and the dominant characteristics of their information-handling activities with the data that are amenable to computerization. The latter dimension distinguishes those with "high" pervasiveness of data-handling in work, meaning that their data-handling tends to be direct, continual, and multimodal (that is, involving considerable generation and manipulation, as well as use of data) from those with "low" pervasiveness, meaning that their data-handling tends to be indirect, intermittent and use-oriented (relative to generation and manipulation of data). Figure 2.2 indicates the four role-types that have been specified on the basis of these two dimensions. The actual classification of 2,537 respondents in our study is presented in the appendix.

- *Managers* are those top department-level administrators who are responsible for establishing the broad performance guidelines of their functional area and for implementing and monitoring performance. They have substantial discretion in decision and action and tend to have a very wide array of information sources provided to them. Their involvement with the kinds of data in automated files tends to be occasional, purposive, and use-oriented. In our sample, the managers are primarily department heads and division heads.
- *Staff professionals* are those relatively professionalized groups who serve top managers in a mainly staff capacity, analyzing data and providing information and advice. They have a relatively high level of discretion in the performance of their tasks, and they tend to be extensively involved with the generation and manipulation as well as the use of the kinds of data that might be in automated systems. In our sample, the staff professionals are primarily planners, policy analysts, budget and management analysts, and accountants.
- *Street-level bureaucrats* are those line personnel who directly provide public goods and services to citizen-clients. Their decisions and actions are gen-

Figure 2.2.   Taxonomy of Roles Among End Users

Pervasiveness of Data
Handling in Work

		High	Low
Autonomy in the organization's hierarchy	High	Staff professionals	Managers
	Low	Desk-top bureaucrats	Street-level bureaucrats

NOTE: High means that data handling (for the kinds of data amenable to computerization) tends to be direct, continual, and multimodal; low means that data handling tends to be indirect, intermittent, and use-oriented (relative to generation and manipulation).

erally guided by standard operating procedures, although they do have some discretion in dealing with clients "in the field." Their information needs tend to be somewhat specialized, and they are typically users of the kinds of data in automated systems on an indirect, case-by-case basis. This role type includes such personnel as welfare workers, building inspectors and health care workers and, in our sample, is primarily composed of police detectives and patrol officers.[4]

* *Desk-top bureaucrats* are those administrative and clerical employees in departmental staff positions who provide general administrative assistance for internal government operations or in support of the provision of goods and services to clients. They are continually involved in the recording, processing, searching, and use of basic operational data. They tend to perform highly routinized and rule-following tasks and have limited discretion in decision and action and in their data-handling activities. In our sample, the desk-top bureaucrats are mainly administrative assistants, bookkeepers, traffic ticket clerks, and records clerks.

Comprehensive analysis of the effects of the context of computing use entails the use of many operational indicators to capture the complexity of each element. But manageable and tractable analysis is best served by the limitation of the independent variables to a few key indicators. We have attempted to circumvent this dilemma, although our ultimate bias has been in favor of a more comprehensible and parsimonious set of representative variables. Our approach was initially to generate a substantial list of operational indicators for the context of computing use. This selection of variables was based on our judgment of the variables for which a reasonable theoretical case could be made, guided by the nature of variables that appear most frequently in the empirical literature and tempered by the reality of the indicators for which we were able to gather data. Through this process, we developed a relatively extensive set of measures, which are fully described in the appendix. Certain organizational environment variables have been excluded because this study focuses upon a single type of organization, American municipal governments, which share many basic structural and functional characteristics.

We then undertook two data-reduction techniques. First, we combined a number of indicators into indices (see the appendix for an explication of these indices) and deleted a few variables with high multicollinearity. Second, we took the remaining nine organizational environment variables, thirteen computer package variables, and eleven user trait variables and subjected each set to factor analysis. We then selected the variable that was most representative of each factor (the variable with the strongest factor loading in nearly every case) and used that variable for the analysis. Table 2.3 reveals the outcome of this selection process. In this manner, several hundred original indicators (or more, for multiple computing installation sites) were reduced to the twelve variables identified in the table. In our analyses and discussions, we refer to the variable by the name we have given to the factor, not to the specific variable that is actually used in the analysis. We believe that this approach enhances the cogency of our findings and discussions, but the reader should judge whether the use of specific variables to represent the contextual factors and whether the name used are reasonable.

We have now identified all the key concepts that structure the analyses that follow. We do not assume that computing will necessarily be a homogenizing technology, having virtually the same impacts on individuals regardless of role or context of use. Nor do we assume that the impacts will be consistent, either in the sense that some roles always benefit more than others or that the crucial element of the context of use will be the same across all roles and all impacts. To be scientifically "proper," all our analyses begin from the orientation of null hypotheses: that there are no systematic patterns in the data. Indeed, given the great complexity of the phenomena we are analyzing, the many unmeasured or weakly measured variables and the limited power of the findings in most empirical social scientific research examining macrolevel phenomena, we will not be surprised to discover many instances where the null findings predominate. Our overall objective is to add some insights to the limited knowledge about the impacts of computing on individuals in organizations, and both positive and null findings can usefully serve this objective.

Although the analyses are structured on a null hypothesis formulation, we do have expectations about the patterns of relationships that will emerge from the analysis. First we expect that there will be notable within-role differences in the level of all four types of computing impacts. There are likely to be particularly large differences in levels of problems and job performance effects, since these seem the areas where the impacts of computing will be particularly re-

Table 2.3. Selection of Variables to Represent Aspects of the Context of Computing Use

A. Organizational Environment

	Factors		
Variables	*I*	*II*	*III*
Number of departments in government	.69	.27	.59
Size of legislative body	.67	.29	−.22
Government employees per citizen	.64	.01	−.06
Land area served	−.12	.88	.35
Population served	.46	.51	.10
Partisanship in local politics index	.27	.51	.10
Reform government structures index	−.36	−.38	.75
Professional practices of government depts. index	.10	.10	.58
Central management control index	−.19	.09	.26
Percent Variance Explained	32%	22%	14%

Factor I: Complexity of government
Variable selected: number of departments in government
Factor II: Scale of service environment
Variable selected: land area served
Factor III: Government professionalism
Variable selected: reform government structures index[a]

B. Computer Package

Variables	*I*	*II*	*III*	*IV*	*V*
Total applications	.97	.01	.01	.05	.22
Level of applications development index	.72	−.03	−.17	.15	.11
Total on-line applications	.72	.17	.10	.13	−.01
Number of technical skills among staff	.56	.11	−.09	.35	−.06
Computing expenditure per capita	.36	.79	.36	.11	.12
Computing budget as % of gov't budget	−.06	.74	−.11	.03	.22
Number of computing installations in gov't	−.04	.04	.77	−.06	.11
Sophistication of operating system hardware	.30	.26	.13	.51	.23
Total core capacity	.51	.24	.42	.53	−.05
Use of computer policy board	.06	−.03	−.08	.46	.02
Year computing began in government	−.26	−.23	−.05	−.27	−.55
Independent computing department	.30	.02	−.39	−.02	−.47
Charges for computing services	.04	.06	.02	−.01	.27
Percent Variance Explained	32%	15%	9%	9%	8%

Factor I: Extensiveness of computing
Variable selected: total applications
Factor II: Resource support for computing
Variable selected: computing expenditure per capita
Factor III: Centralization/decentralization of computing
Variable selected: number of computing installations in gov't
Factor IV: Sophistication of computer package
Variable selected: sophistication of operating system hardware
Factor V: Routinization of computing
Variable selected: year computing began in government

Table 2.3. *(continued)*

C. User Characteristics

	Factors			
Variables	*I*	*II*	*III*	*IV*
Member of computer application design group	.57	.14	.13	.04
Computer courses taken	.56	.12	.22	.13
Believes does not understand computing	−.56	.02	.02	.04
Interested in computing	.53	.08	.16	−.21
Year of birth	.01	−.82	.00	.17
Years in type of job	.06	.62	−.01	.03
Years involved with computing	.32	.50	.01	.17
Member of work-related organization	.10	.20	.70	−.06
Recent courses related to work	.11	−.16	.38	.00
Highest educational level	.33	−.03	.34	.27
Evaluation of data processing unit service	−.03	.00	.01	.48
Percent Variance Explained	24%	16%	11%	10%

Factor I: User's competency with computing
 Variable selected: member of computer application design group
Factor II: User's age (and work experience)
 Variable selected: year of birth
Factor III: User's professionalism
 Variable selected: member of work-related organization
Factor IV: User's orientation to data processing staff
 Variable selected: evaluation of data processing unit service[b]

[a] Includes indicators of presence of manager/CAO, extent of at-large elections, power of mayor.
[b] Includes user's appraisal of the quality of computer services and the responsiveness of computing staff to the user's needs.

sponsive to the quantity and quality of computing services provided to a user. Second, we expect that the between-role differences in impacts will be clear, and that they will be related to the two role-type dimensions specified above. In general, those in positions higher in the organizational hierarchy will have more discretion about utilization and thus have higher proportions of low users or nonusers and, among users, have higher proportions of individuals reporting job performance benefits. In contrast, those in roles with more pervasive information-handling and less discretion about computing use will report relatively higher levels of problems with the technology and more substantial effects on their work environments.

Third, we assume that the patterns of relationships between the impacts of computing and the context of use will vary across roles in a relatively complex manner. Broadly, we anticipate that utilization will be most affected by user traits and the organizational environment among those roles with greater discretion and by the nature of the computer package among those with limited discretion. Problems with computing will primarily be related to the nature of the computer package across all role-types, with user traits also being quite significant for those with greater discretion. The effects of computing on the work environment will be most strongly related to user traits for those in more discretionary roles and will be related to features of the computer package for those in less discretionary roles. And job performance impacts will be contingent upon both the computer package and the user's traits.

At the most general level, table 2.4 summarizes our expectations about the direction of the relationship between each impact and each measure of the context of computing use across all roles. We stress that the discussion in the last several paragraphs is best understood as our "hunches," based on our reading of the (limited and somewhat inconsistent) empirical and theoretical literature and our field ex-

Table 2.4.   General Patterns of Relationships Hypothesized Between Computing Impacts and Context of Use

	Utilization	Problems	Work Environment Effects	Job Performance Impacts
Organizational Environment				
Complexity	+	+	−	+
Scale service environment	+	+	+	+
Government professionalism	+	−	+	+
Computer Package				
Extensiveness	+	+	+	+
Resource support	+	−	+	+
Centralization	−	+	−	+
Sophistication	0	+	+	+
Routinization	+	−	+	+
User Characteristics				
Computing competency	+	−	+	+
Work experience	−	+	−	0
Professionalism	+	+	+	+
Orientation to computing staff	+	−	+	+

perience. We recognize that plausible arguments can be made for alternatives to nearly any of the predictions we have presented. The systematic empirical analyses that follow should clarify these expectations. We begin in chapter 3 with an examination of the types and levels of computing use by end users.

3. Utilization of Computing

Our inquiry into the impacts of computing on end users begins with the question of utilization. It seems obvious that if one policy analyst uses computing routinely on problem-solving tasks and another never uses it on such tasks, the impacts of the technology on the work of the two individuals could be quite different. Similarly, we might expect different impacts if one manager directly utilizes an automated system by sitting at a terminal and "playing" with the data while another manager only examines a set of data that has been generated from the automated system in a report produced by someone else. These examples highlight two central dimensions of computer utilization—*how* a person makes use of computing and *how often* such use occurs. Thus our analysis of computer utilization will examine both the qualitative dimension measuring the *style of use* and also the quantitative dimension measuring the *extent of use*. In this chapter, we shall address three types of questions: (1) Do levels of computing use vary within roles for a given mode of use? (2) Do levels of computing use vary across roles? and (3) Can within-role differences in levels of use be accounted for by key features of the organizational environment, computer package, or user's characteristics?

We distinguish three broad modes of use of computing by end users in service-oriented organizations. First, a person can examine information that has been generated by others from computerized files. Such information can appear in the form of computer printouts or in other material that incorporates the information produced from an automated file. Second, a person can obtain specific information from a computer-based system by requesting someone else (in person, by memorandum, by telephone, or by radio) to generate the information (in a batch request or from a terminal). Third, a person can directly obtain information from an automated system by use of a terminal. We shall term these three alternative modalities of computing use as "passive" use, "indirect" use, and "direct" use, treating each mode as an increasingly direct and intentional involvement with computing in order to acquire information available from automated systems. We recognize that there will be some instances where indirect use is the most active mode possible, because a relevant on-line system is not available for the user.

We also distinguish varying levels in the frequency of computing use in a given mode, ranging from continual, daily use to the opposite extreme of nonuse, in the case where a person never employs that mode of computing. Most of our later analyses of computing impacts will focus on people who report at least some use of computing and who have some direct involvement with the computer package. But for our analysis of utilization, the nonusers are also an interesting category, and thus this chapter includes those "potential" end users in the four role-types who report no actual involvement with the computer package, although their governments do have computing. Our operational measures of the frequency of computing use are explicit questions regarding how often the respondent uses computing or computer-based information in each of the three modes. For passive, indirect, and direct use, the respondent reported whether he/she uses computing daily, a few times per week, a few times per month, several times per year, at least once per year, or never.

Although we shall structure our empirical analyses of these questions in terms of null hypotheses positing that there are no systematic differences within or between roles, we do expect that differences in computing utilization will appear. In general, we assume that there will be quite substantial variation in use within roles. We hypothesize that passive use will be most frequent, followed by indirect use, and that direct use will be least frequent, a pattern that we expect across all roles. We also expect that the variation within role will be greater on direct use, since the level of direct use is likely to be particularly responsive to differences in both the available technology and the traits of the individual. Regarding between-role differences in utilization, we again hypothesize significant variations. We expect that utilization levels will increase as the role involves more pervasive data-handling activities, given the basic notion that such activities will stimulate greater use of computing as a tool to facilitate their efficient and effective completion. In addition, roles lower in discretion are likely to have flexibility in choosing not to use computing on a given task, and hence utilization levels will tend to increase as the role is lower in the organizational hierarchy. These assumptions lead to the prediction that computing utilization will be highest among desk-top bureaucrats and lowest among managers. In comparing staff professionals and street-level bureaucrats, greater utilization by the former is expected, since the pervasiveness of data handling in a person's work is assumed to be more critical than discretion in affecting the level of computer utilization. And we assume that these between-role differences will be more distinct as the mode of computing use moves from passive use to direct use.

Finally, we expect that within-role differences in levels of computing utilization will be associated with all elements of the context of computing use. Regarding the organizational environment, we hypothesize that as the scale and complexity of the government and its information environment increase, there will be greater utilization of computing. The effect of the organizational environment on computing use is likely to be particularly strong for those in roles characterized by pervasive data handling, desk-top bureaucrats and staff professionals in our study. The aspects of the computer package that are likely to be most strongly associated with increased computing utilization are the greater extensiveness and routinization of the computer package. And for direct use, greater sophistication and decentralization of the computer package also should increase the level of use, especially among those with more discretionary data-handling needs, the managers and the street-level bureaucrats. Regarding user characteristics in the context of use, the user's sense of computing competence and a positive orientation toward the computer specialists should particularly increase an individual's propensity to use computing. And we expect the effect of user characteristics to be stronger among those in roles with greater discretion, the managers and the staff professionals.

FREQUENCY OF COMPUTING UTILIZATION

Table 3.1 reports the frequency of computing utilization in the passive, indirect, and direct modes by local government personnel in each of the four role-types. This table enables us to assess the differences across modes of use within each role, and aids our analysis of the between-role differences in use patterns. In terms of within-role levels of computing use, the table generally supports the hypothesis that frequency of use increases from the direct to the indirect to the passive mode. This pattern is very strong for managers, staff professionals, and desk-top bureaucrats, with the mean increasing about our frequency level for each mode of use.

The exception to this pattern is the street-level bureaucrats, where indirect use is considerably higher than passive use. While the "modal" street-level bureaucrat (that is, the most commonly occuring) makes both passive and indirect use of computing on a daily basis, fully 60 percent use computing indirectly each day. This high level of indirect computing is best understood in terms of the recurrent needs of street-level bureaucrats for computer-based information while operating in the field. If they do not have access to a terminal at the location where they are providing service (many in our sample do not have such access), they must rely on indirect computer use. For example, when a patrol officer stops a speeding vehicle, he is likely to use the radio to request computer-based information from an operator at headquarters regarding the status of the automobile (stolen?) and driver (warrants?). While about one-third of the street-level bureaucrats do use a computer terminal at least a few times per week, nearly half never use a terminal. Thus, because of the substantial number of nonusers of terminals and the continual need for information in the field, the street-level bureaucrats are heavy users of computing in the indirect mode. They also use computing passively on a frequent basis, with the largest proportion (44 percent)

Table 3.1.   Frequency of Computing Utilization by Mode of Use

	Managers (N=708)	Staff Professionals (N=428)	Street-Level Bureaucrats (N=850)	Desk-Top Bureaucrats (N=449)
Direct Use				
Never	78%	67%	48%	58%
Once per year	1	7	2	1
Several times per year	5	4	6	2
Few times per month	4	5	7	4
Few times per week	5	7	11	8
Daily	7	9	26	26
Mean[a]	.95	1.17	2.28	1.91
Coefficient of Variation[b]	1.18	1.23	.95	1.19
Indirect Use				
Never	16%	13%	3%	24%
Once per year	6	6	1	5
Several times per year	26	35	4	16
Few times per month	23	21	10	19
Few times per week	17	13	23	18
Daily	12	11	60	19
Mean	2.91	2.68	4.34	2.68
Coefficient of variation	.49	.54	.24	.66
Passive Use				
Never	6%	3%	9%	11%
Once per year	2	4	3	1
Several times per year	21	21	8	10
Few times per month	37	36	14	26
Few times per week	17	16	21	13
Daily	18	20	44	39
Mean	3.39	3.38	3.73	3.67
Coefficient of variation	.33	.34	.42	.38

[a] Variable scores calculated on the basis of these values: Never = 0; Once per year = 1; Several times per year = 2; Few times per month = 3; Few times per week = 4; Daily = 5.
[b] The coefficient of variation is the ratio of the standard deviation to the mean (s ÷ m).

making daily use of routinely produced computer-based information and two-thirds using such information at least a few times per week.

The level of computing use among the desk-top bureaucrats does fit the anticipated pattern, with increasing use in each less direct mode. Like the street-level bureaucrats, this group's "modal" frequency of passive computing use is daily, and the majority make passive use of computing at least a few times each week. But the indirect use of computing by desk-top bureaucrats is considerably lower than passive use and has the greatest variation of any role (as indicated by the high coefficient of variation). About 1 in 4 desk-top bureaucrats never request computer-based information and about 1 in 5 report indirect use at each frequency level above the once-per-year category. Direct use of computing by desk-top bureaucrats is particularly surprising, given the intensive, in-house information environment within which they work. While about 1 in 4 use computer terminals on a daily basis, about three-fifths never use computing in the direct mode. These data suggest that direct use by desk-top bureaucrats remains an all-or-nothing proposition at this point.

Table 3.1 suggests that the frequency of computing use by managers and staff professionals is quite comparable. For both roles, the great majority never use computing in the direct mode. And the "average" manager and professional request others to provide computer-based information and make passive use of computer-based information a few times per month, with a somewhat higher frequency of passive use. For these two roles, it is perhaps most surprising that the utilization of computing is at such moderate levels for the staff professionals. While there is considerable interest and attention in increasing the use of computing by top managers, there is often an implicit notion in discussions of computing utilization that staff professionals such as those in our analysis are frequent and purposive users of computing. While these data do not indicate that most professionals are completely insulated from computing, less than 1 in 5 directly use computing as frequently as a few times per week, less than 1 in 4 make indirect use of computing this often, and less than 3 in 5 make even passive use of computing a few times per week.

To evaluate the hypothesis that the within-role variation in frequency of computing use is greater as the mode moves from passive to direct use, the coefficients of variation (the ratio of the standard deviation on the mean) must be examined. In general, the data support this hypothesis for every role except the street-level bureaucrats. Once again, the extensive indirect use of computing by street-level bureaucrats seems to be crucial, since there is considerably less between-individual variation among street-level bureaucrats in indirect use than in passive use. It is also notable that for all four roles, the level of variation within-role is very substantial on direct use, and rather more similar on indirect and passive use. This might be accounted for by the unavailability of on-line computing to some individuals; but it is probably more importantly related to the major increase in computing competency necessary to use a terminal as opposed to requesting others to provide one with computer-generated information or to examining routinely produced information.

Table 3.2 indicates several interesting between-role differences in computing utilization, as measured by the chi-square statistic. First, it is clear that there *are* significant differences in the patterns of computing use across the four roles and all three modes of use, with only one exception (passive use by managers and staff professionals). This seems an important empirical validation for the conceptual decision to differentiate between the four role-types.

Second, as suggested above, street-level bureaucrats are the most frequent users of computing in all three modes of use. Our field research revealed, and chapter 6 will substantiate more fully, that the street-level bureaucrats in our study, mainly police, are supported

Table 3.2. Differences Between Roles in Frequency of Computing Utilization

	Mode of Use		
	Staff Professionals	*Street-level Bureaucrats*	*Desk-top Bureaucrats*
Managers	↑Direct***(.09)***[a] ←Indirect* (.04)	↑Direct***(.32)*** ↑Indirect***(.63)*** ↑Passive***(.30)***	↑Direct***(.21)*** ←Indirect***(.05) ↑Passive***(.17)***
Staff Professionals		↑Direct***(.21)*** ↑Indirect***(.57)*** ↑Passive***(.24)***	↑Direct***(.15)*** ←Indirect***(.06)* ↑Passive***(.16)***
Street-Level Bureaucrats			←Direct***(.07)** ←Indirect***(.51)*** ←Passive***(.09)***

[a] All role pairs listed where chi-square is significant, with first asterisks indicating probability. Arrow indicates role in which use is relatively higher (for example, direct use by staff professionals is significantly higher than for managers). Statistic in parenthesis is Kendall's tau, with appropriate significance level.

  * $p < .05$
  ** $p < .01$
  *** $p < .001$

by relatively simple, directly useful automated applications which offer substantial improvement over the information available in manual files.

Third, the desk-top bureaucrats are the second most frequent users of computing in both the direct and the passive modes, although they are the lowest users of computing in the indirect mode. It seems that, given their high information needs but their low organizational position, they tend either to do their own computing or to accept what has been produced routinely by others, but they cannot/do not request others to provide computing to them. Fourth, it seems that managers exercise their authority by often requesting others to provide them with computer-based information, while they are low in their direct and even their passive use of computing. Finally, it is surprising that staff professionals are relatively low users of computing in every mode, since their pervasive data-handling needs would suggest higher computing use.

Table 3.3 summarizes the expected and actual levels of computing utilization by those in the four roles. There is broad support for our predictions regarding within-role patterns. As hypothesized, there are generally higher levels of computing utilization as the mode of use changes from direct to indirect to passive. And there is also more within-role variation within a mode of computing use as the mode is more active.

However, the comparisons of computing between roles are often contrary to our predictions. First, we had hypothesized that frequency of use would be greatest among those with both higher data handling needs and also lower organizational discretion. In fact, it seems that higher use levels are more strongly associated with lower discretion than with pervasiveness of data-handling, especially because of the low utilization levels among staff professionals and the very high use levels among streel-level bureaucrats. The high level of indirect use by managers is also inconsistent with this general hypothesis.

Second, our assumption that there are greater between-role differences in use as the computing mode becomes more active is also unsupported. As measured by the chi-square values, the greatest differences are on indirect use, between the street-level bureaucrats and all other roles, and this role has its smallest differences from other roles on active use. And overall, it seems that the most

Table 3.3. Expected and Actual Frequency of Computing Utilization

Levels of Computing Use Within Roles

Expected	Actual
• Passive use > indirect use > direct use —especially for roles with greater discretion • Variation on direct use > indirect and passive use	• As expected —except street-level bureaucrats: indirect use > passive use > direct use —especially for roles with greater discretion • Variation on direct use > indirect use > passive use —except street-level bureaucrats: direct use > passive use > indirect use

Levels of Computing Use Between Roles

Expected	Actual
• Greater utilization as role involves more pervasive data handling and, to a lesser extent, less discretion Desk-top bureaucrats > staff professionals > managers	• Utilization by role varies across modes of use, role discretion is more important than pervasiveness of data handling Passive: Street-level bureaucrats > desk-top bureaucrats > managers and staff professionals —generally higher where less role discretion Indirect: Street-level bureaucrats > managers > staff professionals > desk-top bureaucrats —generally higher where less data-handling Direct: Street-level bureaucrats > desk-top bureaucrats > staff professionals > managers —generally higher where less role discretion
• Between role differences on direct use > indirect use > passive use	• Between-role differences on passive use > direct use > indirect use (except street-level bureaucrats) • Between-role differences relatively low on indirect use except in comparisons with street-level bureaucrats, where differences are very high

substantial between-role variations tend to occur on passive use, the exact opposite of our expectation. This is surprising, since it seems plausible to assume that passive use of computing would be most widespread and least contingent upon matters of choice or upon the context of computing use.

EXPLAINING VARIATIONS IN FREQUENCY OF COMPUTER UTILIZATION

While our null hypotheses hold that there is no systematic association between the frequency of computing utilization within a given role and the context of computing, we have suggested relationships that we do expect. Table 3.4 enables us to evaluate the effects on utilization levels of the three elements in the context of computing use. It is evident that the null hypotheses must be rejected, in the sense that there are statistically significant regression equations between the variables representing the context of use and the between-individual differences in the frequency of computing use for every role in every mode of use. But the explanatory power of the independent variables is modest, since less than 20 percent of the total variance within a role is accounted for (measured as the R^2 statistic) in any case and less than 10 percent is accounted for in 7 of the 12 cases.

The top part of table 3.4 allows assessment of the three contextual elements as *competing explanations.* The set of variables representing each contextual element is regressed on the mode of use, and the table indicates the total variance explained by that element. The organizational environment has the strongest explanatory power in only one instance, passive use by managers. Aspects of the computer package are the most important contextual element in five instances, including all three modes of use for desk-top bureaucrats. And the characteristics of the user account for the greatest amount of variation in six instances, including two of the three modes of use for managers, staff professionals, and street-level bureaucrats. If one looks for patterns between a mode of use and a contextual element, the only clear case is on indirect use, where the computer package has the greatest explanatory power for every role except managers and is statistically significant for all four roles.

Table 3.4. Explanatory Power of Context of Use Elements for Utilization of Computing, Within Role

	Managers	Staff Professionals	Street-Level Bureaucrats	Desk-Top Bureaucrats
Competing Explanations				
Percent of within-role variation in use explained by:				
Organizational environment				
direct use	3***	1	1	1
indirect use	3**	7***	6***	2
passive use	5***	2	0	1
Computer package				
direct use	2*	2	2	5**
indirect use	5***	11***	15***	4*
passive use	2*	3	2	3**
User characteristics				
direct use	5***	10***	6***	1
indirect use	7***	7***	4***	3
passive use	4***	7***	3***	3
Alternative Explanations				
Percent of within-role variation in use explained by:				
All conceptual elements combined:				
direct use	11***	18***	19***	8*
indirect use	8***	12***	8***	7*
passive use	9***	13***	5**	7*
Percent of total accounted for by:				
Organizational environment				
direct use	28	39	30	50
indirect use	52	6	16	18
passive use	52	16	5	29
Computer package				
direct use	0	24	55	50
indirect use	0	20	0	80
passive use	0	20	29	0
User characteristics				
direct use	72	37	14	0
indirect use	48	94	84	0
passive use	48	64	64	71

* $p < .05$
** $p < .01$
*** $p < .001$

The lower part of table 3.4 facilitates evaluation of the contextual elements as *alternative explanations*—that is, as complementary aspects of an overall pattern of effects by the context of use on the level of computing utilization. Given our conceptual framework, the organizational environment variables are first entered into a regression equation on computing use, since they are the broad context within which the technology and the user exist, and then the remaining variables are entered, using a stringent criterion for including a variable in the analysis.

The regression equations are significant in all twelve instances, and the results yield a mixed set of inferences. At least two of the three elements of context of computing use contribute importantly to the explanation of variance in seven instances. This fact, plus the substantially higher total explained variance in those cases where several elements are important, lend support to the notion that the elements of the context of use often produce interdependent impacts on computing use. However, there are four instances where one of the three contextual elements accounts for more than two-thirds of the explained variance, a level of explanatory dominance where the notion of complementary effects has only minimal appeal. The dominant contextual element is the characteristics of the user in three cases (direct use by managers and indirect use by staff professionals and street-level bureaucrats), and is the computer package in one case (indirect use for desk-top bureaucrats). It is notable that the computer package is insignificant in five instances, including all three modes of use for managers, and that the user characteristics element is insignificant on computing use by desk-top bureaucrats. This suggests that when an individual has very high role discretion, it is the individual's own traits rather than the available technology that are most strongly associated with utilization; but personal characteristics have minimal systematic effect on computing use among those with very low discretion, where use is mainly contingent upon the available technology.

Table 3.5 indicates the specific contextual variables that are significantly associated with variations in computing use. User characteristics occur most frequently among the key explanatory variables. Of particular importance are measures of the sociotechnical interface, especially the positive orientation of the user to the computer specialists, which is significant in eight cases, including higher levels of passive use for all four roles and higher levels of direct use among managers, staff professionals, and street-level bureaucrats. For those in more discretionary roles, greater use also tends to occur among users who feel more competent with computing.

Aspects of the computer package are generally more important for those in less discretionary roles, with the linkage between greater use and greater resource commitment to computing being more frequent. While the extensiveness, sophistication, or decentralization of computing are related to direct use for most roles, it is somewhat surprising that these key features of the computer package are not more consistently associated with modes of use, since they usually receive considerable attention in the literature on the utilization of computing. Finally, greater complexity and scale of the government's operations are the features of the organizational environment that most frequently appear, especially for higher use levels among those with greater discretion.

The overall pattern of relationships is compared to our initial expectations in table 3.6. While there is no single, consistent pattern in these relationships, a few broad generalizations are possible. First, *the context of computing use seems to have the most systematic effect on the levels of computing utilization among those in roles with greater discretion.* It is interesting that the context of use has greatest explanatory power for those with both discretion and pervasive data handling, while it has least explanatory power for those with pervasive data handling but the most limited discretion. These findings are partially at variance with our original assumption that pervasiveness of data handling would be a more critical dimension of differences in computing use than role discretion would be. While the level of a person's information processing needs does affect the level of computer utilization, the variation in use is more substantially altered by whether the person's role allows greater freedom to choose the level at which computing will be employed.

A second, and related point is that *the explanatory power of the context of use tends to increase as the mode of use becomes more active, regardless of role.* This suggests, as we expected, that decisions to use computing in the more active modes are more strongly influenced by the milieu, the available technology, and the user's own traits. Computing use does seem more intentional and purposive as the involvement required of the user becomes greater.

Table 3.5. Explanatory Power of Variables in Context of Use for Utilization of Computing, by Role

	Managers	Staff Professionals	Street-Level Bureaucrats	Desk-Top Bureaucrats
		Direct Use		
Organizational environment	+Gov't complexity (.11)**			−Gov't complexity (−.16)**
Computer package		+Scale of service env. (.12)* +Extensiveness of computing (.18)** +Routinization of computing (.12)*	+Scale of service env. (.12)** +Resource support for computing (.32)*** Decentralized computing (.10)* +User orientation to computing staff (.15)***	+Sophistication of computing (.15)*
User characteristics	+User orientation to computing staff (.13**) Younger user (−.13)** −User professionalism (−.14)*** +User computer competency (.11)**	+User orientation to computing staff (.14)* +User computer competency (.21)***		

Table 3.5. (continued)

	Managers	Staff Professionals	Street-Level Bureaucrats	Desk-Top Bureaucrats
		Indirect Use		
Organizational environment	−Gov't professionalism (−.11)** +Gov't complexity (.10)* +Scale of service env. (.09)*		−Gov't complexity (−.08)*	+Resource support for computing (.18)** Less extensive computing (−.15)*
Computer package				
User characteristics	+User computing competency (.17)***	+User computing competency (.21)*** Older user (.20)*** +User professionalism (.11)*	Younger user (−.22)*** +User orientation to computing staff (.09)*	

Table 3.5. (continued)

	Managers	Staff Professionals	Street-Level Bureaucrats	Desk-Top Bureaucrats
		Passive Use		
Organizational environment	−Gov't professionalism (−.12)** +Gov't complexity (.15)*** +Scale of service env. (.08)*	+Scale of service env. (.12)*		
Computer package		Routinization of computing (.17)**	+Resource support for computing (.12)**	
User characteristics	+User orientation to computing staff (.13)** +User computing competency (.12)** −User professionalism (−.10)**	+User orientation to computing staff (.23)*** −User professionalism (−.15)**	+User orientation to computing staff (.14)*** Younger user (−.08)*	+User orientation to computing staff (.15)*

* $p < .05$
** $p < .01$
*** $p < .001$

Table 3.6. Comparison of Expected and Actual Linkages Between Computer Utilization and the Context of Use

Expected	*Actual*
Increased computing use where:	
• Increased scale and complexity of government operations	• As expected, but only limited linkages
—especially for roles where data handling is pervasive	—not contingent on pervasiveness of data handling
	—most evident for managers
• Computer package is more extensive, routinized and sophisticated	• Direction generally correct, but clear support for expectation only among staff professionals
—especially for roles where data handling is pervasive	—not supported
—especially for more active modes of use	—direct use > passive use > indirect use
• User has positive sociotechnical interface with computing	• As expected, consistent pattern
—especially for more discretionary roles	—as expected
—especially for more active modes of use	—no clear pattern between modes of use
• User is younger, more professional	• Inconsistent, limited linkage

Third, *the characteristics of the user are the most consistently important aspect of the context of computing use.* As expected, greater use is consistently associated with a more positive sociotechnical interface, in that the user has both a favorable view of the responsiveness of the computing staff and also a sense of his/her own competency in using computing. Higher utilization levels are also more prevalent among people who are younger and more professional. Although we predicted that user characteristics would become more critical as use became more active, they have particularly strong explanatory appeal for more passive modes of use. It is true, however, that user characteristics are also clearly linked to the direct use of computing by managers.

Fourth, *the nature of the computer package is clearly related to level of use in some instances, especially among those with less discretion.* This is contrary to our expectation that the computer package would be more significant among those with greater discretion regarding use. But there is some support for our assumption that a more developed computer package (in the sense of being more routinized, extensive, and sophisticated) would be associated with greater direct use and with higher utilization among those in roles with more pervasive data-handling responsibilities, the staff professionals and desk-top bureaucrats. Finally, *greater use is associated with increased scale and complexity of the organizational environment in some cases,* especially for managers and for direct use in most roles.

CONCLUDING OBSERVATIONS

Utilization of computing is the pivot upon which all other impacts of the technology turn. Thus we have begun our study of the effects of computing on people in organizations with an assessment of the nature and extent of computing use. We have identified quite distinctive modes of use, varying from the active and personal use of a terminal to the relatively passive scanning of computer-based information that "appears" in one's work domain to the total nonuse of any computer-generated information.

As we anticipated, there is considerable variation in the level of computing use among potential end users in the public organizations we studied. More than 3 out of 4 managers never use computing in the direct mode, while less than 1 in 30 staff professionals never makes passive use of computing. In general, as the mode of computing use entails more active involvement by the user, the total level of use declines and the within-role variation between users increases. It is also evident that there are broad differences in both the modes and levels of computing use across the four role-types in our analysis. In fact, there is a statistically significant difference in level of computing utilization in 17 of 18 role pairings, with those in the more "bureaucratic" roles tending to make the most frequent use of computing.

Our examination of the impact of the context of use on the level of computing utilization provided mixed results. It is clear that a considerable amount of the between-individual variation in the level of computing use cannot be accounted for by the explanatory variables in our study. This might mean that there are only limited systematic associations between the level of computing use and the organizational environment, the computer package, and the user's characteristics. Or it might indicate that the explanatory variables which we employ are not the one that most powerfully associated with use levels.

However, the variables in the analysis do account for between 10 and 20 percent of the between-individual variation in use for most roles and most modes of computing use. Thus it seems reasonable to conclude that the context of computing use does have some effect on the level of utilization. End users in some roles seem more responsive to the context of computing use than others, particularly those in roles with greater discretion and, as a consequence, with greater freedom to choose how and when to use computing in their work. In some cases, each of the three elements of the context of computing has a significant effect on the level of use. The characteristics of the user, especially the person's view of the responsiveness of computing staff and the person's own computing competency, are the aspects of the context of use that are most frequently important. A more established and developed computer package and a more extensive information processing environment also seem to stimulate greater use of computing in some end-user roles.

Overall, then, the nature and extent of computing use by people in public organizations is neither uniform nor random. There are clear and distinguishable patterns of utilization. Computing use is contingent upon the discretion attached to a person's work, to the pervasiveness of data handling in that work, and to aspects of the context within which the person uses the technology. To understand why different people use computing more or less in their work, one needs to be sensitive to the characteristics of their roles, to the computer package available to them, to the information processing environment within which they operate, and, perhaps more importantly, to their own personal orientation to computing.

Although characterizations of the impacts of computing in organizations often tend to imply that similar groups of people are affected by the technology in about the same manner, this examination of individual end users provides a cautionary note to such sweeping assumptions. We find clear and substantial differences in computing utilization among end users, both within roles and, even more, between roles. Such findings support the decision to examine individuals as the units of analysis.

Subsequent chapters will indicate that such differences are evident in many, but not all, impacts of computing. And the most powerful explanations of variations in computing impacts will occur when we focus intensively on end users who share a common set of role responsibilities. We begin such intensive analyses in chapter 4, where we undertake a special study of computing utilization among staff professionals. We have selected this role, which has both high discretion and pervasive data-handling responsibilities, because staff professionals seem to deviate from our expectations that they would be extensive users of computing and would be especially responsive to the context of use.

4. Staff Professionals and Computers: Types of Utilization by End Users

Chapter 3 indicates that staff professionals use computing no more extensively than the managers they serve, and considerably less than desk-top and street-level bureaucrats (see table 3.1). This finding is surprising for several reasons. First, the result is inconsistent with conventional images of staff professionals as relatively young, educated, tool- and technique-oriented information workers who handle extensive data and are naturally oriented towards computers and information systems. Second, it is inconsistent with images of the computer as a vital aid to problem finding and problem solving, two key aspects of any staff professional's job. And third, such modest levels of use seem inconsistent with images of the computer's impact on the staff professional's role in the organization, since the literature predicted an early and substantial impact, even the eventual elimination of the staff professional's role along with the middle manager's role (Leavitt and Whisler 1958; *Business Week* 1983).[1]

In short, our broad findings on the use of computing in chapter 3 seem at variance with the image of staff professionals as "leading edge" end users. Thus this chapter provides a more detailed examination of computer use among staff professionals in order to enhance our understanding of this type of end user.

Staff professionals are, as their name suggests, both professionals by training and staff by virtue of the functions they perform in the organization. As professionals, most are trained in some functional area, such as policy analysis, planning, accounting, finance, economics, or budgeting. As staff, they use their specialized training to select, analyze, and interpret data which aid them in problem solving and in providing information and advice to the policymakers or managers they serve. In the context of our study, staff professionals are: administrative aides to the mayor, city council, or chief administrative officer; urban planners; data-base custodians (in the planning, housing and urban renewal, fire, engineering, or public works departments); central budget analysts (in the budget, finance, or accounting offices); accountants (in finance, accounting, comptroller, or budget offices); and manpower allocation analysts (in the police).

COMPUTERS IN STAFF PROFESSIONALS' WORK

As suggested by the variety of roles above, the nature of staff professional work and of computer use in that work is varied. Three examples are presented below which illustrate the variety involved. The examples—budget monitoring, manpower allocation, and policy analysis—generally represent only a portion of the staff professionals' work and of the computer support available and/or used by them in their work.[2]

Budget monitoring is a key activity of both central and departmental staff, usually budget analysts, accountants and administrative analysts. It involves the examination of the "current balance report" for variances or differences between departmental budgets and expenditures that warrant investigation. The current balance report is a periodic (usually monthly) accounting of budgets and expenditures, usually broken down by department and by line item of expense, although more elaborate breakdowns and data sometimes are reported. The variances of interest may be differences in levels or in rates of expenditure or both.

Computerized budget monitoring systems tend to vary in terms of whether they are primarily helpful to control of department expenditures by central staff or by department staff. Some budget monitoring systems are aimed primarily at producing detailed information on a weekly or daily basis for use by central staff in monitoring department expenditures. Department staff receive only monthly summaries and these usually are several weeks old by the time of receipt. Consequently, the summaries are used by department staff only for reconciling departmental bookkeeping systems and not for controlling expenditures. Other computerized systems produce summary and detailed information on a weekly basis and get that information out to department staff, as well as to central staff, within a day or two after the close of the accounting period. Consequently, these summaries can assist department staff in controlling their own expenditures and also serve central staff.

The physical output of budgeting monitoring systems is almost always a very large computer printout; in some instances however, considerably more detailed data also might be available in a computer database that can be queried by staff via remote terminals. When they receive the printouts, the staff professionals immediately scour them for unusual patterns of expenditure, and take follow-up action as required by the situation. That action might involve a request to the computing staff for additional computer reports, or direct query of a computer database to inspect particular transactions. In addition to this comprehensive monthly review, the computer reports and files are usually referenced when reviewing department requests for funds transfer, change in expenditure, additional budget, new staffing, and so forth. Thus, the pattern of computer use in budget monitoring can be briefly intensive once a month and then light but continuous throughout the month. Of course, the actual pattern of use in any particular organization will be influenced by the nature of the computer package available to these staff professionals and by the traits of the individual budget analyst, accountant or administrative analyst.

The second example of computer support for staff professionals, manpower allocation, is a more complex and sophisticated use of computing. Computerized manpower allocation is primarily used by police planners and analysts for allocating police patrols to city neighborhoods. Patrol allocation is aimed at ensuring that the allocation of police officers is based on some objective definition of need, which turns out to be a highly complex matter. It is complex because there are a large number of alternatives that might feasibly accomplish the same objectives. Departments can redraw the boundaries of police districts, change the manpower levels per district, change the length or phasing of patrol shifts, move special patrol units around, or change the activities of patrol officers.

Police manpower allocation is further complicated by the uncertainty surrounding the outcomes of any particular allocation scheme. Most allocation schemes embedded in the computer models are aimed at decreasing response times and increasing manpower levels in high crime areas. However, some research suggests that this allocation scheme only results in relocating where crime occurs rather than reducing crime because criminals simply skip to other neighborhoods in response to increased patrol in any one neighborhood. Therefore, other schemes have been developed which keep manpower levels relatively steady but reallocate the "activities" of patrol officers. For example, "law enforcement" activities might be increased in high-crime areas, whereas "crime-prevention" activities might be increased in low-crime areas.

Finally, patrol allocation is complicated by the difficulty of measuring service need and delivery. Calls for services, crime incidents, traffic accidents, population density, street miles and similar measures are among the best available indicators of a need for police services but are inadequate in themselves. Even more difficult to measure is the adequacy of police service delivery. Here most police analysts are left with clearance rates, response times, and citizen complaints as crude indicators of service delivery. Yet only a small proportion of police calls for service require an immediate response, most are not for serious crimes, and most service delivery takes place after the police arrive at the scene.

In this context, computerized manpower allocation is aimed at providing police planners and analysts with tools that allow them to analyze crime patterns, assess patrol needs, assign patrols to neighborhoods based on need, and simulate the likely impacts of different allocation schemes in advance of commitment to redeployment. The computer support usually includes detailed databases about crime, statistical packages for analyzing crime patterns, and computer models for assigning patrols and simulating likely impacts. The analyst's task is to discover patterns in the crime data that indicate differential need for patrol among urban neighborhoods, and then try out different patrol allocation schemes to respond to that need. The intensiveness of crime analysis and modeling in an organization can vary considerably depending upon the nature of the available computer package and the traits of the individual police analyst.

Because of the complexity of analyzing crime patterns and running the simulation models, patrol allocation tends to be done in this highly formal manner only periodically, and sometimes episodically (i.e., in response to a clear indication that the current allocation scheme is not working). As such, patrol allocation is characteristic of the use by staff professionals of other computer models such as population, transportation and land use forecasting models, facility location models, or revenue and expenditure forecasting models.

The third example of computer support for staff professionals is urban databanks for policy analysis by urban planners and analysts (e.g., demographers, economists). Urban databanks pool facts about a city's people and their environment (e.g., population, land use, housing, and economy). In turn, this information is aggregated and analyzed to determine environmental conditions (e.g., the adequacy of housing, the state of repair of infrastructure, the health of the economy). These analyses can be used as a guide by urban planners and analysts in identifying problems, determining needs, developing programmatic remedies, and applying for outside financial assistance. In some instances, information also is being fed into computer models that mimic the behavior of some aspect of the environment (e.g., land use change and economic development). These analyses and models can be used by urban planners and analysts to pretest the effects of various public actions, which can then be presented to public officials as an aid to deciding among alternative policies. Also, information about people can be used to assess the political feasibility of development and financial plans.

The computer support available to urban planners in this work is the most varied of any available to staff professionals. It generally consists of urban databases, various statistical, mapping, and graphics packages to manipulate the databases, and urban development models. The databases can be few or many; the packages simple or sophisticated; the models coarse or fine-grained and detailed. Computer support might be batch processing, online inquiry, interactive analysis, or all of these. Usually, the level of computer support available is somewhat related to the nature of the planners' demands; it is generally unlikely that greater capability will be available than is demanded by the planners and analysts themselves.

The foregoing examples of computer support for staff professional work illustrate both the great variety in the nature of staff professionals' work and the equally great variety in the nature of the computer package which might support that work. These examples also suggest the considerable variety that staff professionals might exhibit in their patterns of computer use.

CONCEPTUALIZATION

In order to get at the central concerns of this chapter, we need to distinguish different types of computing use among staff professionals and then to examine the characteristics of each type of end user. Thus we categorize staff professionals on the basis of their total configuration of computing use, considering both their modes of computer use (direct, indirect, and passive) and the frequency of computer use in each mode (frequently, occasionally, seldom, or never). Four types of end users among staff professionals result from this categorization:

1. The *total user* makes some direct use of a computer terminal to obtain information, and both requests others to provide computer-based information (indirect use) and also receives information that has been generated by others from computerized files (passive use) on at least an occasional basis;
2. The *instrumental user* never makes direct use of a computer terminal, but requests others to provide computer-based information and receives information that others have generated from computerized files at least occasionally;
3. The *reactive user* never makes direct use of a computer terminal, seldom or never requests others to provide computer-based information, and seldom or occasionally receives information that has been generated by others from computerized files;
4. The *nonuser* has virtually no conscious involvement with computers or computer-based information (i.e., never makes direct, indirect, or passive use of computing).

Of these four types of end-user computing, it is readily apparent that the "total user" most closely fits the image of the staff professional in the literature. Table 4.1 displays the distribution, across these four types of computing users, of the 346 staff professionals in our study. Nearly one-half (44 percent) of the staff professionals are reactive users, with the remainder split between instrumental users and total users (27 percent each). Less than 3 percent of the staff professionals are nonusers, such a small group that they are eliminated from the subsequent analyses in this chapter. Thus only one-fourth of the staff professionals in our study fit the image of the total user with frequent hands-on use of computing. Moreover, nearly one-half of the staff professionals are characterized by the opposite image. These reactive users are distinguished from the nonusers only by the occasional, passive receipt of information generated by others from computer files.

In our subsequent analyses, we seek to understand what distinguishes the total user—our expected "model" staff professional as an end user—from the other two types of computer users. In addition, we attempt to determine whether differential computer use can be accounted for by: (a) the characteristics of staff professionals as computer users, (b) the nature of the computer package available to them, and (c) the demands and supports of the organizational environment in which they work, including the task-specific environment of their job.

In general, we begin with the assumption that certain characteristics of the individual staff professional will affect computer use. For example, staff who are younger, more professionally oriented, more computer competent, and more positively oriented toward computer specialists might be expected to use computing more than those who are older, less professionally oriented, less computer competent, and less positively oriented toward computer specialists.

Table 4.1. Staff Professionals by Taxonomy of End-User Types

Nonuser	2.6%	(9)
Reactive user	43.8	(153)
Instrumental user	27.0	(93)
Total user	26.7	(91)
Totals	100.0	(346)

It also seems reasonable to expect that the nature of the computer package affects each staff professional's type of computing use. For example, we assume more active end users where there is a more extensive computer package, which might increase the likelihood that data needed by staff professionals will be in the organization's automated systems, and where there is more sophisticated computing, which might increase the likelihood that the staff professionals will have greater capacity to manipulate available data to meet their perceived information needs. Computing utilization might be further facilitated by greater resource support for computing, decentralization of computing, and routinization of computing.

Finally, the organizational environment might influence the use of computing by staff professionals. A larger scale service environment and more complex government environment might increase the need for quantitative and symbolic representations of both the urban milieu and the governmental system by means of computerized data and models which aid analysis and decision making. In the more professionalized governments, there might be greater demand for and use of computing, since its analytic capabilities might simplify and order the complexity of the environment with which the staff professionals deal.

To assess whether any of these expectations are correct, we employ the twelve variables representing the context of computing use in a discriminant analysis,[3] because we want to understand what distinguishes or discriminates between the various types of end users— in this case, between the total user, the instrumental user, and the reactive user. In particular, we want to determine: (a) whether the different end user types are associated with specific roles; (b) whether the end-user types are empirically distinguished in terms of the context of computing use; and (c) which (if any) contextual variables best discriminate between these types of computing users.

FINDINGS

Specific Roles of Staff Professionals within Each End-User Type. Table 4.2 classifies staff professionals by role and by our type-of-end-user taxonomy. The specific role of the staff professional does seem to be associated with end-user type. In general, the reactive users are mainly comprised of administrative aides and the planning staff. The instrumental users are comprised of manpower allocation analysts and accountants. And the total users are primarily manpower allocation analysts, central budget analysts, and data-base custodians.

The data needs of staff professionals are likely to vary depending upon their task-specific environment. It is possible that most data needs of some staff professionals cannot be met by computer-based systems because the required data are not in the automated systems of the organization and they cannot reasonably be put there. This might help account for the fact that fully three-fifths of the administrative aides to the mayor, council, or chief administrative officer are reactive users. Our case study work has shown that, generally, there are few if any computer applications in local government that directly serve these aides. Usually, they must attempt to adapt the data in some operating system or general database of the government to their purposes. While they might engage in specialized data collection to meet their information needs, their perceived or imposed time frame for producing results is often too short to encourage such special collection.

Table 4.2.   Breakdown of Staff Professionals by End-User Types

Task	Nonuser	Reactive User	Instrumental User	Total User	(N)
Administrative Aides					
Mayor staff	6%	65%	18%	12%	(34)
Council staff		75	25		(8)
CAO staff		57	28	15	(53)
Central Staff					
Planning staff		80	20		(15)
Central					
budget analyst	5	39	22	34	(64)
Data-base					
custodians	5	38	17	40	(65)
Department Staff					
Accountants	1	38	41	20	(71)
Manpower					
allocation					
analysts		17	36	47	(36)
Totals (N)	(9)	(154)	(95)	(94)	(352)

Thus some data needs of such staff professionals as administrative assistants to the chief executive are too ad hoc or too dynamic to be economically maintained in automated systems. Moreover, other data might be too judgmental or subtle to be automated, involving selective tapping of the knowledge and experience of peer professionals which are then brought to bear on the local problem. While there are current efforts to develop computer-based systems for tapping expert opinion (e.g., the PTI network of science advisers; the LOGIN computer network by Control Data Corporation), these are not generally available to staff professionals in local governments. All these features of the data needs of policy-oriented aides (and perhaps of policy-oriented planners as well) might provide a partial explanation for why these role types have not yet become extensive users of computing.

Whereas administrative aides are predominantly reactive users, the central budget analysts and data base custodians exhibit an interesting split, between reactive users and total users. These role-types, who are frequently found in central staff agencies, tend to be more directly served by computing. For example, many budget analysts have access to computerized current balance reports which enable them to track spending patterns for the departments they monitor. Similarly, data-base custodians usually have access to computer files on many characteristics of the organization's environment (in the case of local government, these data might measure aspects of the citizens' demography, housing stock, employment, transportation, business, and industry, and even public opinion data.) Given these data and the relatively straightforward information-processing tasks these roles typically undertake, the substantial number of total users are more easily accounted for than the equal number of reactive users.

The remaining two roles in table 4.2 are also split between our types of computer users, but each is split differently. Accountants are divided between reactive users and instrumental users, with about two-fifths in each category. Manpower allocation analysts are divided between instrumental users and total users, again with about two-fifths in each category. The data needs and information processing tasks of accountants seem comparable to those of central budget analysts, yet there are few total users. And the manpower allocation analysts seem similar to problem-solving aides, yet there are many total users. Can the context of computing use help classify these patterns by distinguishing between end user types?

Contextual Elements That Characterize Each Type of Staff Professional Computer User. Table 4.3 shows that when staff professionals are categorized according to our taxonomy of end-user types, they are indeed distinguished from one another on the thirteen variables representing the context of computing. In particular, the total user is clearly distinguished from the instrumental and reactive user. Approximately 30 percent of the variance between total users and both instrumental and reactive users is explained by these variables. The instrumental user is less distinct from the reactive user, however, with only 10 percent of the variance explained.

Table 4.4 shows the specific contextual variables that distinguish between the three end user types among staff professionals.[4] The total user is clearly distinguished from other end-user types by individual characteristics—he/she tends to be a member of a professional work group, has a positive evaluation of computer staff, has personal competency with computing, and is older. The total user operates in a work environment where the computer package has become a routine part of work life, is decentralized to end users, and is extensive. Finally, the total user operates in a complex, professionalized organizational environment and a large-scale service

Table 4.3. Discriminant Analysis of Staff Professionals by End-User Types

	Total User			Instrumental User		Reactive User
	Instrumental user	*Reactive user*	*All*	*Reactive user*	*All*	*All*
Canonical correlation	.52	.55	.45	.32	.27	.37
Total explained variance (R^2)	27%	30	20	10	7	14
Percent cases correct	75%	74	70	62	62	64
Wilks lambda*	.728	.697	.801	.901	.926	.861

* Significant at < .001.

environment. Thus only two of the thirteen contextual variables are not significantly associated with the total user (greater resource support and, interestingly, greater sophistication of the computer package) and only one key variable is associated with the total user in a possibly counter-intuitive way (total users are older rather than younger staff professionals). In short, there is compelling evidence that *the total user emerges in a context of computing that is most fully supportive of extensive end-user computing.*

In contrast, the reactive user has minimal computer competency, has a negative evaluation of the responsiveness of computer staff, is not a member of a professional work group, and is in an organization with few computer applications and brief experience with computing. The instrumental user can be characterized between the two extreme types of computer users. The instrumental user is a

Table 4.4.   Characteristics Typifying Staff Professionals in Each End-User Type

Reactive User	*Instrumental User*	*Total User*
Organizational Environment		
	Smaller scale service environment	Larger scale service environment
	Less complex government environment	Complex government environment
	Professionally oriented government	Professionally oriented government
Computer Package		
Less routinized computing		More routinized computing
	Less sophisticated computing	
Less extensive computing		More extensive computing
		Decentralized
User Characteristics		
Negative orientation toward computing staff		Positive orientation toward computing staff
Lower user competency with computing		Higher user competency with computing
Lower user professionalism	Higher user professionalism	Higher user professionalism
	Younger	Older

NOTE: Based on the standardized canonical coefficient.

member of a professional work group, is younger, is in an organization that lacks sophisticated computing, and operates in an organizational environment that is smaller scale, less complex, and more professionalized.

Variables That Best Discriminate Between Types of Professional Staff Computer Users. There are six key variables in the context of use that distinguish between the three types of computer use among staff professionals (based on discriminant function analyses for each pairing of end-user types). Four of these are characteristics of the user: his/her professionalism, age, orientation toward computing staff, and competency with computing. One of these variables is a feature of the computer package, the routinization of computing within the organization. The last variable is a feature of the environment, the scale of the organization's service environment. Using these six variables, we can describe the major differences between each paired comparison of end-use types among staff professionals. These differences are illustrated schematically in table 4.5.

The total user is distinguished from both the instrumental user and the reactive user on four of the six variables. The total user has the most positive appraisal of the responsiveness of computing staff, has the highest level of computer competency, works in the most routinized computing environment, and deals with the largest scale service environment. In addition, the total user, along with the

Table 4.5. Discrimination Across Pairs of Staff Professional End-User Types

User's orientation toward computing staff	Total user > instrumental user > reactive user[a]
User competency with computing	Total user > instrumental user > reactive user
Scale of the service environment	Total user > reactive user > instrumental user
Routinization of computing	Total user > instrumental and reactive user
User's professionalism	Total and instrumental user > reactive user
User's age	Total and reactive user > instrumental user

[a] This notation (>) means that there are significant differences: the total user feels more positively oriented toward computing than the instrumental user who is more positive than the reactive user.

instrumental user, is the most professionally oriented and, along with the reactive user, is older.

There are three variables that distinguish the reactive user from other end users. In general, the reactive user is the least professionally oriented, has the most negative appraisal of computing staff, and has the least computer competency. Finally, the instrumental user is youngest, works in the least complex service environment and, along with the reactive user, works in the least routinized computing environment.

To further simplify the analytic distinctions, we performed a three-type discriminant function analysis, which specified two key elements that significantly distinguish among the three end-user types (table 4.6). The first factor, which we call the user's "computing experience" is comprised mainly of two variables: orientation toward computing staff and competency with computing. The second factor is the user's age, and we term it the user's "work experience." What is most significant about this analysis is that both factors tap characteristics of the users, rather than features of the technology or the organizational environment. Thus it appears that *the type of computer use among individual staff professionals is more powerfully influenced by the professionals' own characteristics than by the technological or organizational environments within which they work.*

When compared on these two dimensions, it is clear that the total user is characterized as having moderate work experience and the most positive computing experience (figure 4.1). It seems that the total user is one who has more or less grown up with computing in his/her work environment, has achieved computer competency in that environment, and has experienced positive working relation-

Table 4.6. Tri-Type Discriminant Function Analysis

Function 1: "Computing experience"		Function 2: "Work experience"	
User's orientation		User's age	.51
toward computing staff	.61		
User computer competency	.56		
Total variance explained	25%		7%
Percent cases correct	55%		55%
Wilks' lambda	.701***		.933***

*** Level of significance < .001.

ships with computing. In contrast, the reactive user has the most extensive work experience and the most negative computing experience. The reactive user probably had well-established work routines prior to the growth of computing, has developed little competency with computing, and has not developed constructive relations with computing staff. The instrumental user tends to have the most limited work experience although professionally oriented, and is "in the middle" regarding sense of computing competency and evaluation of the computing staff. It is possible that the "model" instrumental user will evolve toward the total user over time, increasing (naturally) in work experience and (developmentally) in experience with computing.

CONCLUDING OBSERVATIONS

Many staff professionals in large service sector organizations are yet not extensive computer users. In our study, only one in four fits the conventional image of the hands-on, frequent user of computers

Figure 4.1. Mapping of End-User Types Among Staff Professionals on Discriminant Functions

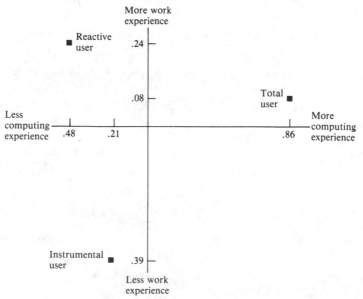

and computer-based information. In contrast nearly one-half of the staff professionals fit the opposite image—that of passive users of computing who occasionally receive computer-based data or reports based on such data. These reactive users are spread across the staff professional roles, although their incidence is highest among the administrative aide and central staff roles (table 4.7). Similarly, the total users tend to cluster in the central staff roles of data-base custodian and central budget analyst. And the instrumental users tend to cluster in the department staff roles of accountant and manpower allocation analyst.

While there are interesting role clusterings among the staff professionals, the differences among staff professionals as end users are not simply due to differences in the task-specific nature of their roles. That is, although some roles such as administrative aides are mainly clustered in one end-user type, other roles exhibit a major division between two major types of computer user. The most interesting split is that between those data-base custodians and central budget analysts who are reactive users and those who are total users. What

Table 4.7. Summary Comparison of Staff Professionals, by End-User Types and Staff Roles

	End-User Style		
Role	*Reactive User (14%)*	*Instrumental User (27%)*	*Total User (27%)*
Administrative aides	Mayor staff Council staff CAO staff 38%	27%	13%
Central staff	Planners Data-base custod. Central budget analysts 40%	26%	Database custod. Central budget analysts 51%
Department staff	Accountants 22%	Accountants Manpower alloca- tion analysts 47%	Manpower alloca- tion analysts 36%
	100%	100%	100%

is significant about this division is that these two homogenous subgroups of staff professionals are discriminated (in an analysis whose data are not reported) by the same variables as the overall comparisons among staff professional user types. This fact lends support to both our end-user taxonomy and our analysis of the variables that discriminate one type of staff professional from another as computer users.

The total user fits the conventional image of the staff professional as an individual using computing in a frequent, multi-modal manner. Despite the vision of a microcomputer "revolution," recent field research confirms that the charcteristic end-user pattern emerging among staff professionals is comparable to that of the total users in

Table 4.8.   Characteristics Typifying Staff Professionals in Each End-User Type (coefficients for table 4.4)

Variable	Reactive User	Instrumental User	Total User
Organizational Environment			
Scale of service environment		−.43[a]	.40
Government professionalism		.26	.25
Complexity of government		−.35	.40
Computer Package			
Extensiveness of computing	−.31		.24
Sophistication of computing		−.28	
Routinization of computing	.30		−.42
Centralization of computing			−.27
User Characteristics			
User's orientation to computing staff	−.52		.62
User competency with computing	−.65		.46
User professionalism	−.32	.27	.15
User work experience		−.52	.15

[a] Reported values are the significant standardized canonical coefficient.

our taxonomy. Large organizations, and particularly public organizations, have generally resisted the introduction of truly stand-alone systems for staff professionals. Even where such systems have been introduced, we have observed that staff professionals rarely rely upon a single system. Also, for reasons of central control of both data-bases and of the use of those data-bases, evolving computer packages in these organizations are arranged to insure that staff professionals remain linked into a more centralized computing/data-base network. Thus our analysis has emphasized the total users, since this group will become the dominant end-user type among staff professionals.

The total user has a positive orientation toward computer staff, has considerable competency with competing, and displays active professionalism. In contrast, the reactive user finds the computer staff unresponsive, lacks competency with computing, and is less professional. *The computer package of the total user is extensive and routinized,* whereas that of the reactive user is neither extensive nor routinized. Because the sophistication of the technology is the element of the computer package that is often emphasized as a key to enhancing the value of computing in the workplace, it is noteworthy that technological sophistication *never* discriminates between types of end users.

While the technology is quite important in discriminating between the total and reactive user, the critical differences between these two types of computer users seem to stem particularly from differences in the characteristics of the individual. Overall, user characteristics are both the most frequently occurring discriminant variables in the analyses and also exhibit the strongest, most consistent, and most significant relationships. The evidence here indicates that *the staff professional who most closely matches the image of an activist end user of computing tends to emerge where the computer package is well established and where the end user's sociotechnical interface is positive and reinforcing.*

5. Performance Benefits from Computing

There are symbolic reasons why an organization might adopt computer technology. The organization might adopt computing in order to symbolize its commitment to modern management practices or to advanced technology. Or it might want to indicate that its decisions and actions are guided by rational criteria rather than by political criteria. But the major rationales for utilization usually involve expectations that computing will generate real benefits in information processing and, ultimately, in individual and organizational performance. This chapter examines the extent to which the end users to our study have experienced performance benefits from computing and it also explores whether differences in the level of these benefits are related to differences in the context of computing use.

In general, we find that a large majority of end users in all four roles report effectiveness benefits from computing and that most enjoy some information benefits; but many of the individuals in each role are unconvinced that computing has generated broad efficiency benefits for their department. The overall pattern of benefits is comparable for those in all four roles, although street-level bureaucrats report somewhat greater benefits. And the context of computing use seems to influence the level of benefits most for staff professionals who, like all other roles, report the most substantial benefits from computing when they experience a positive sociotechnical interface, especially as this is manifest in the responsiveness of the computing specialists.

MEASURES AND HYPOTHESES REGARDING COMPUTING BENEFITS

Among the benefits that might be anticipated from the use of computing in organizations, those that improve the information environment are perhaps the most obvious. The extensive information-handling capabilities of computer technology are often enumerated to indicate the value of computing. We have measured these potential information benefits by gathering the assessments of end users regarding the extent to which computing has improved four aspects of their information environments: (a) the speed with which information can be obtained; (b) the ease of access to information; (c) the availability of new information; and (d) the timeliness of the information. These four aspects of computing's effect on information are combined into the *information benefits* index analyzed below.

While one can infer performance benefits from an improved information environment, the most widely predicted gains for computing have primarily involved productivity improvements. Such improvements entail an increase in the ratio of outputs to inputs in the production of a good or service. While precise and rigorous measures of the impact of computing on productivity are desirable, they have proven elusive, except on the most narrow task (Mason 1977). The people in organizations can judge from their own work experience whether computing has altered staff levels, costs, and work in their departments. Thus we employ these assessments to construct an index of *efficiency benefits* from computing, combining the extent to which computing has reduced departmental staff, has reduced the cost of departmental operations, and has enabled the department to increase its work volume without corresponding increases in cost.[1]

The recent literature of assessing organizational performance has stressed that effectiveness measures are no less important than efficiency measures. For the kinds of end users of computing in our study, a pivotal aspect of effectiveness is how well services are provided to the citizen-clients of the government. Thus our analysis of the potential benefits from computing also includes an evaluation by end users of whether computer technology has improved their department's *effectiveness* in serving the public. The nature of citizen service varies across roles, since some employees, such as police and clerks, deal directly with clients in the provision of services, while other employees primarily serve the public indirectly, through their administrative functions or through supporting service-providers.

While our organizing framework posits no systematic relationships in the data, we do expect that distinctive patterns will be evident. In the first place, we hypothesize that information benefits will be the impacts of computing most widely identified, since these are the most straightforward and direct benefits that should emerge with the utilization of computing. We also predict that these benefits will be most extensive among end users in roles with pervasive data-handling responsibilities, the desk-top bureaucrats and the staff professionals. Second, given the high costs associated with the provision of computing and the potentially ambiguous effects of computing on service sector jobs, the efficiency benefits from computing are likely to be reported by the smallest proportion of the respondents. To the extent that efficiency benefits are identified, they might be perceived most frequently by those in managerial roles, since they have an overall perspective on the functioning of their departments, and by desk-top bureaucrats, since staffing levels and cost per unit of service on their intensive, data-handling tasks seem most subject to improvement due to the use of computing. Third, the impacts of computing in relation to our service effectiveness measure are the most difficult to predict. We do anticipate that effectiveness benefits will tend to be reported by end users in each role in lower proportions than information benefits.

Among the elements in the context of use, we hypothesize that the computer package will be most strongly associated with information benefits. As computing is more extensive and routinized, there should be more substantial information benefits for users in all roles, and the sophistication of the technology might also improve the quality of information, especially for staff professionals. While the computer package might also be related to efficiency and effectiveness benefits, these are likely to be most strongly associated with the characteristics of the users, and particularly with the sociotechnical interface. End users should identify higher levels of these benefits for themselves and their departments where they deal with computer specialists who are responsive to their task needs in the provision of automated applications and where they have a stronger sense of their own competency to use computing with effectiveness and efficiency. The organizational environment might be related to any of these performance measures, but we assume it will be most strongly associated with efficiency benefits, since it is reasonable to predict that the efficiencies from computing use will be particularly evident in governments of greater complexity and service scale.

ACTUAL PATTERNS OF COMPUTING BENEFITS

Table 5.1 indicates the extent to which end users in the four roles attribute job performance benefits to computing. The key conclusion to be drawn from the table is that the use of computing has resulted in considerable benefits for most people. About three-fourths of those in each role report that computer use has resulted in effectiveness benefits in departmental service delivery, a higher incidence of this impact than we expected. And a substantial majority in every role has enjoyed information benefits from computing. While only about 6 in 10 managers and staff professionals report that computing has enhanced their information environments, this benefit is reported by 8 in 10 street-level bureaucrats and 7 in 10 desk-top bureaucrats. Of the three computing benefits measures, the smallest proportions of end users attribute efficiency benefits to computing, although even in this case the majority in every role indicates that computing has improved departmental efficiency.

According to table 5.1, the street-level bureaucrats are consistently the role in which the largest proportion of individuals report benefits from computing and the staff professionals are the role in which the largest proportions tend to indicate that they and their department have not enjoyed such benefits. A more precise analysis of the between-role differences in the distribution of job performance benefits indicates that the impacts of computing are quite comparable across roles. An examination of paired role comparisons by means of chi-square and tau statistics indicates that street-level bureaucrats

Table 5.1.   Level of Performance Benefits from Computing

	Managers (N=355)	Staff Professionals (N=195)	Street-Level Bureaucrats (N=143)	Desk-Top Bureaucrats (N=130)
Information Benefits				
Agree	25%	21%	36%	28%
Somewhat agree	39	42	46	42
Somewhat disagree	28	29	16	21
Disagree	8	8	3	9
Mean[a]	1.78	1.78	2.07	1.83
Coefficient of variation[b]	.44	.43	.34	.45
Efficiency Benefits				
Agree	18%	13%	22%	13%
Somewhat agree	40	38	40	38
Somewhat disagree	29	36	27	34
Disagree	14	13	11	14
Mean[c]	1.63	1.50	1.69	1.51
Coefficient of variation	.54	.54	.56	.56
Effectiveness Benefits				
Agree	48%	46%	53%	47%
Somewhat agree	26	29	24	26
Somewhat disagree	15	14	14	14
Disagree	12	12	9	12
Mean[d]	2.21	2.19	2.10	2.15
Coefficient of variation	.54	.59	.53	.57

[a] Mean based on index scores, with Agree=3.00–2.50; Somewhat agree=2.25–1.50; Somewhat disagree=1.25–.75; Disagree=.50–.00.
[b] Coefficient of variation is the ratio of the standard deviation to the mean (s ÷ m).
[c] Mean based on index scores, with Agree=3.00–2.67; Somewhat agree=2.33–1.67; Somewhat disagree=1.33–.67; Disagree=.33–.00.
[d] Mean based on scores, with Agree=3.0; Somewhat agree=2.0; Somewhat disagree=1.0; Disagree=0.0.

differ significantly from all three other roles regarding the extent of information benefits from computing and that they differ from staff professionals on the extent to which they identify efficiency benefits from computing. But the between-role distributions are not significantly different for any other pairings. Thus, contrary to our hypotheses, it seems that computing does not produce sharply contrasting impacts on job performance for those in the various roles.

Rather, *the application of computing to the work of end users with quite different role responsibilities in public organizations results in remarkably similar arrays of performance effects.*

EXPLAINING DIFFERENTIAL PERFORMANCE BENEFITS

Given our analytic framework, we are also interested in whether key features of the context of computing use seem to account for variations in the extent to which end users experience computing impacts on job performance. Table 5.2 reveals that the context of use has modest explanatory power for the between-person variations in these impacts with R^2 values in the 10 to 20 percent range.

Staff professionals, the role whose members are least likely to attribute performance benefits to computing, are also the role whose members are most responsive to the context of computing use, especially on efficiency and information benefits. When assessed as competing explanations, user characteristics are the most adequate explanatory element in nine of the twelve cases, including all three types of computing benefits for managers and staff professionals. In the other three cases, the key contextual element is the computer package—for information and efficiency benefits among desk-top bureaucrats and for efficiency benefits among street-level bureaucrats.

In some cases, an alternative explanations approach, incorporating all aspects of the context of computing use, provides a fuller explanation of variation in the impacts of computing on job performance benefits. This is quite clear for both "bureaucratic" roles, where either the organizational environment or the computer package add significantly to an explanation of variation based on user characteristics. However, for the managers and the staff professionals, it is generally the case that virtually all (between 98 percent and 72 percent) of the total explanatory power is due only to the user characteristics.

Table 5.3 enables us to identify the particular variables in the context of computing use that are most important in accounting for differences in the benefits of computing. For both managers and staff professionals, the crucial user characteristics are those measuring the user's sociotechnical interface, particularly his/her orientation to the computing staff. For managers, the user's sense of computing com-

Table 5.2. Explanatory Power of Context of Use for Computing Benefits, by Role

	Managers	Staff Professionals	Street-Level Bureaucrats	Desk-Top Bureaucrats
Competing Explanations				
Percent of within-role variation in use explained by:				
Organizational environment				
information	0	3	1	1
efficiency	2	2	1	4
effectiveness	0	3	3	1
Computer package				
information	2	0	2	5
efficiency	3	7**	10*	5
effectiveness	1	2	6	8
User characteristics				
information	12***	18***	7**	3
efficiency	7***	17***	7*	4
effectiveness	9***	14***	9*	10**
Alternative Explanations				
All contextual elements combined:				
information	13***	21***	8*	n.s.
efficiency	10***	22***	15***	12**
effectiveness	9***	14***	7*	14***
Percent of total accounted for by:				
Organizational environment				
information	3	15	16	n.s.
efficiency	16	11	8	39
effectiveness	2	14	42	10
Computer package				
information	8	0	0	n.s.
efficiency	13	14	59	30
effectiveness	0	0	0	25
User characteristics				
information	89	85	83	n.s.
efficiency	72	74	33	30
effectiveness	98	86	58	65

* $< .05$
** $< .01$
*** $< .001$

petency is also quite important. As we hypothesized, greater benefits from computing are consistently linked with a positive orientation to computing staff and to the end user's computing competency.

While the computer package is not always a significant explanatory element, its effects present a most interesting pattern. More decentralized computing is associated with higher levels of benefits in two instances. But the most intriguing data reveal that, for every role, a computer package that is more *modest* in scale or sophistication is associated with greater efficiency benefits from computing. This is clearly contrary to the conventional wisdom, which holds that more extensive and sophisticated computing will generate greater benefits in job performance for the large majority of people in most white collar roles. As we shall see below in chapter 7, fewer problems with computing, as well as greater benefits, are quite consistently linked with a more modest and routinized computer package. Such findings are a provocative challenge both to the notion that "more is better" and to the view that shortcomings can be alleviated by a "technological fix." At least, end users seem as sensitive to the high costs of computing as they are to its benefits.

In general, we can infer from table 5.3 that greater benefits from computing are particularly associated with a context of use in which the user has a very favorable sociotechnical interface with computing. These users characteristics dominate the impact of the context of use for those in roles with the greatest discretion. Among those in roles with less discretion, both roles we term "bureaucratic," the computer package and/or the organizational environment also tend to have a significant effect on the impact of computing on a person's job performance. Thus the technology and the environment seem to have the greatest effect on job performance benefits among those who are likely to have least choice about whether to use computing and how it will be integrated into their work life.

It will be more possible to suggest why greater benefits are associated with a more modest computer package when we also have examined the relationship between the context of use and the problems that people have with computing. One might argue that as the computer package becomes more extensive and sophisticated, there is a substantial rise in the cost of computing services and, as a consequence, the efficiency benefits from computing become more

Table 5.3. Key Contextual Variables for Performance Benefits, Attributed to Computing, by Role

Element of Context of Use	Managers	Staff Professionals	Street-Level Bureaucrats	Desk-Top Bureaucrats
Information Benefits				
Organizational environment	+Government complexity (.10)*a	+Government professionalism (.17)**		n.s.
Computer package	Less computing expenditure (−.10)*			
User characteristics	+User orientation to computing staff (.23)*** +User computing competency (.21)*** Less user professionalism (−.11)*	+User orientation to computing staff (.35)*** +User computing competency (.19)*** Less user professionalism (−.13)**	+User orientation to computing staff (.27)***	
Efficiency Benefits				
Organizational environment	Less government professionalism (−.10)*		+Government complexity (.22)***	+Government complexity (.20)***
Computer package	Less sophisticated computing (−.12)**	Less extensive computing (−.22)***	Less extensive computing (−.33)*** Decentralized computing (−.30)***	Less computing expenditure (−.19)***
User characteristics	+User orientation to computing staff (.18)***	+User orientation to computing staff (.37)***	+User orientation to computing staff (.20)***	

Table 5.3. (continued)

Element of Context of Use	Managers	Staff Professionals	Street-Level Bureaucrats	Desk-Top Bureaucrats
	+User computing competency (.16)**	Younger user (−.21)**		Younger user (.20)***
Effectiveness Benefits				
Organizational environment				
Computer package				Decentralized computing (−.29)***
User characteristics	+User orientation to computing staff (.22)*** User computing competency (.19)***	+User orientation to computing staff (.35)***	+User orientation to computing staff (.21)***	+User orientation to computing staff (.25)*** Younger user (−.20)***

[a] Standardized betas from regression equation are in parentheses, with statistical significance based on the T statistic:

* $p < .05$
** $p < .01$
*** $p < .001$

ambiguous. In a related manner, it might be that a more complex computer package is no longer directed so explicitly to the kinds of basic automated applications where the most obvious and demonstrable benefits on job performance are located. Minimally, there is no evidence here to support the view that a highly developed computer package will necessarily, or even usually, generate greater benefits for the job performance of users, whether managers or clerks.

CONCLUDING OBSERVATIONS

Table 5.4 summarizes the relationships between our hypotheses and the empirical findings presented in this chapter. On balance, there are as many instances which confound our expectations as ones which conform to them. First, as we have hypothesized, *efficiency benefits attributed to computing are the least extensive impacts reported by end users in all four roles.* But information benefits due to computing are less widely enjoyed than are broad improvements in the delivery of service to the clients of the government. Second, although we hypothesized notable differences between roles in the level of performance benefits, *only the street-level bureaucrats differ significantly from any other role in the extent to which performance impacts on work emerged,* with the street-level bureaucrats reporting efficiency and information benefits at higher levels than one or two other roles. Ironically, these were types of performance impacts where we assumed that other roles would have greater benefits, and only on service effectiveness, where we did posit relatively greater benefits for street-level bureaucrats, was that role not differentiated from other roles.

Third, *the organizational environment is a less important aspect of the context of computing use than we had expected.* It seems particularly surprising that the size of the information and service environment, measured both as government complexity and as scale of service, has virtually no systematic relationship to the level of computing impacts on information benefits, efficiency, or service effectiveness. Fourth, *there are fewer instances than we hypothesized where the nature of the computer package has a substantial effect on job performance benefits.* The computer package is most significant for those whose work allows relatively less discretion and, contrary

Table 5.4. Comparison of Expected and Actual Benefits from Computing

Expected	Actual
Overall	
Information benefits > effectiveness benefits > efficiency benefits	Effectiveness benefits > information benefits > efficiency benefits
Information Benefits	
Desk-top bureaucrats and staff professionals > managers and street-level bureaucrats	Street-level bureaucrats > desk-top bureaucrats, managers and staff professionals
Within-role differences most strongly associated with:	Within-role differences most strongly associated with:
—computer package, especially with extensiveness and routinization of computing	—user characteristics, especially with positive STI
	—computer package, only for desk-top bureaucrats
Efficiency Benefits	
Managers and desk-top bureaucrats > street-level bureaucrats and staff professionals	Street-level bureaucrats > staff professionals, only significant between-role difference
Within-role differences most strongly associated with:	Within-role differences most strongly associated with:
—user characteristics, especially with positive STI	—user characteristics for managers and staff professionals, especially positive STI
—organizational environment, especially with larger scale and scope of governments' environment	—computer package for street-level bureaucrats and desk-top bureaucrats, especially less extensive, more decentralized computing

Table 5.4. (continued)

Expected		Actual
	Effectiveness Benefits	
Street-level bureaucrats > managers, desk-top bureaucrats, staff professionals		No significant between-role differences in benefits levels
Within-role differences most strongly associated with:		As expected
—user characteristics, especially with positive STI		

to our assumption, *greater* benefits are associated with a *less* developed computer package and are unrelated to the routinization of the technology. And finally, we were correct in positing that *the characteristics of the individuals end user, and especially the quality of the sociotechnical interface, are substantially linked with the level of performance benefits that the particular user experiences.* In fact, the relationship between perceived benefits and the responsiveness of computing staff is exceptionally strong, in comparison to that for the other aspects of the context of use. The nature of the end user's STI is systematically related to the presence or absence of performance benefits from computing.

It is clear that the end users in our analysis are not uniformly impressed with the efficiency benefits from computing. A large minority in every role indicated that computing has not resulted in cost and staff savings, and nearly half of the staff professionals and desk-top bureaucrats hold this view. For the staff professionals, one might argue that their work "outputs" are not subject to quantification and thus it is difficult to gauge how the productivity of those outputs might have been altered by computing. And managers might be more sensitive than most to the relatively high costs of computing, as well as to its cost efficiencies. But it is particularly difficult to explain why desk-top bureaucrats would not identify efficiencies due to computing, since their activities seem the type that are especially well-suited for the kinds of staff reductions and cost savings per unit of work output for which computing is widely touted.

It is interesting that those desk-top bureaucrats who do attribute efficiencies to computing tend to be in contexts of use characterized by more modest computer packages. When an organization develops its computing applications, it typically begins with those information processing tasks that are straghtfroward and cost-efficient. But the continual expansion of computing increasingly results in the automation of information processing tasks for which the direct efficiency-based benefits are less and less clear. And even the simple applications are redesigned to provide more sophisticated and complex capabilities (e.g., additional data, supplementary tasks) on which cost-benefit ratios are less favorable. The clearest support for this dynamic between net benefits and development in the computer package is found in the fact that, *for each role, the significant relationship between greater efficiency and an aspect of the computer package is with a variable that reflects less sophisticated or less extensive computing.*

Indeed, this expansion dynamic might explain why the effectiveness benefits are the most frequently identified benefits in the analysis. While computing might be a costly enterprise, in terms of both the computer package itself and also the new work demands that it places upon end users, it does seem to generate a steady overall increase in the level and quality of operational activities and service provision in most instances. Thus about three-fourths of the end users in every role recognize effectiveness benefits generated by computing. Despite their quite different needs from and uses of the technology, all roles report effectiveness benefits at about the same level. Moreover, this broad indicator of the benefits of computing in the provisions of services to citizen-clients is most strongly linked with the quality of the user's sociotechnical interface. Effectiveness benefits are higher when the end user finds that the computer staff are concerned about and responsive to the user's needs, the most significant explanatory variable in the context of computing use for every role. For those in roles with the least discretion in their work, not only the STI but also the nature of the computer package and the organizational environment are systematically linked with the level of job benefits attributed to computing.

In sum, these data suggest a population of end users who are neither universally enthusiastic nor utterly skeptical about the benefits of computing for their job performance. There is general recognition that computing has enhanced their capacity to serve the citizens who are their clients and that this effectiveness benefit is directly related to the responsiveness of computing specialists to their task needs. But many are unconvinced that the current cost-benefit balance sheet from the application of computing is clearly positive. A large minority of users do not attribute net cost and staff efficiency to the impacts of computing on their department's operations. And nearly one in four managers and staff professionals are not even convinced that they have enjoyed the most straightforward contribution of computing to job performance—significant information benefits.

Among the information worker roles we have examined, street-level bureaucrats consistently report the greatest benefits in job performance from computing and the staff professionals report the lowest levels of benefits. Since the future economic viability of postindustrial society is often linked explicitly to the productivity benefits generated by computing, it seems particularly important to examine the conditions under which such benefits are most likely to occur. As a consequence, the next chapter offers a detailed analysis of the effects of computing on the productivity of detectives—the street-level bureaucrats in our analysis who report the most substantial computing benefits and who share relevant job performance characteristics with many other information workers.

6. Police Detectives and Computers: Productivity Impacts

The promise of productivity improvements has always been high in the litany of benefits predicted for computer use in government. Particular attention has usually focused on increased productivity at the clerical levels, where the "brawny" capabilities of computing are applied by means of large-scale and repetitive data processing and office automation (see chapter 8). Substantial promise has also been associated with managerial utilization of computing, where its more "brainy" capabilities are employed in various types of decision support systems (see chapter 10).

There has been greater uncertainty about the effects of computing on the productivity of those professional workers at intermediate levels in the organizational hierarchy. Thus it is particularly interesting that the empirical evidence in chapter 5 revealed that some of the professionals in our sample, the staff professionals, report relatively low levels of job performance benefits due to computing, while other professionals, the street-level bureaucrats, report the highest benefits. Since professionals are widespread in all service industries, both public and private, it is important to assess the conditions under which computing does seem to have made an important contribution to job performance.

Hence in this chapter we undertake a careful, empirical assessment of the effects of computing on the performance of one major subset of the street-level bureaucrats, police detectives. In particular, we analyze the detectives' level of computing use, the productivity effects of computing on criminal investigation activities, and the importance of the context of computing use on the individual-level effects of computing.

Professionals operate in an information-rich environment where there are substantial data that might be relevant and where decisions and actions must be based on an appraisal of the best available data. The processing of information is so central to the work of some professionals, such as planners, stock brokers, accountants, and journalists, that the work seems well-suited to productivity gains from computing. But for many other professionals information processing is a more peripheral support task as the professional provides direct service to clients. Therefore, such professionals as lawyers, social workers, insurance agents, probation officers, health officers, and police detectives have seemed less likely candidates for striking productivity gains from computing.

Yet the problems facing service-providing professionals are not unlike those facing managers and others for whom computerized systems are relevant: (a) the existence of a data base so large that the individual has difficulty accessing and making conceptual use of it; (b) the necessity of manipulation or computation in the process of deriving useful information; (c) the existence of some time pressure, either for the final answer or for the process by which the decision is reached; (d) the necessity of judgment, either to recognize or decide what constitutes the problem or to choose a solution; and (e) the need to facilitate responses to families of problems that are frequent and require direct action as well as decision (Keen 1980:23–44).

Police detectives are an interesting case study of the impacts of computer-based systems for several reasons. First, detective work is information intensive in theory and practice; yet detectives are among those service-providing professionals for whom productivity gains from computer technology have seemed less likely. Second, the predominance of highly discretionary field work involving multiple sources and modes of information places detectives low, even among the "street-level" professionals, in the presumed centrality of a computerized system to work. Third, however, police detectives have been supported by some of the most extensive and decentralized computer-based aids available to any professionals in the public sector. This has been the result of both the general automation of law enforcement records and also the provision of specific systems tailored to their investigative tasks. And fourth, detectives seem an illuminating precursor of what other case-oriented professionals, both within and outside government, will experience with the extension of computing and especially with the rapid spread of microcomputers that enable individual workers to communicate with large organizational data bases. Thus, in the final section of this chapter detectives' uses and experiences with computing are the basis of a general characterization of computer-based systems for professionals.

COMPUTERS IN DETECTIVE WORK

Most people have a broad understanding of the nature of police detective work, because the detective is among the professions most widely portrayed in contemporary American media. In some of these characterizations (e.g., Colombo, Joe Friday, Cagney and Lacey) detectives undertake slow, plodding searches for rather mundane types of information; in others (e.g., Baretta, Belker, Kojak) the detectives seem constantly involved in dramatic undercover work full of excitement and violence. In reality, the former description is representative of most police detectives, most of the time, although there are a few of the latter type of detectives in many departments. While the work styles of detectives vary, all undertake the same basic tasks:

After a preliminary investigation and report has been completed by patrol officers, the detective: (1) gathers additional information and evidence to establish the facts of a crime and identify the suspects; (2) attempts to arrest the suspects if criminal prosecution is warranted and feasible; (3) attempts to connect the suspects with other crimes; and (4) helps the prosecutor prepare the case for prosecution. (ICMA: 1982)

The centrality of information to these tasks is clear. The essence of detective work is the gathering and manipulation of information, whose many sources include personal knowledge, networks of informants, interviews, and existing organizational files. Among the organizational files that might be available to a detective, in either a manual or computerized mode, are ones that contain: detailed descriptions of potential suspects (e.g., physical characteristics, last known address, criminal history, and so on); alias names; M.O. (modus operandi); inventories of pawned and/or stolen property (including serial numbers); characteristics of uncleared cases; and lists of warrants outstanding at local, state, national, and international law enforcement agencies (see Kraemer, Dutton, and Northrop 1981: ch. 5).

Given the extent and variety of information processing in detective work, it is clear that the computer might be a valuable tool to detectives because of its potential to store, retrieve, and combine organizational data at levels of comprehensiveness, speed, and sophistication that far surpass human processing of manual files and even surpass human cognitive processing capacity. One can imagine how a detective might make use of a range of investigative support information that is computerized. For example, the detective might use a computer terminal to get a copy of the preliminary incident report containing the key facts regarding a case, then begin to "play" with the information in the automated files by checking for a similar M.O., or by identifying an individual or automobile from any features noted by witnesses (such as a physical description of a suspect or a partial auto license number), or by checking recently pawned property, or by determining the most recent address of someone the detective might wish to interview. Clearly, the detective's decision to use such automated information systems would depend on a variety of circumstances, including the quality of the data-bases, the ease of access to the system, the detective's own inclination to use the system, the department's standard operating procedures, and so on.

CONCEPTUALIZATION AND HYPOTHESIZED RELATIONSHIPS

The central focus of this chapter is to assess how the computer package has affected the productivity of individual detectives in their work.[1] We treat the concept of productivity broadly here, to reflect an improvement in job performance that involves effectiveness more than efficiency. The performance standards we use to tap detective work center in individual-level impacts of computing on available information and on the number of workable cases, arrests, and clearances. We use detectives' own assessments of the effects of computing on their job performance as indicators of these performance standards.[2]

We view the linkage between computing and the individual detective's productivity at two levels. The first is a straightforward link between the *extent of computer use* by individual detectives and productivity shifts. We expect that detectives' productivity will be greater with higher levels of computer use. The second linkage is rather more complex, involving the *effects of the context of computer use* on productivity. The *organizational environment* is the broadest context within which the detective uses computing. The government's greater size and complexity, the increased scale of the service environment, and a higher level of professional practice in the government all might be linked to increased detective productivity due to computing. The *nature of the computer package* available to the detective is perhaps the most obvious contextual element that might affect the relationship between computing and the detectives' productivity. We posit that as the technology is more extensive, more sophisticated, more decentralized, and more routinized, productivity gains attributable to that computer package will increase. Finally, among the *characteristics of the individual* detective, greater computing benefits might be enjoyed by those who are younger and more professionally oriented, and thus more likely to utilize an innovative technology. We also hypothesize that productivity improvements attributed to computing will increase as the user's sociotechnical interface with computing is more positive.

We ask four questions regarding detectives and computing: (1) To what extent do detectives use computers in their work?; (2) Do the detectives attribute productivity shifts in their own work to the utilization of computers?; (3) Are there systematic associations between detectives' level of computer use and measures of the "output" from the detectives' work?; and (4) Can we account for between-detective differences in the impact of computing on detectives' productivity by features of their organizational environment, of the computer package available to them, or of their personal traits? Of the total sample in the data base, this chapter examines the 374 detectives who provided information regarding their use of the computer or of computer-based information.

We assess the first two questions by tabular analyses of the responses of the detectives to specific queries regarding the utilization of computing in their work and regarding objective measures of the impacts of computing on their productivity. We assess the third question using Pearson's correlation coefficient, in order to examine whether there is a strong relationship between the individual detective's level of utilization of computing and the kinds of productivity shifts that the detective experiences. Finally, we analyze whether there are systematic relationships between productivity shifts and important features of the context of use of computing.

FINDINGS

Detectives' Use of Computers. Clearly, the availability of computerized information is a necessary condition for its utilization by detectives. There has been a strong and continuing effort by federal, state, and local government agencies to support the development of police information systems (Colton 1978; Laudon 1974). While few detectives have access to every type of automated police file, the 40 police departments in this study had computer access (batch or online) to an average of 6.2 of the 14 major police investigation data files that are automated, and detectives in every department in the study had access at least to state and national computerized data banks on outstanding warrants, criminal histories, and drivers' license and motor vehicle registration.[3] These detectives do make quite substantial use of such computer files in their work (table 6.1). About 2 out of 5 detectives report that they use computer files for *all* of their active cases, and almost two-thirds of the detectives use computers in the majority of their cases. While some do not use the technology, the "average" detective uses computing on about 60 percent of his/her cases.

Table 6.1.   Utilization of Computing by Detectives

Number of last ten active cases where computer used:	Percentage of detectives
0	20
1–4	17
5–9	24
10	39
	100
The "average" detective was assisted by the computer on	5.94 of every 10 cases

NOTE: 374 detectives in 40 municipalities.

Productivity Shifts from Computer Use. Two categories of productivity improvement can be assessed: (a) improvements in the information available to detectives; and (b) improvement in specific measures of each detective's workable cases, arrests, and clearances.

It is typically assumed that if the performance of professional workers will be higher if their information is of higher quality, greater quantity, easier accessibility, and richer manipulability. Thus, for those as information-dependent as detectives, a significant improvement in the information environment due to computing could be viewed as an indirect productivity gain. Our measure of information improvements (table 6.2) is an index combining four aspects of the benefits that computing might provide: new information, more up-to-date information, increased speed in obtaining information, and ease of access to information. More than 80 percent of the detectives have experienced these information benefits from computing, with strong confirmation of these benefits reported by about 30 percent of the detectives. It is clear, then, that a large majority of the detectives have enjoyed the kinds of improvements in their information-handling environments that are among the most fundamental benefits expected from computer technology.

Table 6.3 displays our more direct indicators of the effects of computing on detectives' productivity. More than 1 in 3 detectives reports that some cases would have been unworkable (that is, cases where further investigation after the initial case report would not have been possible) were it not for the use of computing. About half of the detectives used the computer to link persons in custody to uncleared cases. And nearly two-thirds of the detectives indicated

Table 6.2. Information Benefits Attributed to Computing by Detectives

Incidence of information improvements from computing[a]	Percentage of detectives
Nearly always	29
Frequently	51
Sometimes	16
Almost never	4
	100

NOTE: 374 detectives from 40 municipalities.

[a] This indicator is an index combining and averaging the detective's responses to four questions: (1) The computer makes new information available to me which was not previously available; (2) The computer provides me with more up-to-date information than that available in manual files; (3) Computers have made it easier for me to get the information I need; (4) Computers save me time in looking for information. The values of responses of each question were: Nearly always = 3; Frequently = 2; Sometimes = 1; Almost never = 0. In the table, the ranges on the index are: Nearly always = 3.00 − 2.50; Frequently = 2.25 − 1.50; Sometimes = 1.25 − .75; Almost never − .50 − 0.0.

that the computer assisted them in some of their arrests and clearances. (Although not shown in the table, this benefit of computing occurred in the majority of instances, i.e., between 5 to 10 cases, for 41 percent of the detectives on clearances and 34 percent on arrests.) From a different angle, computing assisted the "average" detective on two-fifths of his/her clearances and one-third of the arrests, helped the detective link 1 in 4 in-custody suspects to uncleared cases, and saved 1 in every 5 cases from being totally unworkable. While some detectives report minimal effects of computing on their productivity, the most reasonable conclusion from these data is that *detectives have experienced major and positive productivity shifts that are attributed to computer technology.*

Extent of Computer Use and Productivity. While our foregoing analysis clearly indicates that computing has enhanced the performance of detectives as a group of professional workers, it also indicates that the computer revolution has not touched all the detectives in our sample of police departments; nor has it touched the detectives evenly. Table 6.4 displays the (Pearson's R) correlation coefficients between the level of utilization of computing, measured as the number of the last ten actively investigated cases on which computing was used, and the various measures of detective perfor-

Table 6.3.   Detectives' Individual Performance Benefits From Computing

Percent of detectives reporting that, on some of their last 10 cases, the computer assisted in:

Making the cases workable	*Arrests*	*Clearances*	*Linkages between persons in custody and uncleared cases*
37%	64%	66%	45%

On the last 10 cases, the "average" detective was assisted by the computer on:

1.8 otherwise un- workable cases	3.6 arrests	4.1 clearances	2.6 in custody linkages

NOTE: 374 detectives in 40 municipalities.

Table 6.4.   Relationship Between Detectives' Utilization of Computing, Information Benefits, and Performance Measures

	Pearson's r with:	
	Number of last 10 active cases where computing used	*Information benefits from computing*
Cases unworkable without computing	.34***	.34***
Arrests where computing assisted	.50***	.36***
Clearances where computing assisted	.56***	.41***
Linkages of those in custody to uncleared cases	.39***	.33***
Information benefits from computing	.36***	

NOTE: 374 detectives in 40 municipalities.
*** = p < .001

mance. There is a highly significant (in statistical terms) relationship between level of computer use and the effects of computing on *every* measure of the detective's productivity related to information benefits, arrests, clearances, and number of workable cases. The linkages are exceptionally strong between computer utilization and the frequency with which computing assists on clearances and arrests.

   At first glance, table 6.4 seems merely to confirm the interesting but unsurprising expectation that detectives who make more extensive use of computing enjoy substantially higher productivity gains from the technology than those who do not. From a slightly different perspective, the data yield a more intriguing point. A detective has a choice regarding the use of computing on each case he/she is assigned. Either the detective can use the computer selectively on those cases where he/she decides there is a reasonable chance that some useful information can be derived or the detective can use computing on virtually every case in the hope that a "hit" may occur. While use of a computer-based decision support system is usually depicted as selective, *it is actually the detective who routinely "goes prospecting" on every case who reaps great benefits from the technology than the selective user.* Table 6.4 also provides support for the inference that improvements in the information environment caused by computing are strongly linked with more direct job performance benefits attributed to computing.

The Context of Use and Productivity. We have now established that detectives do enjoy productivity gains from the use of computer systems in their work and that such gains increase with higher levels of utilization of those systems. Our conceptual framework holds that both the computer package and the user operate within an organizational environment, and that any combination of these three contextual elements might account for variations in individual detectives' productivity. Table 6.5 shows that the context of use does account for a significant amount of between-detective variation on most of our measures of productivity attributed to computing (row 1). Thirty-six percent of the variation across detectives in the level of *information benefits* from computing can be accounted for by the explanatory variables. And from 10 to 18 percent of the variation across detectives in *individual performance benefits* attributed to computing on arrests and clearances can be accounted for by the explanatory variables. Only the differential impacts of computing on workable cases are not significantly associated with our measures of the context of computing use.

It is clear that the individual elements of the contexts of computing use vary in their explanatory power. The nature of the organizational environment does not have much explanatory appeal on any of the productivity measures; at most, only 28 percent of the total explained variance is accounted for by such variables (row 2a). This is somewhat surprising, since it is reasonable to predict that computer-based decision support systems will be especially valuable to detectives in jurisdictions with larger populations, given the greater difficulty of

Table 6.5. Explanatory Power of Context of Use Elements to Account for Between Detective Variation in Productivity Shifts Attributed to Computing

	Information Benefits	Individual Performance Benefits			
	Information Improvements	Unworkable cases	Computing assists: arrests	Computing assists: clearances	Computing assists: linkages between persons in custody and uncleared cases
1. Total explained variance (R^2):	35.8%***	n.s.[a]	14.7%***	17.7%***	10.0%***
2. Percentage of total explained variance (above) accounted for by variables measuring:					
a. Organizational environment	11%		28%	4%	3%
b. Computer package	7		41	60	12
c. User characteristics	83		24	37	85
3. Most powerful explanatory variables:					
a. Organizational environment	−Government complexity (.19)**		Government professionalism (.16)*	−Government complexity (.15)*	−Government complexity (.13)*
b. Computer package	Decentralized computing (.19)**		Decentralized computing (.25)*** Sophisticated computing (.22)***	Decentralized computing (.31)*** Sophisticated computing (.25)***	Sophisticated computing (.13)*

Table 6.5. (continued)

	Information Benefits		Individual Performance Benefits		
	Information Improvements	Unworkable cases	Computing assists: arrests	Computing assists: clearances	Computing assists: linkages between persons in custody and uncleared cases
c. User characteristics	+User orientation to computing staff (.53)***		+User orientation to computing staff (.15)* +User professionalism (.14)* +User competency with computing (.12)*	+User orientation to computing staff (.13)* +User professionalism (.22)***	Older user (.19)*** +User competency with computing (.17)***

NOTE: 374 detectives in 40 municipalities.

* $p < .05$ Statistical significance for repression equation is

** $p < .01$ the F statistic, and for the explanatory variables

*** $p < .001$ is the T statistic (with standardized beta in parentheses).

[a] n.s. = Not significant

knowing one's field environment directly and personally. Moreover, some version of the size variable is typically the most powerful explanatory variable in contingency analyses of organizational structure and performance (Blau and Schoenherr 1971; Child and Mansfield 1972), and we have employed two strong measures of size in this analysis. For these reasons, it is particularly surprising that in the three cases where a size variable is significant, greater benefits from computing are associated with governments with *less* complexity. It is difficult to explain this pattern.

The nature of the computer package is quite important in accounting for between-detective variations in the value of computing. It is the dominant explanatory element, accounting for 41 percent and 60 percent respectively of the impact of computing on arrest and clearance levels (row 2b). In particular, computing improves the productivity benefits to detectives where it is decentralized to users and where it is more sophisticated (row 3b).

The contextual element with the greatest capacity to account for differences in the effects of computing on detective performance regarding information benefits and in-custody clearances is the characteristics of the individual user, and particularly the sociotechnical interface between the user, the technology, and the technologists (row 2c). User characteristics also have significant explanatory power on the role of computing for detective's arrests and clearances. Productivity benefits from computing are higher where the detective is more professional, older, and more competent with computing, and where the detective has a more favorable assessment of the responsiveness of the computing staff (row 3c).

TYPES OF COMPUTERIZED SYSTEMS-IN-USE

Traditional Images of Computer Support. Taken together, these data yield an intriguing point: the systems-in-use by detectives are at odds with conventional images of the nature and role of computerized systems for professionals and managers. They suggest that a new concept may be warranted for professionals like detectives whose work is primarily case-oriented. We will first review the conventional images in the literature of computerized systems for professionals and managers and then introduce another type of system-in-use derived from our empirical analysis of detectives' use of computing.

In chapter 1 (table 1.1), we briefly outlined two conventional images of computerized systems: model-based and operations-based systems.[4] The first and most traditional concept, the *model-based system,* is largely tied to the theoretical and professional literature of operations research, management science, and decision science and usually appears under the decision support system (DSS) label (see table 6.6). This concept stems from theories which posit "problem solving" as the essence of professional work and prescribe model building as a means of solving problems. Information for decisions, then, is the output of formal analytical models and simulations (e.g., models for police manpower allocation, for service demand, or for projecting revenues and expenditures). By definition, information use is selective in such model-oriented systems because the model prescribes the relevant data and provides "the answer."

Systems based on the problem-solving concept incorporate both the mathematical operations and the data required to support the model. The data and operations are defined by the theory underlying each particular model and usually are distinctly different from anything found in the current operations and data of the organization. Therefore, decision support systems must be built that are separate from the computer applications serving routine organizational operations and they must be supported by data collection procedures and data flows that are tailored to meet the unique needs of the decision model. The computer package underlying such DSS is one with the capacity to handle many small samples, sophisticated mathematical computations, and large simulations—namely, highly skilled model builders and large computational capacities.

The second type of computerized system, the *operations-based system* has its heritage in the intellectual and practitioner literature of computer science, information systems, and data processing, and most commonly appears under the label of MIS (Management Information Systems). This conception is supported by research that has found "problem finding" to be an important activity of professionals and managers. The information used in problem finding is defined by extremely simple nonanalytical models, mainly involving data comparisons—over time, across organizational and geographic

Table 6.6. Comparison of Types of Computerized Systems

Attributes	Types of Computerized Systems		
	Model-based	Operations-based	Data-based
Activity served	Problem-solving	Problem-finding	Fact-finding, fact-linking
Type of use	"Selective," driven by analytic, optimizing models	"Selective," driven by historical and heuristic models	"Prospecting," driven by fact searches and ad hoc hunches
Mode of use	Indirect through intermediaries	Indirect through intermediaries or computer-based reports	Direct, personal use of terminal
Data used	Information is generated specifically for the model, usually separate from routine operations and transaction processing	Information is a product of routine operations and transaction-oriented data processing	Information is from operational records, but reorganized to aid linkage; *plus* data gathered explicitly as an information base for the user
Nature of computing package	Large computational capability, batch or on-line access; simulation and modeling languages; model building expertise	Sophisticated information storage and retrieval, integrated data files and applications, data-base management, on-line access; computer expertise	Interactive, easy access to multiply data files for both simple and complex retrievals/linkages; data-base management; professional expertise
Examples	Traditional DSS: cash flow models, revenue/expenditure forecasting models, manpower allocation models, facility location models	Traditional MIS: integrated financial systems, cost accounting systems, geographic information systems, personnel/payroll systems	Human–Machine systems: detectives investigation support, case management systems (prosecution, probation, health), case law precedent search, medical diagnosis

boundaries, and between planned and actual achievements. These historical and areal models are illustrated by the many routine reports, exception reports, and ad hoc comparison reports produced in the daily operations of most organizations (e.g., in police, the watch commander's report of criminal incidents and traffic accidents).

Computerized systems based on the problem-finding concept are formed largely from the transaction-oriented applications serving routine operations. The greater the degree and range of such automated applications within the organization, the broader the potential data-base from which relevant information can be generated. Exploiting this potential requires technical capacity for integrating data (i.e., across departmental, agency, account, geographic, and other boundaries), storing large data-bases, and quickly accessing them for various information requests. The computer package supporting such systems therefore includes highly skilled computer staff, data-base management systems, large storage and core capacities, and on-line access.

Clearly, systems based both on the traditional DSS and MIS images can be found in public and private organizations and, specifically, in the police, as the examples already cited and those listed in table 6.6 illustrate. But neither of these two types of computerized systems corresponds to what we have found to be the primary systems-in-use among detectives. Indeed, the actual systems-in-use are considerably at variance with the traditional images of DSS and MIS, and suggest that a new type of system—the "data-based" system—might be a more appropriate characterization of end-user computing among case-oriented professionals.

A New Concept of Computer Support. In contrast to the traditional concepts of DSS and MIS, which are based upon the notion of "selective" use of information, the *data-based system* involves various forms of information "prospecting" in order to find and link relevant facts in the analysis of a given case (in such case-oriented fields as criminal investigation, medical care, legal work, welfare work, investment counseling, and so on). Such prospecting involves direct, personal use of a computer terminal to search collections of information, which are themselves a by-product of operational records that have been organized to aid case retrieval and linkage. The computing package provides interactive, easy access to the organized information via powerful data-base management software which allows direct manipulation by the end user, who brings his/her professional expertise to bear in handling the case investigation.

Computer support for detective investigation provides a good illustration of the data-based system for case-oriented professionals. Detective investigation involves many record searches in many independent files for many different reasons under many varied circumstances. The type of use is best characterized as "prospecting," and it is driven both by the search for individual facts and by ad hoc hunches about how certain facts might be linked to aid a criminal investigation. Such prospecting is illustrated by three main patterns of use. The first is simple fact retrieval, involving the completely structured use of on-line data-bases to search for particular facts about a crime, criminal, or modus operandi. The second use pattern involves more complex, less structured searches with computer support tailored to perform the most frequently occurring searches, such as the search for all field incidents within a particular time period or geographic area, or the search for all individuals with a particular modus operandi. The third use pattern is the most complex and unstructured, involving ad hoc, exploratory search with the aid of a generalized analysis system for search, summary, graphic representation and calculation. It is illustrated by the detective's effort to identify a pattern of comparable phenomena or to link clues from a crime with other incidents or facts—for example, to determine whether a late model blue Chevrolet with a partial license plate of NJP. . . which was observed by witnesses near the scene of a rape can be further identified because it might have been stolen, ticketed for a parking violation in the area, recently changed hands, owned by a suspect in the crime, or owned by someone with an M.O. similar to that for this crime.

Some of the information sought by the detectives is contained in the general law enforcement systems of the government—that is, the record-keeping systems which serve patrol officers, watch commanders, and records clerks, as well as detectives. Information also is drawn from special files designed explicitly to capture and store data that might aid detective investigations, and further information is drawn from the systems of other local, regional, and national law enforcement systems.

The computer package supporting the data-based system is moderately sophisticated, mainly involving computers with large storage capacity and on-line, remote access (sometimes interactive access) to the data-bases. Search of the data-bases from remote terminals is aided by preprogrammed keys, which facilitate routine fact-finding, by special software for frequently occurring searches, and by generalized data-base management software to support ad hoc retrieval and analysis. The computer technology also is decentralized, which, in the context of the police, means: freedom from contention with other departments for access; rapid response on a 24-hour basis; and control over the design and operation of systems by computer professionals oriented toward serving the police. This characterization is consistent with the empirical analysis in table 6.5, where sophistication and decentralization of the computer package and a favorable evaluation of the responsiveness of computing staff are the key variables accounting for variance among detectives in the impacts of computing on their productivity. Finally, in contrast to the other two types of systems, which require a user (or an intermediary) with considerable model and computer expertise, the data-based system requires end user expertise in a substantive area (i.e., crime/criminal behavior in the case of detectives) and some hands-on expertise in using computing. This is also consistent with table 6.5, where user professionalism and user competency with computing are associated with greater computing benefits.

The data-based system is an important and useful conceptualization not only because it defines a major class of professional users of computing, but also because it has implications for worker performance. Our data indicate that the detective who routinely goes prospecting on every case reaps greater benefits from the technology than does the selective user. This finding is consistent with other research on human-machine interaction which finds that decision making by professionals is enhanced when they use computer terminals and easy-to-use retrieval software in an active, "prospecting" mode (see Alter 1980; Kunreuther and Schoemaker 1982). In chapter 11, we further explicate the characteristics and significance of the data-based system in the actual work of information workers generally.

CONCLUDING OBSERVATIONS

From a policy perspective committed to improving productivity of professionals by means of computing, these findings are quite encouraging. There is clear evidence here that computer technology can enhance the productivity of professionals in the service sector. The kinds of performance benefits associated with detectives in this analysis should be generalizable to other professionals who undertake similar semistructured tasks and are dependent on a rich information environment. At minimum, the benefits should be generalizable to other professionals who are engaged in activities that are essentially "case-oriented," e.g., probation officers, lawyers, social workers, prosecutors, court administrators, physicians, investment counselors, and insurance agents (see, for example, the analyses by Dery 1981; Malvey 1981; Meindl 1985 and Weimer 1980). Computing has the capabilities to serve as an integral part of a valuable information/data support system for these kinds of workers.

Moreover, this analysis has suggested some of the major conditions that seem to increase the contribution of computer-based systems to professionals' work. The case of detectives suggests that professionals will derive greater productivity benefits from computing: (a) if the computer package is more decentralized, so it is under the control of end users; (b) if sophisticated computing capacity which permits human-machine interaction is available; (c) if the end users have greater competency and experience with computing; (d) if the technical experts are more responsive to the felt needs of the users regarding the design and operation of the computer-based decision support systems; and (e) if end users routinely rather than selectively utilize the system. This analysis of detectives reveals that all of these conditions are quite crucial in increasing major benefits of computing to work performance. Thus despite continuing images of the computer as a mechanistic and homogenizing technology, its impact is highly contingent upon the technological, the personal, and the interpersonal context within which computing is provided and used.

These findings generally support the notion that improved job performance will result from placing microcomputers in the hands of professionals in organizations. Microcomputers decentralize both the technology and control over its use directly to the professional, while simultaneously providing that professional with access to the organization's data-bases. Microcomputers also provide interactive computing capacity locally while providing access to large computations, storage, and networking capacities of mainframes. Both of these characteristics of the technology—its decentralization and its sophistication—correspond to important contributors to greater information benefits and higher productivity among detectives in our study.

Although the nature of the computer package is important, the most critical variables determining the value of end user computing using data-based systems might lie elsewhere. As with the detectives, they might involve the characteristics of the users and their interactions with the technology and the technologists. The greater the professionals' experience and competence with computing, the more routinely the professionals use computing, and the more that technical experts are available and responsive to the needs of professionals to gain competence and experience, to help with special problems, and to facilitate the professionals' interfaces between their own computing activities and the larger systems and databases of the organization, the greater the productivity benefits from use of computers by professionals. These relationships will certainly hold regarding effectiveness performance criteria and, given the value derived from better exploiting the costly technology, they are likely to obtain for efficiency criteria as well. The importance of expert assistance, in particular, supports the currently popular notion of providing "information centers" (Hammond 1982) within an organization, where professionals and managers can obtain help in evaluating, procuring, using, and maintaining relevant elements of the computer package (whether on mainframes, minicomputers or microcomputers) and the decision systems they support. We return to these themes in chapter 11.

7. Problems with Computing

Almost everyone familiar with the applications of computer technology is aware of the story where computing has caused a monumental blunder such as an incorrect billing for $500,000 instead of $50.00. And those who deal with computing on a regular basis have experienced some inconvenience when a system has been "down" or when the time between a request for computing and delivery of the product has been excessive. While these problems are examined occasionally in the scholarly literature (see, for example, Brewer 1973; Dickson, Simmons, and Anderson 1969; Guthrie 1974; Keen and Gerson 1977; Lee 1973; Lucas 1973, 1975; Mumford et al. 1972), they are more than balanced by widespread claims in the popular and professional literature that computing is a relatively "problem-free" technology. These conflicting images suggest intriguing questions about problems with computing: How common are such problems? What kinds of problems occur most frequently? Do people in different roles experience different problems? Does the context of computing use affect the incidence of these problems? Our data offer a promising empirical base with which to examine these questions in the setting of public organizations.

MEASURES AND HYPOTHESES

Although it might seem straightforward, some discussion of what constitutes a "problem" with computing seems important. In the first place, some impacts of computing that the end user might define as a problem involve a disjunction between expectation and reality. For example, the user might feel that it is a problem if computing has not provided new information beyond what is available in existing manual files. Second, computing might alter the work environment of an individual in ways that he/she finds problematic, but that are desirable from the perspective of organizational goals. For example, an end user might see it as a problem if the use of computing has increased the level of supervision of his/her work. Are these problems? They can certainly be viewed as problems in the sense of Epictetus' observation: "Men are not disturbed by things but by the view they take of them." In other chapters, we examine these types of quasi-problems, such as areas where end users might fail to enjoy certain benefits from computing (chapters 5 and 6), or where computing produces negative impacts on their personal work environments (chapters 9 and 10).

In this chapter, however, we focus on areas where people might experience quite direct problems in the use of automated information and of computing services.[1] The problems with automated information involve the difficulties facing the end user regarding his/her capacity to control the quality and alteration of information in automated systems. And the problems with computing services involve the difficulties facing the end user in receiving desired computing support in a timely and efficient manner. Even in these areas, objective standards of computing "problems" at the individual level are elusive. Thus we rely upon people's own reports of the frequency with which they personally experience these kinds of difficulties with automated information and computing operations available to them.

From our analysis of the benefits from computing (chapters 5 and 6), it is evident that most end users have enjoyed such information benefits as speedier and easier access to information, the provision of new information, and the availability of more timely information, relative to the information in manual files. From these responses, it seems reasonable to infer that few users in our study believe that they have major problems due to the failure of computing to provide them with information benefits. In this chapter, we assess aspects of a person's involvement with information where he/she might experience computing problems regarding either control of or quality of automated data and information. Specifically, users indicate how often they have difficulties in changing or correcting information once it has been entered into computerized files and in determining and maintaining the accuracy of data in such files. We term these difficulties *"information problems,"* and our dependent variable is an index combining and averaging the frequency with which the end user experiences each kind of problem (across a range of frequencies from "almost never a problem" to "almost always a problem").

From another perspective, there are certain problems that an end user might face in utilizing computing services on a day-to-day basis. Such difficulties include "foul-ups" in computing operations, slow response from the data processing unit on requests for computing services, and unsatisfactory priority level in the use of the computer package. Each user indicated the frequency with which he/she experienced each of these problems with computing services, ranging from "not a problem" to "very often a problem." Our *"operational problems"* index combines and averages the end user's report of the incidence of each of these kinds of problems with computing.[2]

There is very little existing empirical research to inform our expectations about the relative incidence of these two types of computing problems. In general, we posit that operational problems will be cited more frequently within a given role than information problems, primarily because the former problems are likely to be more visible and obvious to most users of computing. Moreover, operational problems should be more common among those whose roles involve more active modes of computing use and more (time-) pressing needs for automated data. On the basis of our analysis of utilization patterns, this suggests that street-level and desk-top bureaucrats will report operational problems at levels higher than staff professionals or managers. Information problems should be associated more directly with pervasive data handling in one's work, and thus we hypothesize that these problems will be reported most frequently by desk-top bureaucrats and by staff professionals.

Among the elements of the context of computing use, it is reasonable to posit that user characteristics, and particularly the variables measuring the sociotechnical interface, will be strongly associated with the level of computing problems. Indeed, an unfavorable appraisal by the user of the responsiveness of the computing staff is itself a problem with the computer package, and thus it should be substantially correlated with operational problems and also correlated, if less powerfully, with information problems. We also assume that as a person is more competent regarding computing, he/she will be more easily dissatisfied with operational shortcomings in the functioning of the computer package, and thus report more frequent problems.

The most intriguing linkages are those between computing problems and the computer package itself. The conventional wisdom holds that as the computer package becomes more established in a given organization, problems with computing are resolved and there are fewer instances of the kinds of operational and informational problems tapped by our two problems measures. In this view, there are likely to be many more shortcomings with computing in its early period after adoption. But, over time, system "bugs" are reduced, the operations staff becomes more adept at providing computing services in a timely manner, the applications software is improved, data gathering and information flows are tailored to better meet organizational needs, and so on.

This suggests the hypothesis that as computing is more routinized and more extensive, problems experienced by users will be less frequent. It is also reasonable to predict that as the computer package is more decentralized, the technology will be more responsive to users' needs and thus there will be a reduction in the incidence of operational and information problems.

There is, however, a contrary hypothesis, argued persuasively in some of the recent empirical literature (see King and Kraemer 1985). In this view, as the computer package becomes more routinized, it also becomes more extensive and more sophisticated. Although this more developed computer package might generate greater benefits, such features might also increase the potential for operational and information problems facing end users. These problems emerge from the magnitude and complexity of the computing operation and also from the sheer size of data files whose quality must be maintained. Given the empirical evidence, we take this contrary view as our working hypothesis and assume that greater computing problems will be reported where the technology is more extensive and more sophisticated and, as a corollary, where it is more routinized. It is not clear that there will be between-role differences in the pattern of associations between computing problems and the computer package, although the frequency of problems might be highest among those with the most pervasive data-handling tasks, and particularly the staff professionals (who also tend to use more sophisticated automated applications).

In predicting the effects of organizational environment on the frequency of computing problems, we begin with the premise that larger scale and complexity in the organizational environment will be associated with a more extensive and interdependent information environment. With greater scale and complexity, it is likely that there will be more problems regarding data management and data quality, particularly where data files are very large or where they are shared among various organizational units with differing needs and interests. And it also might result in more frequent operational problems, because complex automated information systems will be more fragile and prone to foul-ups and because competing demands for priority in computing services are more likely. Thus we hypothesize that increasing scale and complexity of the organizational environment will be associated with more frequent computing problems among end users in all roles, and especially those who have the most pervasive data-handling needs (that is, desk-top bureaucrats and staff professionals).

ACTUAL LEVELS OF PROBLEMS WITH COMPUTING

Table 7.1 provides data with which to assess the level of computing problems reported by end users in the four roles. Most broadly, there is support for our prediction that operational problems are experienced more frequently than information problems. High levels of operational problems are reported by between one-third and one-fourth of those in each of the four roles. But high levels of information problems are rare for end users in any role, ranging from 14 percent of the desk-top bureaucrats to only 6 percent of the staff professionals. From a different angle, the modal problem level for each role is "moderate" on operational problems, but "low" on information problems with 48 to 58 percent of the people in this category. A staff professional is ten times more likely to have low than high information problems, and the ratio is 6:1 among managers and 4:1 among street-level bureaucrats and desk-top bureaucrats. In contrast, about as many end users within each role experience high operational problems as experience low operational problems.

In examining between-role differences in the level of computing problems, table 7.1 suggests that, unlike our hypothesis, there is little difference in the frequency of problems across roles. This inference is further supported by statistical analysis (not show, using chi-square), in which there are few significant between-role differences.[3]

Table 7.1. Level of Problems with Computing

	Managers (N=395)	Staff Professionals (N=230)	Street-Level Bureaucrats (N=179)	Desk-Top Bureaucrats (N=170)
Information Problems[a]				
High	9%	6%	12%	14%
Moderate	36	36	41	36
Low	55	58	48	51
Mean	.70	.70	.86	.75
Coefficient of variation	.91	.91	.83	.96
Operational Problems[b]				
High	24	32	27	25
Moderate	50	42	52	48
Low	26	25	20	27
Mean	1.01	1.18	1.13	1.09
Coefficient of variation	.71	.68	.64	.72

[a] The respondent assessed these two statements: Information is difficult to change or correct once it has been put in a computerized file; Computerized data are less accurate than data in manual records and files. The response values were: Almost never true = 0; Sometimes true = 1; Frequently true = 2; Nearly always true =3. This index combines and averages the responses to the two questions. On the index, High = 2.0–3.0; Medium = 1.0–1.5; Low = 0–.5.

[b] The respondent reported the frequency with which he/she experienced these problems within the last year; (a) foul-ups in day-to-day computer operations; (b) slow response of data processing to requests; (c) difficulty in getting priority for computing. The response values were: Not a problem = 0; At times a problem = 1; Often a problem = 2; Very often a problem = 3. This index combines and averages the responses to the three questions. On the index, High = 1.67–3.0; Medium = .67–1.5; Low = 0–.5.

Given the quite different levels of computing use and styles of computing use across the four roles, it is surprising and interesting that end users in the four roles indicate such comparable levels of problems with computing. In contrast to our analyses of use, benefits, and work environment impacts, problems seems that one area where computing has been homogenizing, in the sense that the levels of impact are independent of role.

Despite the overall comparability across roles in table 7.1, it is interesting that the incidence of computing problems among desktop bureaucrats is not distinctively high. We assumed that end users in this role would be most susceptible to computing problems, since their responsibilities are continuously linked with the handling of detailed data, and thus such issues as data accuracy, computing foulups and slow response time could result in particular sensitivity to shortcomings with computing. While marginally more desk-top bureaucrats report "high" information problems than those in other roles, there is no evidence in these data that they have experienced substantially greater problems with computing than other end users. It might be that the computer package handles the mundane information processing needs of desk-top bureaucrats with few problems. Or these end users might be disinclined to complain because computing is providing them with information-handling assistance that is relatively problem-free, in comparison to information-handling in their precomputing standard operating procedures.

While there are minimal between-role differences in the level of problems with computing, we also want to assess whether the context of computing use is systematically associated with the level of computing problems within any role. The regression analysis data in table 7.2 indicate that the context of use is associated with the frequency of computing problems. There are statistically significant relationships between the context of use and both types of computing problems for all four roles. The context of use is relatively more important in accounting for variation in the incidence of operational problems, explaining between 20 and 31 percent of the total within-role variance.

The most striking finding in table 7.2 is the dominance of user characteristics in explaining differences in the frequency of computing problems. The associations between problem level and user char-

Table 7.2. Explanatory Power of Context of Use Elements for Computing Problems Within Role

	Managers (N=391)	Staff Professionals (N=229)	Street-Level Bureaucrats (N=176)	Desk-Top Bureaucrats (N=160)
Competing Explanations				
Percent of within-role variation in problems explained by:				
Each contextual element alone:				
Organizational environment				
information problems	1	5**	3	4
operational problems	3**	10***	2	6**
Computer package				
information problems	3*	2	5	3
operational problems	5***	0	0	2
User characteristics				
information problems	12***	13***	12***	20***
operational problems	19***	27***	18***	14***
Alternative Explanations				
Percent of within-role variation in problems explained by:				
All contextual elements combined:				
information problems	13***	15***	16***	24***
operational problems	23***	37***	20***	22***
Percent of this total accounted for by:				
Organizational environment				
information problems	6%	29%	20%	15%
operational problems	14	29	12	34
Computer package				

Table 7.2. (continued)

	Managers (N=391)	Staff Professionals (N=229)	Street-Level Bureaucrats (N=176)	Desk-Top Bureaucrats (N=160)
information problems	8	0	18	0
operational problems	9	0	0	0
User characteristics				
information problems	85	71	61	85
operational problems	77	70	88	66

Key Explanatory Variables

Greater Information Problems

	Managers	Staff Professionals	Street-Level Bureaucrats	Desk-Top Bureaucrats
Organizational environment Computer package	+Computing expenditure (.11)*	+Scale of service environment (.12)*	−Scale of service environment (−.23)** +Computing sophistication (.22)**	−Scale of service environment (−.21)**
User characteristics	−User orientation to computing staff(−.29)*** −User professionalism (−.11)*	−User orientation to computing staff (−.33)***	−User orientation to computing staff (−.29)***	−User orientation to computing staff (−.45)*** Older user (.24)***

Greater Operational Problems

	Managers	Staff Professionals	Street-Level Bureaucrats	Desk-Top Bureaucrats
Organizational environment	−Govt. professionalism (−.12)***	−Govt. professionalism (−.10)*	−Govt. professionalism (−.14)*	
Computer package	+Computing expenditure (.11)*			+Routinized computing (.16)*
User characteristics	−User orientation to computing staff (−.44)***	−User orientation to computing staff (−.50)*** +User computing competence (.12)*	−User orientation to computing staff (−.43)***	−User orientation to computing staff (.36)***

*** < .001
** < .01
* < .05

acteristics are highly significant for all four roles on each type of computing problem. Moreover, as we predicted, the crucial variable is the responsiveness of the computer specialists to the end user. In all eight instances, it is the most powerful explanatory variable, accounting for as much as half the between-individual variance explained by all the significant variables. It is not unreasonable to argue that this variable can be interpreted as another kind of problem with computing—in this case, a problem grounded in the behaviors of the technical staff in responding to the needs of the user. But from the end user's own perspective, this variable is at the heart of the sociotechnical interface, and thus it remains a prior and, clearly, a powerful explanator of specific operational and information problems with computing. In short, *both information and operational problems with computing occur more frequently among those end users who find that computer specialists are more intrigued with the technology than with serving users' needs and are unwilling/unable to communicate in the users' language.* The user's orientation to computing staff is the only aspect of the user characteristics that is consistently associated with the incidence of computing problems.

In a competing explanations framework, computing problems is the first impact variable where the explanatory power of one element in the context of use has clear dominance across all roles. There is no instance where either the organizational environment or the computer package approaches the level of explanatory power of the user characteristics. Indeed, there is only a single case where either element of the context of use accounts for as much as ten percent of the between-individual variance—the organizational environment on operational problems among staff professionals.

The explanatory dominance of the user characteristics element is underlined in the alternative explanations framework. There are only two instances where including all three elements of the context of computing use in a single explanation does notably increase explanatory appeal. In both instances, the improvement upon an explanation based only on user characteristics variables is provided primarily by features of the organizational environment.

In these cases, the effect of the organizational environment varies across roles. For staff professionals, the pattern is consistent with our hypothesis—namely, computing problems (particularly operational problems) increase as the scale of the service environment increases. But for desk-top bureaucrats and, in a modest way, for street-level bureaucrats, increased scale of the organizational environment is associated with *lower* levels of information problems. This is consistent with the suggestion above that those in bureaucratic roles, because they face large information processing environments, assess the problems created by computing to be minimal in comparison with the benefits provided by the technology.[4] We shall explore this idea more fully in chapter 8, where problems and benefits attributed to computing by desk-top bureaucrats are examined in more depth.

The most unexpected finding in table 7.2 is the minimal explanatory power of the computer package. *The nature of the computer package has virtually no power as either a competing explanation or as a part of an interdependent (alternative) explanation.* In our earlier discussion, we elaborated on the interesting debate about whether a more developed (that is, routinized and extensive) computer package would be associated with diminishing problems or increasing problems. On the basis of table 7.2, we can offer very little empirical resolution to this debate. In general, the answer on the basis of these data is: the nature of the computer package does not much matter.

If one "squeezes" these data hard (by examining the simple correlations as well as the regression coefficients), it seems that operational problems do tend to be more frequent for people in settings where the computer package is more routinized and extensive, although the levels of sophistication and decentralization of the package are not associated with problem level. And the level of information problems does not seem consistently related to *any* variable measuring the computer package.

While one might be able to link the computer package with differential levels of problems measured at the aggregate (e.g., the departmental or organizational) level, we find no evidence of such linkages at the individual level. Whatever inferences one makes, *there is little in these data to indicate that end users' problems with computing will be overcome by a "technological fix."* Rather, problem reduction is best accomplished by policy interventions that improve the quality of the interactions between the providers of technical computing services and the users of the computing package.

CONCLUDING OBSERVATIONS

Despite the hopes of some and the claims of others, there is little evidence that computing is or becomes a trouble-free tool in the service of organizational personnel. About three-fourths of the end users across all roles experience operational problems with computing on at least an occasional basis. And the data suggest that, if anything, these problems become more frequent as the technology is more routinized and extensive. The frequency of these problems related to the day-to-day provision of computing is quite directly associated with the extent to which the user is involved with a computer staff that attempts to be communicative and to emphasize the user's needs rather than the technology's capabilities. The importance of this aspect of the sociotechnical interface is far greater than any other characteristic of the user, of the computer package, or of the organizational environment. These data clearly support the inference that the quality of the sociotechnical interface is the key to understanding the level of continuing operational problems that end users attribute to computing use in organizations.

End users in all four roles report that the instances in which they experience problems related to the handling and quality of information in automated systems are substantially less frequent than the instances in which they face operational problems. About half of the end users indicate that information problems are infrequent, and the extent of such problems is virtually identical regardless of role. Although the linkage is less strong than on operational problems, the level of information problems is also clearly associated with the responsiveness of the computer staff. Despite our expectation that information problems might be more extensive where computing is less developed, the nature of the computer package has no systematic effect on the information problems of the individual end user.

Overall, these data suggest that problems with computing are rather personal phenomena, with differences in the assessment of computing problems being generally unrelated to the person's role responsibilities or data-handling tasks, to the computer package available, or to the organizational milieu within which the individual works. While it might be that people's evaluations of computing problems are not identical to objective measures, such evaluations can have profound impacts on how people utilize computing, how they integrate it into their work, and on how they feel about their jobs, about computer technology, and about themselves. Indeed, the personal assessment of the balance between the benefits enjoyed and the problems experienced with computing is essential to grasping the role and impact of the technology on information workers as end users. It is this balance that we explore in chapter 8.

8. Clerks and Computing: The Problem/Benefit Mix

The initial promise of computing in organizations was premised on the capacity of the technology to process very substantial amounts of data with rapidity and accuracy. Indeed, because of the early emphasis on the "brawny" end of computing, most organizations assumed that computing would be particularly useful in replacing the "army of clerks." Many of the early analytical studies of computing speculated about how those clerks whose jobs were spared by the new technology would react to it. In general, most assumed that the overall reaction of the clerks to the new situation would be negative. In addition to the apparent threat of clerical jobs, there would also be anxiety regarding the utilization of a new technology which seemed complex, rigid, and unforgiving of human error. Thus this innovation was expected to generate uneasiness and even resistance from the clerks (Braverman 1974; Marenco 1966; Mumford and Banks 1967).

The actual impacts of computing on clerks have been quite varied, according to the empirical research that has examined this issue (see, for example, Child et al. 1985; Cooley 1981; Crompton and Jones 1984; DeKadt 1979; Kling 1978). In earlier chapters, we have determined that the clerks in our analysis, the "desk-top bureaucrats," generally report that computing has provided them with considerable benefits in terms of information-handling, and has not resulted in particularly high levels of problems, even relative to other roles.

In this chapter, we shall explore more fully the linkage between clerks and problems with computing. We focus specifically on one group of desk-top bureaucrats in our study—those clerks who are responsible for traffic ticket processing. First, we discuss how traffic ticket clerks can use computing in their work. Next we identify the problems with computing that these clerks might experience and we provide data on the extent to which the clerks report such problems. We then assess whether problems and benefits experienced with computing tend to be "zero-sum." That is, do most clerks experience either high problems and low benefits or low problems and high benefits, or do many clerks report a more complex mix of problems and benefits?

COMPUTING AND TRAFFIC TICKET PROCESSING

The clerks in traffic ticket processing use computing in a manner similar to that of many other desk-top bureaucrats. The work is information intensive, with an emphasis on highly routinized information processing tasks that involve the entry, retrieval, and alteration of records. The traffic ticket clerks typically receive hard copies of the tickets that have been issued for parking or moving traffic violations. The clerks are responsible for holding these records, for retrieving the records when payment is tendered, and for indicating the disposition of the record at various stages. In most local governments, the citizen is able to pay for the violation by mail or in person if he or she does not wish to challenge the citation. Thus, the clerk must be able to locate the ticket, determine the payment required, and enter the payment received. Ideally, the clerks should also be able to identify those citizens who have more than one ticket, to "flag" those tickets which have become delinquent (due to non-payment), and to notify the citizen and/or the law enforcement agencies regarding such delinquency status.

The capacity of computing to facilitate this process is apparent. In an automated traffic ticket processing environment, the relevant information from the ticket can be entered into the system by a clerk at any site with direct or indirect access to the automated system. At all subsequent times, the ticket information can be retrieved on the basis of any of the parameters entered, including the auto license number, the name of the registered owner of the vehicle, the date and location of the citation, the type of violation, the officer who issued the ticket, and the status of the fine. When a citizen tenders payment, this can also be recorded in the file. In addition, the automated system might be able to provide additional services, such as linking the ticket to other outstanding tickets that involve the same automobile or owner, or automatically flagging delinquent tickets. Some automated systems also print a letter notifying the citizen that the ticket is delinquent and even issue a warrant at the appropriate time.

The value of these applications of computing to the traffic ticket processing function was dramatically illustrated in two similar municipalities in the Boston metropolitan area. In each city, the processing of traffic tickets was handled by a limited number of clerks who were increasingly swamped by the quantity of tickets that was being issued. Both cities had a "manual" system, in which the hard-copy tickets were filed by auto license number, were pulled when payment was tendered, and then were refiled in the "paid" file. Ideally, the clerk would notice any other tickets under the license number when retrieving the ticket; but the clerk would not find tickets issued for different automobiles, and moving violations were not filed with the parking tickets. Moreover, the clerks had no time to search the files to determine which tickets had become delinquent or to issue warnings or warrants regarding such tickets. As one might imagine, many citizens who inadvertantly or intentionally did not pay their parking tickets noticed that "the system" seemed to forget about them. This knowledge diffused slowly but steadily, as many people learned that they could receive and ignore parking tickets with impunity. As literal spillover effects, the number of violations grew dramatically and the number of outstanding tickets in the clerks' filing cabinets overflowed into boxes and could not even be filed properly.

It was under these circumstances that one of the cities implemented an automated system for processing traffic tickets. The system had the capabilities outlined above, including the automatic mailing of warning notices and the issuance of warrants on delinquent tickets. As one might expect, the "scofflaw" rate, which had been more than 50 percent, dropped within nine months to less than 5 percent in the automated municipality, and within eighteen months, it had virtually disappeared.

This "natural experiment" regarding the impact of computing on productivity has the kind of denouement that computing advocates find ideal. The automated system proved highly cost-beneficial, generating very large revenues for the city, it made the staff far more efficient in their handling of data, and it even reduced the "lawlessness" of the driving (and parking) public. While the benefits in this case were rather more dramatic than usual, the basic situation is not atypical of many instances where computing has been successfully applied to a basic, routinized clerical task. We have shown in a previous chapter that desk-top bureaucrats enjoy information and operational benefits from computing, and chapter 9 will reveal that they are generally satisfied with the impacts of such applications of computing on their work environment. Our interest here, however, is to assess whether these technological innovations are truly Pareto optimal for the clerks, or whether there are also significant problems associated with the use of computing.

PROBLEMS WITH COMPUTING

Chapter 7 identified two broad types of problems that end users might experience in the use of computing in their work. One type is information problems, which concern the quality and manipulability of automated data. The second type is operational problems, which entail such shortcomings of the technical systems as delays, foul-ups, and unsatisfactory service priorities.

Desk-top bureaucrats such as traffic ticket processing clerks are particularly sensitive to these kinds of problems. The client-bureaucrat relationship involves potentially abrasive interactions and can be particularly unpleasant (for example, the disgruntled citizen paying a traffic fine). Thus, it is important that the clerk utilizes an automated system that provides rapid and accurate information. A situation where the computer is down or where it malfunctions constitutes a very serious problem for the clerk, since many such automated systems involve direct data input as well as on-line retrieval by the clerk. The clerk needs to deal quickly and efficiently over the desk top with clients, and errors can be very serious—for example, the incorrect issuance of a wanted warrant on a driver. In short, the nature of the clerk's work is such that he/she might be quite sensitive to any information problems or operational problems with computing. Figure 8.1 indicates the frequency with which such problems are reported by the traffic ticket clerks who use automated systems.

There is no evidence in these data that the clerks are plagued by problems with computing. On both the information problems index and the operational problems index, the mean incidence of problems is less than 1.0. This can be interpreted to indicate that the "average" clerk in the analysis has occasional problems with computing. This average clerk reports that operational problems occur with somewhat greater frequency than do information problems. About one in ten clerks reports that he/she never has operational problems with computing, while only one in fifty has very frequent problems on all three specific measures (foul-ups, slow response, priorities).

More than one in four of the clerks indicates that he/she almost never experiences information problems with computing on either

Figure 8.1. Level of Computing Problems Among Clerks

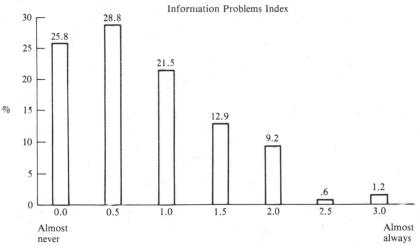

Information Problems Index

Mean = .79

Coefficient of variation = .87

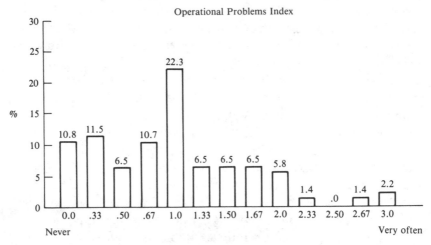

Operational Problems Index

Mean = .96

Coefficient of variation = .71

NOTE: N = 146 traffic ticket processing clerks in 40 municipalities.

ᵃ An index combining and averaging the responses to questions regarding how often each of the following statements is true, with the response categories: Almost never true = 0; Sometimes true = 1; Frequently true = 2; Nearly always true = 3.

For the information problems index, the questions were: Computerized data are less accurate than data in manual records and files; and information is difficult to change or correct once it has been put on a computerized file.

ᵇ An index combining and averaging the responses to a question regarding whether each of the following types of problems had occurred within the last year, with the response categories: Not a problem = 0; At times a problem = 1; Often a problem = 2; Very often a problem = 3.

For the operational problems index, the cited problems were: foul-ups in day-to-day computer operations; slow response to data processing to requests for information; and difficulty in getting priority in using the computer.

of the two specific measures (changing or correcting automated data and determining or maintaining the accuracy of data in those files). Only 1 percent of the clerks reported very frequent problems on both of these measures. While it would be inaccurate to characterize computing as a "problem-free" technology for these clerks in traffic ticket processing, most clerks experience computing problems occasionally rather than constantly. However, if one believes that computing *should* be virtually problem-free for end users requiring accurate and timely automated data, then these data do indicate that computing is a somewhat troublesome factor in the clerk's work. In our analysis below, we shall distinguish among those clerks who experience relatively higher and relatively lower information and operational problems with computing, splitting the group at the mean. This will enable us to explore whether there are characteristics of the context of use that are systematically related to the level of computing problems that a clerk experiences.

PROBLEM CONFIGURATIONS AMONG CLERKS

One interesting question regarding the kinds of computing problems that face clerks, or any other people who work with computers, is whether different types of problems are reinforcing or independent. A plausible argument can be made that those people who experience one type of problem with computing at a certain level will also report other types of computing problems at about the same level. In terms of our analysis, this would lead to the hypothesis that those clerks who report relatively high levels of information problems would also report higher levels of operational problems and, conversely, others would be relatively low on both types of problems. One might predict this either because all computing problems are likely to exist at about the same levels in a given context of use or because a user's perception of problems in one domain of computing use would spill over into other domains.

A competing hypothesis is that there is no systematic linkage between the two types of problems and that clerks will not necessarily cluster into the high-high and low-low categories in a frequency distribution. In this view, the sources of operational problems are likely to be independent of the sources of information problems. For example, operational problems might be attributable to failures in the service provided by computing staff or in the policy decisions of those controlling the uses of the computer package, while information problems might be attributable to such factors as shortcomings in the design of automated applications or the clerk's own behavior and orientations to his/her work.

We find the notion that most clerks will report comparable levels on both information problems and operational problems to be the most compelling hypothesis, and our data facilitate a straightforward test of the question. We have dichotomized the clerks on each problems index at the mean so that half the clerks are classified as having higher levels of each type of computing problems and half the clerks are classified as having lower levels of problems. Figure 8.2 indicates the distribution of clerks in terms of information and operational problems.

The table provides some support for our hypothesis that there is consistency in the levels of computing problems experienced, across problem types. About three-fifths of the clerks report either high levels of both information and operational problems or low levels of both problem types. There is a significant (.22 Kendall's tau) correlation in this predicted direction. The most common situation is for a clerk to experience low levels of both types of computing problems, the pattern for one-third of the clerks.

While 28 percent of the clerks are in the predicted category of high information problems and high operational problems, almost the same proportion, 25 percent, report high operational problems but low information problems. While differences in the marginal distribution of cases across the cells necessitate care in making inferences about this pattern, it seems that both high information problems and low operational problems are clearly associated with the level on the other problem types. Stated another way, a clerk can experience low information problems regardless of the level of operational problems and can experience high operational problems regardless of the level of information problems. Thus from a problem-oriented perspective, high information problems are more closely

Figure 8.2.   Distribution of Clerks on Computing Problems

Operational Problems

		High	Low
Information Problems	High	28%	14%
	Low	25%	33%

Tau = .22 (< .01)

NOTE: N = 132 traffic ticket processing clerks in 40 municipalities.

linked to the level of operational problems than are high operational problems linked to the level of information problems.

A related question is whether those clerks with lower levels of problems or higher levels of problems tend to emerge in characteristic contexts of computing use. We might predict that the high problems people would have more negative sociotechnical interfaces with computing and, on the basis of our (original but unsupported) hypothesis in chapter 7, they might use computer packages that are more sophisticated, more extensive, and more routinized. Those with relatively low levels of computing problems might be characterized by the opposite context of use, in which the clerk has a positive STI and the computing package is less complex and more routinized. To examine these possibilities, we employed discriminant analyses, comparing those with relatively high computing problems versus all the rest and those with relatively low problems versus all the rest, and also comparing the high problems versus the low problems groups. The results of these analyses are displayed in table 8.1.

The table indicates clearly that the context of computing use has a very strong capacity to discriminate among those with high and low computing problems. This is reflected by the canonical correlation coefficients and by the capacity of the selected variables of the context of computing use to classify between 69 percent and 79 percent of the clerks into the "correct" cell.

Among those with *high computing problems,* the computer package is the most important element in the context of use. As we predicted, those people with high computing problems are in contexts where the computer package is more routinized and more extensive, although the level of sophistication is not a significant variable. The most surprising result is that no personal characteristics are among the variables most important in distinguishing those with high computing problems from others. The only other significant discriminating variable is more professionalized governments, which tend to be the contexts in which clerks have more computing problems.

The *high levels of computer problems are far more contingent upon the nature of the computer package with which the end user deals than upon his/her personal characteristics.* And the computer package that is linked with high levels of computing problems is one that is "developed," in the sense that it is routinized and extensive. This

Table 8.1.   Key Variables in Context of Use Discriminating Levels of Computing Problems Among Clerks

	High information and operational problems versus all others	Low information and operational problems versus all others	High problems versus low problems
Group Centroids:	H=.925 0=−.267	L=−.470 0=.266	H=1.030 L=−.638
Context of Use Variables			
Organizational environment	More gov't professionalism (.78[a])		More gov't professionalism (.77)
Computer package	More routinized computing (.87) More extensive computing (.70)		More centralized computing (.78) More extensive computing (1.03)
		Lower resource support for computing (−.51)	Higher resource support for computing (.455)
User characteristics		Positive orientation to computing staff (.87)	Negative orientation to computing staff (−.99) Less user competence with computing (−.74)
Canonical correlation coefficient	.452	.339	.641
Percent cases correctly classified	78%	69%	79%
Wilks' lambda	.796**	.885*	.589***

NOTE: N=132 traffic ticket processing clerks in 40 municipalities. "High" and "low" problems clerks are in top or bottom half on both information and operational problems.

[a] Standardized discriminant function coefficient, with sign changed to accord with appropriate interpretation of data, given the group centroids.

finding gives stronger empirical grounding to our inference, only mildly supported in the last chapter, that computing problems become more extensive, rather than diminishing, as a more developed computer package penetrates the organization.

In at least partial contrast, table 8.1 indicates that clerks with relatively *low levels of computing problems* are distinguished more by their personal characteristics than by the nature of their computing package. The variable most strongly associated with lower levels of computing problems is the quality of the end user's relations with computing staff. In addition to a favorable orientation to computing staff, the clerk with lower problems uses a computer package that is relatively modest, in the sense that computing is allocated a lower level of resource support.

An analysis of particular interest compares those clerks with relatively high and relatively low levels of computing problems. Table 8.1 indicates that these two groups can be very powerfully distinguished by the context of their computing use. Relative to those with low problems, those with high computing problems tend to work with computer packages that are more extensive, more centralized, and supported by more resources. These "problem" people have a negative orientation to the computing staff and toward their own computing competence, and they work in more professionalized governments.

Thus the direct comparison of those end users with high and low computing problems corresponds closely to our original hypotheses and to the data above, especially for those with high levels of computing problems. High problems are more common among clerks in governments that are oriented to professional operations and that have implemented a substantial computer package—extensive, centralized, and expensive. Such clerks also are characterized by a very unfavorable STI, in the sense that they offer a negative assessment of both the computing staff and of their own computing competency.

If the emphasis is on those people with low computing problems, one can reverse this causal characterization of the effects of the context of computing use. That is, clerks who experience relatively few problems with computing work with a modest, less centralized computer package, are in less professionalized governments, and have a generally positive assessment of their own computer competency and the responsiveness of computing staff. Since this analysis is based on relative differences, it cannot determine whether the incidence and level of computing problems is more contingent on one or the other context of computing use. Considering all the data in table 8.1 together, however, it seems reasonable to infer that clerks with high computing problems tend to use a highly developed computer package and that clerks with low computing problems have computing competency and work with responsive computing staff.

In sum, we suggest: *(a) that a favorable sociotechnical interface can reduce the level of problems experienced by the end user, given the existing computing package; and (b) that a more developed computer package tends to generate greater computing problems, given a user's existing STI.*

THE PROBLEMS-BENEFITS MIX

Another intriguing question regarding the impacts of computing on the work of the clerks is the configuration of problems and benefits experienced by the individual. It seems reasonable to assume that those people who enjoy relatively greater benefits from computing will also report relatively fewer problems with the technology, and vice versa. In part, this might relate to the end user's personal scale of measuring problems and benefits and in part it might result from a "halo effect," either negative or positive, depending on whether benefits or problems were more extensive and more salient to the user. This section examines whether levels of computing problems and benefits are systematically associated for the clerks in this analysis.

The variables indicating problems with computing are those we have employed in this chapter—information problems and operational problems. The variables representing benefits from computing are those indices developed in chapter 5 to indicate information benefits, resource efficiency, and service effectiveness. In general, our working hypothesis is that there will be a consistent inverse relationship between the levels of computing problems and computing benefits reported by the clerk. We expect particularly strong relationships between those variables that are most closely associated. For example, we assume a strong inverse correlation between information benefits and information problems and between operational benefits and service effectiveness. Similarly, it is reasonable to predict strong positive correlations between the two problems indices (we have examined this earlier in the chapter) and among the three benefits indices. It is important to reiterate that these predictions are based on the assumption that the effects of computing on a given end user are generally uniform and consistent across a variety of dimensions of problems and benefits in the end user's work. Each problems and benefits index is dichotomized at its mean so that about half the clerks are classified as reporting relatively higher or lower levels on the index.

Table 8.2 presents the relevant data to evaluate these predictions about the mix of problems and benefits. Each problems measure is significantly associated with two of the three benefits measures. In these cases, between 60 percent and 65 percent of all clerks experienced problems and benefits from computing that were in one of the predicted high/low patterns. Thus, for about three-fifths of the clerks, there is an inverse relationship between the level of information problems experienced with computing and the levels of both service effectiveness and information benefits attributed to the technology. The same proportion of clerks report that their level of operational problems with computing is inversely related to the service effectiveness and resource efficiency associated with their use of computing. There is virtually no such pattern between operational problems and information benefits or between information problems and resource efficiency.

Even on the variable pairs that do support the hypothesis, as many as 35 percent of the clerks are contrary to the "consistent" pattern. In none of the six variable pairs is the statistical association remarkably strong, given the "reasonable" assumptions guiding the analysis. Indeed, even the correlation between information problems and operational problems is a modest .22, with almost two in five clerks *not* experiencing either high levels or low levels on both problems (as noted above in table 8.1).

Of all the variable pairings in the table, it is the linkages between different types of benefits from computing that are most fully consistent with our hypothesis. Between 68 percent and 73 percent of the clerks report high or low benefits from computing on each pair of indices, and the correlation statistics are the highest ones in the table. The clerks' appraisal of the impacts of computing on service effectiveness is the variable most consistently related to the other benefits and problems measures. High or low service effectiveness impacts from computing are associated positively with information benefits and resource efficiency and are associated negatively with information problems and operational problems. It might be that the service effectiveness measure is the one (of these five problems/

Table 8.2.   Mix of Computing Problems and Computing Benefits Among Clerks

		Resource Efficiency Benefits[a]		Service Effectiveness Benefits		Information Problems		Operational Problems	
		H%	L%	H%	L%	H%	L%	H%	L%
	H%	32	12	40	11	17	32	24	25
Information benefits	L%	22	34	17	33	29	22	29	22
		.34***[b]		.45***		−.22**		−.09	
	H%			41	14	23	30	30	20
Resource efficiency benefits	L%			18	28	22	26	19	30
				.37***		−.02		−.21*	
	H%					18	38	26	34
Service effectiveness benefits	L%					27	17	27	14
						.29***		.23**	
	H%							28	14
Information problems	L%							25	33
								.22**	

NOTE: N=132 traffic ticket processing clerks in 40 municipalities.
[a] All variables dichotomized at mean score, with table indicating percent of cases in H=high or L=low groups.
[b] Kendall's tau beta correlation statistic, with significance level:
  * < .05
  ** < .01
  *** < .001

benefits indicators) that clerks interpret most broadly as a summary measure of the effects of computing on their work.

For many of the clerks, computing is neither uniformly beneficial nor consistently detrimental. It is interesting, for example, that about 1 in 5 clerks experiences high information problems with computing but also reports high information benefits, or high service effectiveness benefits, or high resource efficiency from computing. An even larger proportion of the clerks report high operational problems with computing and yet also attribute high information benefits and service effectiveness benefits to the technology. Thus the existence of considerable problems in the use of the technology does not necessarily eliminate the possibility that a person will also enjoy major benefits from computing.

It is less surprising, but also the case, that some of the clerks report few problems with computing and also do not attribute great benefits to their use of the technology. About 1 in 5 clerks fits into this category for most problems-benefits variable pairings. We assume that these are people for whom the use of computing technology is not particularly salient in their work. Again, it is the service effectiveness variable where the smallest proportion of clerks report computing problems in the same direction as this benefit.

CONCLUDING OBSERVATIONS

Clerks are among those desk-top bureaucrats in organizations for whom the most obvious and immediate benefits from computing were expected, and also among those for whom the intensive application of computing might generate considerable problems. In this chapter, we have considered the patterns of computing problems experienced by the traffic ticket processing clerks in our study. In general, the clerks report occasional operational problems and quite limited information problems attributable to computing. While their use of the technology has certainly not been problem-free, the level of computing problems reported by the clerks is quite modest.

The use of automated applications has become a central component of the work of many of these clerks. Because clerks' work requires extremely high levels of accuracy in the handling of data and also requires great speed and reliability in the information-processing services which support it, "occasional" problems can be viewed either as a positive or a problematic assessment of the impact of computing on their work. Given the legal responsibilities of traffic ticket-processing clerks, it is probably better that operational problems such as slow response are more frequent than information problems regarding the accuracy and manipulability of data.

A central interest in this chapter has been to examine whether the configurations of different problems and also of problems versus benefits are reinforcing. Very loosely, we might generalize that there is a "two-thirds" rule. That is, in most cases, *about two out of three clerks have the same relative levels of different types of computing problems and have inverse levels of problems and benefits from computing.* Since about 1 in 3 clerks does not fit the pattern, it is our view that these data indicate somewhat less "consistency" in the clerks' evaluations of computing problems and benefits than we had expected. We believe that this is best interpreted as an indication that clerks are sensitive to a complex pattern of impacts of computing on their work. The fact that an end user has experienced substantial problems in using computing does not mean that the user will necessarily deny that considerable benefits have also been enjoyed. Conversely, benefits from computing do not guarantee that an end user will not also be quite aware of the informational and operational shortcomings of the computing environment within which he/she is working.

Our analysis has also made clear the importance of the context of computing use in affecting the level of problems that a clerk experiences. It is the nature of the computer package that has the greatest explanatory power for those reporting relatively high computing problems. More clearly than the data in chapter 7, the analysis in this chapter reveals that computing problems are experienced with greater frequency by end users whose computer package is more extensive and more routinized. Clerks with low levels of computing problems, on the other hand, are most clearly distinguished by their user characteristics, particularly their greater competency with computing and their positive experiences with computing staff.

If one considers our special analyses of the impacts of computing on the street-level bureaucrats and the desk-top bureaucrats, one of the most striking observations is that *both* benefits and problems from computing are more extensive for people who work with a computer package that is more developed. This seems a classic manifestation of the "good news, bad news" phenomenon associated with many major technological innovations. The same aspects of the computer package that seem to stimulate greater benefits, including greater extensiveness, routinization, and sophistication, are also those that produce higher levels of problems. Thus the confidence in a technological fix seems misplaced. The evidence here is that the factors which are most associated with lower levels of problems, relative to benefits, are those relating to an improvement in the quality of the individual end user's sociotechnical interface, factors involving human rather than technical adjustments. The challenge, it seems, is to employ the most productive and extensive computer package while mitigating the problems it generates by improving the manner in which the affected users interact with that package.

9. Computing and Control in the Work Environment

Among the major impacts of computing on the work environment of information workers, an area that has been characterized by uncertainty and even controversy, is the effect of computing on the relative distribution of power enjoyed by different roles and individuals. One view stresses the capacity of computing to increase the end user's ability to influence others, to reduce the time pressures associated with the information processing aspects of work, and to increase the end user's sense of mastery of his/her work. In contrast, those with a broadly negative assessment of the impacts of computing on the individual's work environment assert that the individual worker will generally feel oppressed by the applications of computing. This view stresses the use of computing by superiors to monitor a person's work, and the tendency of computing use to increase the time pressures felt by the worker and to alienate the person from his/her work.

This chapter attempts to examine empirically whether either of these sets of claims about the impacts of computing on the work environment seems to be supported by the experiences of the end users in our study. There are alternatives to the two views suggested above, including the notion that computing has had very little significance for the work environment of most people. It is also possible that computing impacts are quite different across roles or even across individuals within a role. Since all our respondents answered questions relevant to these issues, we are able to assess whether computing does seem to have important effects on the work environment and whether such effects are linked to the context of computing use.

CONCEPTUALIZATION AND HYPOTHESIZED RELATIONSHIPS

In our conceptualization, the linkage between an individual and the work environment can be characterized by issues of control in relation to the individual's job space. There can be shifts of control due to computing either in relation to other people or in relation to the job itself. Thus we employ four variables that measure the effect of computing on the individual-work nexus: (a) control of the individual's work by others, as indicated by the closeness of supervision; (b) the individual's control over others, as indicated by his/her capacity to influence others in the work environment; (c) the constraints imposed by the job itself on the individual's work behavior, as indicated by the level of time pressure on the job; and (d) the individual's overall feeling of control over his/her work life, as indicated by the sense of accomplishment on the job.

These four aspects of control are summarized in figure 9.1. This selection of specific measures has been informed by core dimensions of the "Job Diagnostic Survey" (see Hackman and Oldham 1975), as well as by existing research on computing in organizations. Our indicators are the end user's own assessments of whether these four aspects of control within their work environments have been affected by the computing systems with which they deal.

While there have been many hyperbolic claims about the impacts of computing in the workplace, the effects that are empirically validated are rather more modest. The early empirical research (surveyed by Sartore and Kraemer 1977) and some recent studies suggest that computing tends to reduce the quality of working life, particularly by producing greater time pressure and reducing individual satisfaction with the job. These impacts were seen to be particularly

Figure 9.1. Relationships Between the End User, Computing, and Control in the Work Environment

Impacts of Computing on Control

	Positive	Negative
In Relation to Other People	Increased influence	Increased supervision
In Relation to the Job	Increased sense of accomplishment	Increased time pressure

strong for those in more clerical jobs, but were reported even for those in managerial positions (see, for example, Cooley 1981; Crompton and Jones 1984; Hoos 1960; Mann and Williams 1958; Mumford and Banks 1967; Werneke 1985). Other recent empirical research (Attewell and Rule 1984; DeKadt 1979; Giuliano 1982; Glenn and Feldberg 1979; Menzies 1981; and summarized by Federico, Brun, and McCalla 1980) holds that, overall, computing has had rather limited impacts on the character of white collar working life. It seems to have increased job pressure somewhat, to have had minimal effects on the level of supervision experienced by the worker, and perhaps to have increased slightly the levels of job satisfaction. There is also some indication in this research that the patterns and levels of computer impacts on work vary across roles, with more positive (or less negative) impacts attributed to the computer as the employee's role ascends the organizational hierarchy (see, for example, Child et al. 1985; Guthrie 1974; Kling 1978; Laudon 1974; Mumford 1972; Whisler 1970).

In general, our hypotheses are guided by this recent empirical research. Thus we expect that the effects of computing on the work environment of end users will be modest rather than substantial. More specifically, we hypothesize that:

1. Computing will result in moderate increases in the *supervision of work* by others, particularly among those in what we term "bureaucratic" roles, where job performance involves less discretion, more routinization, and tasks whose quantity and accuracy are amenable to quantititative measurement.

2. Computing will result in differential changes in *influence over others,* with those roles lower in the organizational hierarchy experiencing relative decreases in influence as they lose their capacity to mediate the information flows to those in decision-making and supervisory roles, who will enjoy increased influence.

3. Computing will increase *time pressure* on those in more routinized and bureaucratic information-handling roles, especially desktop bureaucrats and street-level bureaucrats, and it will reduce time pressure on top managers and staff professionals who utilize aggregate and summarized data.

4. Computing will generally increase the overall *sense of accomplishment* with the job for those employees who have enjoyed increases in control over others and have avoided increases in control by others and time pressure—primarily managers and staff professionals, given our prior hypotheses.

As suggested by these specific hypotheses, we expect that the overall impact of computing on control of work life will be differentially distributed among role types. In general, computing will enhance control of work life in relation to other individuals and in relation to the job for those employees who are higher in the organizational hierarchy and who perform more discretionary information processing tasks (managers and staff professionals) while diminishing control of work life for employees lower in the hierarchy and with less discretion (those in "bureaucratic" roles).

With regard to the effects of the context of computing use on work environment effects within roles, we generally hypothesize that more favorable benefits (that is, less pressure, greater job accomplishment, no increase in supervision by others, and greater influence over others) will be particularly associated with an end user who has a positive sociotechnical interface with computing, especially with a user's greater competency with computing, with a computer package that is more routinized and relatively less sophisticated, and with an organizational environment that places substantial information processing demands on the person, due to its greater scale and complexity.

Initially, we examine tabular data that indicate the extent to which computing has, in fact, had any of these effects on the work environments of those working in local governments. Second, we explore the *relative* effects of computing on work, across the four roles in our study, using chi-square and Kendall's tau statistics to measure the significance of between-role differences. Third, the linkages between the context of computing use and the level of effects of computing on people's work environment are assessed, employing regression analysis. Finally, we summarize our findings regarding computing and control in the work environment.

OVERALL IMPACTS OF COMPUTING ON WORK LIFE

Table 9.1 indicates the percentage of end users in each role who attribute impacts on control in their work environment to computing. Two interesting broad generalizations can be derived from these data. First, *the changes in work life caused by computing are widespread, but are not pervasive.* Rather like descriptions of the half-full/half-empty glass of water, there are nine instances where the majority of individuals within a role report no change due to computing and there are seven instances where the majority have experienced a change. In fact, it is most accurate to reformulate this generalization to emphasize that the incidence of change caused by computing varies considerably with the nature of the work impact. On the two impact measures tapping control in relation to others, the majority in each of the four roles have experienced no significant impact of computing on their work environment. The large majority in every role (73–78 percent) find that computing has not altered the extent to which their work is supervised and most (54–68 percent) indicate that computing has not affected their capacity to influence others. In contrast, a majority within each of the four roles does report a notable impact of computing on their sense of accomplishment with work, and only the staff professionals (at 49 percent) fall below a majority among all roles in attributing changes in time pressure to computing.

It is intriguing that substantial majorities of employees, across all roles, report that computing has had no noticeable effect on supervision of their work or on their capacity to influence others. The images of the computer as an effective/pernicious device for careful and precise monitoring of work are prevalent, from the early predictions about the impact of computers in organizations by Leavitt

Table 9.1. Effects on Work Environment Attributed to Computing, by Role

Computing Effect Upon:	Managers (N=498)	Staff Professionals (N=321)	Street-level Bureaucrats (N=343)	Desk-Top Bureaucrats (N=286)
Supervision of work				
More closely supervised	17%	6%	18%	9%
No difference	78	78	73	78
Less closely supervised	5	16	8	13
Influence over others				
Less	2	3	3	4
No change	56	54	68	67
More	42	43	30	28
Time pressure				
Increased	22	34	19	37
Not affected	48	51	36	40
Decreased	29	15	45	24
Sense of accomplishment				
Lower	4	3	5	6
Not affected	44	46	40	42
Raised	52	52	55	51

NOTE: Respondents are 1,448 professional service workers who indicated that they use computers or receive computer-based reports. Precise wording of these variables is in the appendix.

and Whisler (1958) to more recent ones by Pfeffer (1981). Why has computing not altered the level of supervision of municipal personnel?

Our intensive case study fieldwork offers several explanations. While computing systems offer great potential for the collection of work performance data which facilitate closer supervision, that potential has been only partially realized. For example, in situations where work was not monitored before automation, it tends not to be monitored after automation. When a new automated system is installed, managers have enough difficulty getting people to adopt and use the automated system, without adding objectionable monitoring features. Moreover, to this point there is an absence of computerized work monitoring systems with sufficient sensitivity to merit extensive use. Finally, many superordinates are disinclined to place reliance upon automated data, as opposed to other kinds of information personally gathered in their supervisory functions.

It is also unexpected that so many of those involved with computing do not feel it has altered their capacity to influence others. Virtually all the literature on automated data systems predicts that these systems will importantly change the manner in which those in particular information-handling roles will access, manipulate, and utilize data and, as a consequence, that automated systems will lead to what Anthony Downs (1967) termed "power shifts." Yet the majorities in each of the four roles report that computing has not altered their influence. However, the data actually do suggest a pattern of differential effects of computing on influence and we shall explore this more fully when we examine between-role differences below.

The second broad generalization that emerges from table 9.1 is that *the effects of computing on work life are largely job-enhancing.* This is most evident on the overall measure of the impact of computing on the information worker's sense of accomplishment. About half of those in every role find that computing has raised their sense of accomplishment on their job, while most of the rest indicate that computing has had no effect. Similarly, while the majority in every role report that computer technology has not altered their capacity to influence others, nearly all those who have experienced an impact report that they have greater influence due to computing, ranging from 28 percent to 43 percent across the roles. Less than 1 in 5 employees in any role reports that computing has increased the level of supervision of their work. And even the impact of the computer on time pressure has been generally benign, with 64 percent to 81 percent reporting that computing either has not affected or has actually decreased the pressure they experience on the job. Overall, there is little support in these general measures for the view that computer technology, at least in its current modes of implementation and use, has been a dehumanizing or demoralizing force in the work life of professional service workers.

BETWEEN-ROLE DIFFERENCES IN IMPACTS

A fuller understanding of these data on computers and the work environment can be achieved by an analysis of the between-role variations. Table 9.1 is useful for addressing this issue, and table 9.2 adds precision to the assessment, identifying the between-role variations that are statistically significant, as determined by chi-square and Kendall's tau measures. Table 9.2 indicates all those instances where the distribution of effects attributed to computing by any two roles are significantly different on both statistical measures and it also identifies the role that has experienced the greater increase.

Two broad findings are quite evident from the analysis of between-role differences in the impacts of computing on the work environment. First, there are no significant differences between any two roles in the extent to which computing has altered the overall feeling of accomplishment with work. Since table 9.1 indicates clearly that computing does raise the sense of accomplishment of most workers, this finding merely reveals the absence of systematic differences in such effects across role-types. The second broad finding is that computer technology produces quite substantial differential effects across roles on the other three aspects of control of the work environment examined in the analysis. Of the eight possible role pairings, there are significant between-role differences in five instances regarding time pressure, and in four instances regarding both su-

Table 9.2. Significant Between-Role Differences in Effects on Work Environment Attributed to Computing

	Staff Professionals	Desk-Top Bureaucrats	Street-Level Bureaucrats
Managers	←Supervision[a]*** ↑Time Pressure***	←Supervision*** ←Influence*** ↑Time Pressure***	←Influence*** ←Time Pressure***
Staff professionals		←Influence**	↑Supervision*** ←Influence*** ←Time Pressure***
Desk-top bureaucrats			↑Supervision** ←Time Pressure***

NOTE: Table 8.2 indicates only those role pairings where the between-group difference is statistically significant for *both* the chi-square and the Kendall's tau statistics, with the significance level for tau: ** = p<.01, *** = p<.001

[a] Arrow indicates the role with the higher direction on the indicator—that is, the role at which the arrow points experiences relatively greater supervision, influence, or time pressure attributable to computing.

pervision and influence. The subsequent paragraphs characterize these differences.

Supervision. Our hypotheses were guided by the assumption that the capabilities of automated systems are best suited to provide work-monitoring data and supervisorial control over those whose work is most routinized and has standardized outputs amenable to quantitative measures of accuracy and workload. Thus, among our roles, we expected the increases in supervision due to computing to be greatest for desk-top bureaucrats, next greatest for street-level bureaucrats, and least for staff professionals and managers. But table 9.2 indicates that it is managers and street-level bureaucrats who experience increases in supervision that are significantly higher than those for the other two roles.

We can suggest possible explanations for these rather surprising findings. It might be that employees in the most routinized information-processing work, the desk-top bureaucrats, find that computerized systems now perform some of the more mechanical aspects of their work, reducing their responsibility for some kinds of data-handling errors, thereby reducing the need for close supervision of their work and perhaps even increasing the proportion of their time allocated to more discretionary activities. For example, Kraemer, Dutton, and Northrop (1981) found that automation enabled clerical staff in traffic ticket-processing agencies to improve their accuracy in handling tickets and also increased their ability to provide discretionary services, such as sending reminder/delinquent notices to citizens.

In contrast to these desk-top bureaucrats, computing might increase the level of supervision felt by street-level bureaucrats because automated systems capture data that reduce the insulation of their activities "in the field" from those who monitor their performance. For example, patrol officers in the field are routinely assigned calls for service by computer-aided dispatchers who continuously monitor the status of the call until it is completed. When patrol officers stop a citizen or respond to a field situation on their own, they notify the dispatcher and further complete a field incident report, offense report, or other report, which is placed on the automated data system. When patrol officers take a break they call in to the dispatcher at both ends of the break. Thus the automated data systems of the police department contain a comprehensive and detailed portrayal of the patrol officers' activities. While the data in these systems are not routinely used to monitor individual performance, they can be used to reconstruct a detailed portrait of an individual officer's activities when something goes wrong. It is this ever-present surveillance and potential for performance assessment that might account for the patrol officers' feeling of increased supervision.

The increased supervision experienced by managers relative to other roles might be due to the greater access to operational data about their departments' operations that computing provides to others responsible for centralized monitoring (top managers) and control of resource use (budget officers, finance managers). Support for the notion that computing can increase the supervision of managers is provided by Markus' (1979) study of a financial information system in a multidivisional corporation, where a new automated system gave corporate managers greater control over divisional expenditures.

Influence. Table 9.2 indicates that on four of the eight role pairings there are significant between-role differences in the effects of computing on individuals' influence. As we expected, managers and staff professionals have enjoyed relatively greater increases in influence attributable to computing in comparison to those in the two "bureaucratic" roles. This seems to offer empirical support to Downs' (1967) power shift hypothesis in the sense that those higher in the organizational hierarchy and in more policy-oriented roles seem to credit computing with affording them the greatest increases in influence (see Dutton and Kraemer 1977). However, this support is qualified by the fact that while power is normally viewed as a zero-sum phenomenon, no more than 1 in 20 employees in any role felt that their influence over others had been reduced by computing (see Table 9.1). It might be that the power "losers" are in roles other than those in our analysis or that the losers do not recognize their loss. Alternatively, influence can be viewed as a form of power that need not be zero-sum (see Neumann 1950). From this perspective, when computing has had any notable effect, it has been influence-enhancing, especially for those in more discretionary, policy-oriented roles.

Time Pressure. Time pressure is the dimension of work life in our study where the effects of computing produce the greatest variation within and across roles. Although the changes in time pressure are most prevalent among the two bureaucratic roles, the directions of change are not fully consistent with our hypothesis. Along with desk-top bureaucrats, staff professionals also report increased time pressure rather than decreased pressure by ratios of about 2:1. As expected, managers are more likely to experience decreased time pressure due to computing; but the street-level bureaucrats experience the highest incidence of decreased pressure, by a ratio of more than 2:1. This last point is underscored in table 9.2, where the street-level bureaucrats report decreased time pressure significantly more often than any other role. And managers enjoy reduced time pressure relative to the two remaining roles. One can, of course, reverse this characterization, observing that desk-top bureaucrats and staff professionals experience work effects from computing that tend to increase time pressure much more frequently than street-level bureaucrats and managers.

As with the effects of computing on supervision, we find the unexpected grouping of managers and street-level bureaucrats versus the other two roles. In this case, our fieldwork suggests that the best explanation of this particular pattern of impacts on work lies in the dominant styles of data-handling that characterize the different roles. Managers and street-level bureaucrats are essentially *users* of automated data, and this use tends to be indirect (that is, mediated by others) and occasional (that is, on a periodic or case-by-case basis). For example, the patrol officers who comprise part of the street-level bureaucrats in our sample require rapid, straightforward fact retrieval in response to a field incident such as a speeding driver. In such situations, they obtain specific information by radio from headquarters dispatch staff who search computerized files for them. Since patrol officers can detain citizens for only a limited time, the rapid response provided through a computerized information system can actually decrease the time pressures that officers feel.

In contrast, the incidence of increased job pressure from computing occurs among staff professionals and desk-top bureaucrats—role-types who are not only users, but also generators and manipulators of considerable amounts of data amendable to automation. These roles are more likely to be involved with computing directly and on a frequent basis. For example, the work of such desk-top bureaucrats as departmental bookkeepers and traffic clerks is dominated by data-handling activities, and they are likely to have substantial "hands-on" involvement with computers and computer-generated data. For those working in such roles, the automated system can increase time pressure in a variety of ways—by increasing the demands for more extensive and timely data entry, by expanding the amount of data that must be considered on a given task and, where interactive systems are used, by forcing the user to conform to the rhythms of the automated system. Such intensification of information processing tasks can substantially increase the time pressure experienced by an employee.

WITHIN-ROLE EFFECTS OF CONTEXT OF COMPUTING USE

As in earlier chapters, an important concern is whether the context of computing use seems to influence the impacts of computing on end users in the organization. We hypothesized that all three aspects of the context would be associated with the effects of computing on users' work environments. Tables 9.3 and 9.4 provide data with which to assess the relationships between the context of use and these effects.

When considered as competing explanations, it seems clear that none of the three aspects of the context of computing use is particularly powerful in accounting for the differences among those within a role. Of the sixteen cases, the set of user characteristics are significantly associated with these differences in only five cases, the computer package is significant in only four cases, and the organizational environment is significant only three times.

Moreover, there are only two instances where an element of the context of use accounts for as much as 10 percent of the between-individual variance in the effects of computing on the work environment. To the extent that the context of use is important, it is generally the user characteristics that have greater explanatory power for those in more discretionary roles and it is the computer package or the organizational environment that has greater explanatory power for those in the more "bureaucratic" roles. This is consistent with our expectation that the effects of computing on the work environment of those is less discretionary roles would be more "driven" by the milieu and that personal characteristics would be more important for those with greater discretion regarding use of the technology.

When the aspects of the context of use are combined as alternative explanations, there is some increase in their explanatory power. Yet even here, the full set of variables is significant in only seven of the sixteen cases. Again, there are important differences among the roles. the context of use has significant explanatory power for managers on all four effects on the work environment and for none of the four effects for desk-top bureaucrats. Thus the level of organizational discretion is also critical when all aspects of the context of computing use are considered together. However, contrary to our general as-

Table 9.3.   Explanatory Power of Context of Use for Effects of Computing on the Work Environment, By Role

Competing Explanations: Percent of within-role variation in effects explained by		*Managers*	*Staff Professionals*	*Street-Level Bureaucrats*	*Desk-Top Bureaucrats*
Organizational environment	a	1	1	1	6*
	b	2	0	1	2
	c	2	1	6*	1
	d	2	2	5*	4
Computer package	a	5**a	2	2	3
	b	1	1	3	2
	c	2	7**	13***	2
	d	3	1	3	9**
User characteristics	a	2	2	0	2
	b	7***	4	3	6
	c	7***	7**	6	5
	d	11***	13***	5	1

Table 9.3. (continued)

Competing Explanations: Percent of within-role variation in effects explained by		Managers	Staff Professionals	Street-Level Bureaucrats	Desk-Top Bureaucrats
Alternative Explanation: (all contextual elements combined)	a	8***	ns	ns	ns
	b	10***	ns	ns	ns
	c	10***	11**	20*	ns
	d	13***	15	13**	ns
Percent of this total accounted for by Organizational environment	a	9	ns	ns	ns
	b	17	ns	ns	ns
	c	26	11	38	ns
	d	16	15	47	ns
Computer package	a	91	ns	ns	ns
	b	0	ns	ns	ns
	c	0	56	40	ns
	d	0	0	0	ns
User characteristics	a	0	ns	ns	ns
	b	83	no	ns	ns
	c	72	33	22	ns
	d	85	85	53	ns

NOTE: a = Supervision by others
    b = Influence over others
    c = Time pressure
    d = Sense of job accomplishment
[a] Significance for regression equation based on F statistic:
  * $p < .05$
  ** $p < .01$
  *** $p < .001$

sumption, the context is more important for those with greater discretion rather than for those with least discretion.

It is also interesting that the context of use is significant for staff professionals and street-level bureaucrats only on those elements of the work environment that concern the relationship of the person to his/her job, not those involving control in relation to other people. And the only variable that is consistently associated with work

Table 9.4. Key Contextual Variables for Work Environment Effects Attributed to Computing, by Role

Aspect of Context of Use	Managers	Staff Professionals	Street-Level Bureaucrats	Desk-Top Bureaucrats
		Greater Supervision by Others		
Organizational environment				
Computer package	Centralized computing (.29)**a	n.s.	n.s.	n.s.
User characteristics				
		Greater Influence over Others		
Organizational environment	+Gov't complexity (.14)**			
Computer package	+User computing competency (.19)**	n.s.	n.s.	n.s.
User characteristics	+User orientation to computing staff (.14)** Younger user (−.11)*			
		Greater Time Pressure		
Organizational environment	+Gov't complexity (.11)*		−Gov't scale (−.18)*	
Computer package		Routinized computing (.17)**	More extensive computing (.28)**	n.s.
User characteristics	−User orientation to computing staff (−.24)***	−User orientation to computing staff (−.16)*	−User orientation to computing staff (.19)*	

Table 9.4. (continued)

Aspect of Context of Use	Managers	Staff Professionals	Street-Level Bureaucrats	Desk-Top Bureaucrats
		Greater Sense of Job Accomplishment		
Organizational environment	−Gov't professionalism (−.11)*		+Gov't scale (.19)*	n.s.
Computer package				
User characteristics	+User orientation to computing staff (.28)***	+User orientation to computing staff (.24)***	+User orientation to computing staff (.25)**	
	+User computing competency (.12)*	+User computing competency (.20)**		
		Younger user (−.15)*		

[a] Standardized beta in regression equations is in parenthesis, with significance based or T statistic.

* $p < .05$
** $p < .01$
*** $p < .001$

environment effects across the different roles is one related to these job control variables. Where the person has a positive assessment of the responsiveness of computing staff, he/she also reports the computing has resulted in a greater sense of accomplishment with work and no increased time pressure on the job.

On balance, the capacity of the context of use to account for differences in the impacts of computing on end users is lower for work environment effects than for utilization, benefits, or problems. The context of use seems most strongly associated with the work environment experienced by those with the greatest organizational discretion and on those work environment effects tapping the relationship of the worker to his/her job rather than to control issues involving the worker and other people. No specific variables in the context of use are consistently associated with most work environment effects across most roles.

CONCLUDING OBSERVATIONS

In assessing the array of data and findings above, several general conclusions are quite apparent. The first overall conclusion is that, for the end users in our analysis, *computing has not yet caused the kinds of dramatic impacts on the work environment that have been suggested* in the mildly empirical analyses that informed our study. In table 9.1, the modal response was no change/no effect attributed to computing in eleven of the sixteen pairings of a role with a feature of the work environment. In fact, the majority in *every* role reports no change due to computing on the key issues of control of work by others and control over others in the work environment. And the modal response on the effect of computing on time pressure is no change for every role except street-level bureaucrats.

But a second general conclusion, qualifying the first one, is that *computing has had notable effects on some aspects of the work environment.* The majority of those in all four roles have experienced a change they attribute to computing in their sense of accomplishment with work, and a majority in three of the four roles report such changes on time pressure. Substantial minorities in several roles also report that computing has altered their capacity to influence others. A third general conclusion is that *where computing has altered the individual's control in the work environment, the change tends to be job-enhancing.* In twelve of the sixteen cases the proportion within a role experiencing a favorable change due to computing is greater than the proportion reporting a negative effect.

Finally, a fourth broad conclusion is that *the context of computing use has only limited explanatory appeal in accounting for within-role variations on work environment effects.* The context of use is most strongly associated with the work environment impacts on managers, where user characteristics, and particularly a positive STI are associated with more favorable effects. But in general, none of the three contextual elements is consistently associated with work environment effects, and even a combination of the elements can account for more than 15 percent of the variance in only one of sixteen cases.

Table 9.5 summarizes some of the major comparisons between expected and actual effects of computing on the work environment. Perhaps more than in any previous chapter, the findings here tend to be at variance with our expectations. The context of computing use has very limited explanatory power in accounting for within-role differences in the effects of computing on people's work environments. The effects reveal seemingly subtle patterns of between-role differences rather than the kinds of broad distinctions we predicted regarding positive and negative effects. What might account for the variance between our expectations and reality? It seems that the existing empirical research and the conventional wisdom resulted in several assumptions that are not supported by our analysis.

First, we assumed that the impacts of computing on work would vary considerably across roles, with some roles experiencing quite positive effects and others experiencing negative effects. As we have noted, this was true for the measures of supervision and time pressure, where changes were positive for some roles and negative for others; but it was not true for the measures of influence and sense of accomplishment, where all four roles indicated that changes were essentially positive. Second, we assumed that the pattern of directionality in the changes would be hierarchical, in the sense that the distribution of effects from computing would scale from those roles higher in the organization and with greater job discretion to those roles lower in the organization and with less job discretion. In fact,

Table 9.5.　Comparison of Expected and Actual Effects of Computing in the Work Environment

Expected	Actual
Overall	
• Substantial effects for most people	• Majority report no change on influence or supervision
	• Majority report change on accomplishment, time pressure
• Effects beneficial for those with greater discretion, negative for those with less discretion	• Most effects job-enhancing for all roles
	• More negative effects on supervision and time pressure for roles with *less* pervasive information-handling
• Context of computing use substantially associated with within-role differences	• Minimal associations between context of use and level of effects
Person-Job Effects (accomplishment, time pressure)	
• Greater negative job effects on those with least discretion	• No between-role differences on accomplishment
	• Greater time pressure: staff professionals > desk-top bureaucrats > managers > street-level bureaucrats
• Developed computer package most important contextual element, associated with increased job effects	• No clear pattern; computer package and user characteristics each most important in 3 instances
Person-Others Effects (influence, supervision)	
• Greater positive control effects from those with high discretion	• Staff professionals but not managers enjoy greatest control benefits
• Positive STI most important contextual element associated with positive control effects	• Minimal and unpatterned associations between control effects and any aspect of the context of use

the data in table 9.2 provide a strong case that there are clusters of roles within which rather similar patterns of effects from computing are reported. Moreover, these clusters are composed of different roles on different aspects of control in the work environment. These varying clusters were characterized for each aspect of control in the work environment in our explication of table 9.2. Is there an underlying structure in these intriguing and somewhat surprising patterns of effects of computing on the work environment?

While the absolute levels of computing effects on control in the work environment serve as the base for discussing this question, we stress the *relative* effects between end-user role-types in order to focus attention on the differential impacts of computing on work. Two different clusters of roles emerged in the between-role analysis in table 9.2. When the issue is the individual's control over others, as measured by the level of influence, managers and staff professionals enjoyed greater increases in control attributed to computing than did those in either of the two "bureaucratic" roles. However, when the issue is the control of the individual by others, as measured by the level of supervision, or when the issue is control by the work context itself, as measured by time pressure, the impacts of computing on managers and street-level bureaucrats are similar and vary significantly from the impacts of computing on staff professionals and desk-top bureaucrats. Broadly, the latter two roles experienced relatively less supervision due to computing and relatively greater time pressure due to computing than did those in the former roles.

Figure 9.2 displays this pattern of relative effects of computing on work for the four end-user roles. Broadly, it shows that one dynamic seems to account for the effects of computing on influence and another for its effects on supervision and time pressure. The configuration of similar roles on influence over others is generally consistent with our initial notion that the effects of computing on control of work would be contingent on the role's level in the organizational hierarchy. Moreover, this is the one case where the pattern initially hypothesized is at least loosely confirmed. We infer that end users in roles higher in the hierarchy do experience relative increases in influences as computerized systems increase their capabilities for accessing, analyzing, and utilizing data relevant to organizational problem-solving, decision making, and action. With regard to changes in influence, it should be recalled that few in any role reported that computing had actually reduced their control over others. Thus we have argued that computing seems to expand the influence "pie" or, at least, it seems to approximate a Pareto optimal situation where some perceive they are better off and few/none perceive they are worse off. But it is also clear that computing has particularly enhanced the control over others of those already in positions higher in the organizational hierarchy, lending some support to the view that computing is a power-reinforcing technology (see Danziger et al., 1982).

To account for the role clusters on supervision and time pressure, figure 9.2 suggests that the second dimension of each role might be crucial. This dimension focuses upon key characteristics of the dominant data-handling responsibilities associated with the role. Our earlier explanations of why these role clusters emerged on supervision and time pressure tended to emphasize the different patterns of data-handling in each cluster. Managers and street-level bureaucrats tend primarily to be users of the kinds of data amenable to automation, tend to use such data on an intermittent or case-by-case basis, and tend to gain access to such automated data through intermediaries. In contrast, such data-handling for staff professionals and desk-top bureaucrats is likely to be far more pervasive in their work. These roles tend to be not only users but also generators and manipulators of the kinds of data in automated systems; they tend to work directly with computers and computer-based data, and such data-handling is a continual feature of their work.

Figure 9.2. Summary of Findings About Relative Impacts of Computing on Control of Work

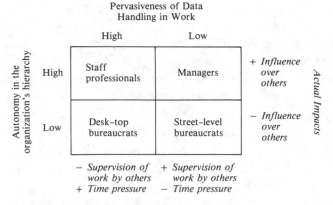

NOTE: High means that data handling tends to be direct, multimodal, and continual; low means that data handling tends to be indirect, use-oriented (relative to generation and manipulation), and intermittent.

[a] Impacts are those effects on an end user's control of work that are attributed to computers. The table indicates those roles which have experienced an impact in a significantly different pattern than the roles with which it is contrasted.

Computing systems are an increasingly crucial force in the work environment of people for whom data-handling is a pervasive job characteristic. The technology can affect and even control the scale and rate of information-processing demands and pressures on the knowledge worker. Continual and multimodal data-handling responsibilities as well as direct involvement with computing are all important factors that tend to increase the time pressure associated with work. In contrast, managers and street-level bureaucrats in the field tend to be buffered from the pressures resulting from continuous and direct involvement with computers; rather they tend to enjoy mainly the job benefits from requesting and receiving from others the timely and relevant information they desire from automated systems.

The data-handling characteristics of the different roles also provide a partial explanation for the role clusters on the effects of computing on work supervision (although it is important to note that the majority in every role indicate that computing has not altered the level of supervision of their work). Since the work of those in roles where data handling is more pervasive, particularly the desk-top bureaucrats, seems most suited to automated work monitoring systems, it is surprising that these groups were more likely to experience *reduced* supervision due to computing than managers or street-level bureaucrats. We suggested that for people whose work is high in data handling there are computerized systems that can fulfill many of the routine calculating, printing, and record-keeping tasks which previously required particularly close supervision regarding accuracy and speed. Indeed, by automating such tasks, computing might reduce not only the closeness of supervision required, but also the proportion of the information worker's time devoted to the nondiscretionary activities where supervision is appropriate. Ironically, it is possible that computing might result in the greatest increases in supervision of people whose work was traditionally insulated from effective data-based monitoring. The relevant examples in our analysis are the role of computing in the supervision of managers by centralized controllers using the data in automated resource utilization systems and the capture and analysis in computerized systems of performance data about street-level bureaucrats whose work was previously buffered from direct supervision because it occurred in the field.

In assessing the "net" effects of computing on control for each role, figure 9.2 illuminates the fact that *no single role has uniformly gained greater control over the work environment as a result of computing.* Clearly, the end users in each role have experienced a mix of positive, neutral, and negative control impacts. But the table does suggest that *computing has particularly benefited the staff professionals on the most crucial components of control in the workplace.* Staff professionals are the only group who have enjoyed both relative increases in their control over others (influence) and also relative decreases in control by others (the level of supervision) of their work. The data on the impacts of computing in table 9.1 are consistent with this interpretation that staff professionals have enjoyed the greatest control benefits. Staff professionals credited computing with more favorable effects on sense of accomplishment than any other role, they reported the lowest level of increased supervision of any role, and they were the role where the highest percentage attributed increases in influence to computing. Only in terms of increased time pressure did staff professionals report a net negative effect from computing.

These beneficial effects of computing for staff professionals regarding control over others and control by others are in accord with the prediction by Downs (1967) and Lowi (1972) that an "information elite" would gain increased control from the expanding use of computers within the organization. The "information elite" combines a high level of technical expertise in their organizational domain with some sophistication in the use of computers and/or computer-based information. Given their organizational position at the center of the policy process, these capabilities enable the information elite to influence, and possibly even to dominate, the nature of policy definition, policy formation, and policy implementation.

The information elite in our sample, as discussed above in chapter 4, is primarily composed of such information workers as policy analysts, planners, and high-level management and budget analysts. Chapter 4 revealed that they are not extensive users of computing; but these groups of technically skilled specialists do provide increasingly sophisticated information services to the organization. Although they are dispersed among different organizational subunits, they tend to share basic norms regarding professional standards of practice and the role that technical expertise ought to play in guiding decisions and actions. Staff professionals, as an information elite, are particularly likely to gain increased control as the role of computing expands within the work environment because this elite serves as the effective broker between the computer elite, who provide data processing services, and the policymakers and managers, who need to tap the extensive capabilities of automated information systems. The information elite gains control over others (influence) and resists control by others (supervision) by a combination of persuading others through the force of their data- and information-based arguments and of serving others as an effective information broker whose competencies are essential.

These findings regarding staff professionals seem especially significant because they are one of the first (if partial) confirmations in a systematic, empirical analysis of the prediction that computer technology will enable an information elite to reap the greatest increases in control within organizations. It is possible that, over time, the spread of computer literacy, of "user-friendly" computer systems, and of personal computers will reduce the relative advantages of the information elite. But the advantages of this elite in the near future seem considerable, and they might continue for quite a long period. Consequently, empirical research on the distribution of control within organizations and on the rise of technocratic elites might well focus on the nature of information elites. In particular, it is important to determine whose interests and agenda will be best served by the actions of the information elite.

10. Managers and Computers: Control

The use of the computer as a tool for managers has been the organizational application of the technology that has received the most extensive attention in the two decades since the introduction of the technology. While the early promise of the computer was closely linked with its value in repetitive, clerical functions, its promise as an aid for management has become the dominant image in the literature. The scholarly literature, beginning with Leavitt and Whisler (1958) and Simon (1960), has consistently and, in most cases, enthusiastically projected the many contributions that computing can make to the effective performance of these management functions.

MANAGERIAL CONTROL

In this chapter, we assess the extent to which computing has affected one crucial management function—managerial control. The manager's control of the work environment involves the formulation and implementation of organizational arrangements through which goals are set and attained using personnel and other resources. Computing can serve managerial control by means of any of the three types of computer-based systems that we specified in chapter 6. First, computing can be the source of model-based DSS that serve as the basis of or as an aid to control-oriented decisions and actions by a manager. Second, operations-based data that are gathered and massaged in computerized systems can provide managers with the information to guide their control activities. These are the systems that are most often associated with the concept "*management* information systems." Finally, the manager can use explicit, ad hoc analyses produced by data-based systems to inform his/her efforts to control organizational action. In our extensive field research, we observed many examples of departmental-level managers using computing in the attempt to gain greater control of resources, of personnel, or of performance goals. Some examples of these uses might help to illustrate their diversity. While these examples are drawn from local government, comparable control functions face managers in most organizational settings.

Resource Control. Because many of the earliest automated applications in local government were in the finance function, managers have often found that their initial opportunities for control by means of computing are related to financial resources. Most directly, computerization of the budget tends to provide managers with more detailed and more timely data about the relationship between levels of authorized expenditure and the actual amounts that have been expended and encumbered in a given budgetary line item. Computing has also facilitated the development of program budgets, usually as a financial information system that supplements the line item budget. Thus, as a by-product of the operations-based data in the computerized accounting systems, managers tend to receive information regarding the status of their financial resources in a form that is more timely and often more rich than that received from manual accounting systems (see Kraemer, Dutton, and Northrop 1981: ch. 7).

Over time, these operations-based computerized budget monitoring systems have tended to become more sophisticated, affording expanded control capabilities to managers. For example, many computerized budget monitoring systems now project the total year-to-date expenditure, by line item (or by program), for the remainder of the fiscal year, and some "flag" any line item where this projection indicates that there will be overspending or underspending that is greater than a specified level (for example, 10 percent of the authorization for the year).

While many cities have developed this type of exception reporting system for fiscal control, some governments have implemented substantially more sophisticated computerized systems to control resources. These are better understood as model-based systems, in the sense that they use complex calculations and even simulations to assess the implications of various resource issues. For example, in one large city on the Eastern seaboard, the system provides more than a simple linear projection of year-to-date expenditure; a computerized model uses the expenditure histories of the previous three fiscal years to develop a projection based on monthly variations in expenditure. While some expenditure items are quite consistent throughout the fiscal year, there are others that are extremely "lumpy." In an obvious example, the street maintenance account involves nearly three times as much expenditure per month in snowbelt cities during some winter months when snow removal is a continual activity. Managers in some departments in this city observed that as many as half of their line-item accounts are characterized by patterns of expenditure that are sufficiently irregular in some cyclical fashion that straight-line expenditure projections are deceptive tools for financial resource control. While many of these systems for managerial control deal with financial resources, they can also be applied to other material resources as well. To cite one example, a few governments have computerized models indicating when to do certain maintenance activities on the equipment in the vehicle pool, and even calculating when it becomes cost-effective to sell equipment rather than repair it.

It is important to note that in these operations-based and model-based automated systems, as in most automated applications supporting managerial control, top managers (or some staff personnel) must make the crucial decisions regarding both the specification of goal parameters and also the actions to be taken in response to variations from those goals. In the city discussed above, the mayor instituted a policy that prohibits further expenditure (including encumbrances) in any line item that has surpassed 115 percent of its projected allocation for the month. Further expenditure is allowed only by special permission of the financial controllers, who can reduce authorized expenditure in a future month by the amount of the overspending, or by the mayor and council, who can authorize a supplementary allocation.

Another type of resource control that has been facilitated by computing is the determination of the real costs of programs. As a function of combining data on performance with data on expenditure, managers can develop relatively accurate measures of cost per unit of service. In many instances, this type of managerial control involves a form of what we have termed a data-based system—an ad hoc request that certain data be collected or restructured to answer a specific question posed by the manager.

In one county, for example, the department head of human and environmental services requested a computer-based analysis which cross-tabulated data from his pest eradication staff on the number of rats killed with data indicating the hours of personnel time involved and the relevant staff salaries. He discovered that the program was costing more than $100 per "confirmed kill," and he commented jocularly: "And I thought that steak was expensive!" In this case, discussion with the staff persuaded the manager that there was little that could be done to reduce the cost of providing the service and that the public health rationales for the program justified its continuation. But the manager was made sensitive to the actual costs of the program because of his decision to take advantage of the capacity of the computer to collect and restructure performance and cost data into meaningful information for managerial control.

Personnel Control. Managerial control of personnel is clearly linked to control of resources, since staff-related expenditure constitutes more than three-fourths of the total operating budget in most local governments. The manager's responsibilities include the rational allocation of available staff to accomplish the goals of the organizational unit and also the monitoring of staff activity to ensure that performance is consistent with those goals.

Clear examples of managerial use of computing to allocate staff are evident in many police departments. Computing is now widely used to inform the decisions regarding the deployment of patrol officers. Police managers have considerable discretion in deciding how to allocate patrol officers in terms of beats (that is, geographic zones), shifts (time periods), and activities (such as foot patrol, car patrol, undercover surveillance, and so on). Minimally, computing can restructure operations-based data to provide the managers responsible for allocation with recent criminal statistics data, such as the locations and times of criminal activities, and with patrol officers' activities such as arrests. This information might then be included in the considerations that determine how patrol will be deployed.

In more sophisticated computerized "manpower allocation models," results of the model-based system indicate how patrol officers should be distributed, by linking such data as criminal activity and officer performance. Even in departments where such models exist, it is rare that police managers merely implement the recommendations of the models, because there are usually other criteria that must be considered. For example, there are often "political" criteria, such as the demands from owners of central business district shops, transmitted to the police via the elected officials of the government, for foot patrol police to provide psychological assurance to customers regarding the safety of the shopping area.

In general, there are few instances where model-based computerized systems *determine* rather than merely support managerial control decisions regarding material or personnel resources, since these organizational environments are characterized by patterns of demands and supports that are independent of a pure, statistical assessment of "rational" or "optimal" allocation. Indeed, analysts have provided persuasive evidence that crucial assumptions and priorities are embedded in any automated model and that the notion these models are free of human choice is misleading (see, for example, Brewer 1973; Dutton and Kraemer 1984; King 1984; Kraemer 1985; Pack and Pack 1977). Thus managerial discretion is evident in all these cases, beginning with the setting of parameters, and centering in decisions about how completely the computer-based recommendations will be revealed and/or implemented.

Given an allocation of personnel, a second important area where computing might affect managerial control of personnel is in monitoring their performance. Many automated systems capture, as a by-product of operations-based data collection, data that can be restructured to provide indicators of staff performance. For example, workload statistics can reveal to the manager the types of activities and the units of work being completed by each person under the manager's supervision. In a small Southern town, the sheriff decided to assess the activities of his two parking wardens. Since traffic tickets were automated, he requested a printout indicating the time of day and location of each ticket issued by each warden. He found that, while each was issuing a quite satisfactory number of tickets, the great majority of those tickets was for parking violations in the late morning and late afternoon in the streets adjacent to the town's only movie house. He quickly deduced how his traffic wardens were spending their afternoons, and they were obliged to bring their behavior in line with his expectations about a proper day's work. This example characterizes the manner in which a computerized system can utilize operations-based data to aid the manager in monitoring the performance of subordinates and, if appropriate, in taking managerial action to alter that performance.

Computer-based data on personnel performance can provide information on the nature of activities and also on the quantity and even the quality of those activities. It is not always the case that these data are the best indicators of effective staff performance. Most currently available computer-based indicators of performance give managers far stronger answers to the question "how much?" than to the question "how well?" Indeed, many personnel complain that computing had resulted in overreliance by managers on the amount of work they perform (e.g., how many tickets issued, how many clients handled, how many units processed) rather than consideration of their ability to achieve service effectiveness. Thus some argue that managers should avoid the temptation to act on the basis of the kinds of easily quantified indicators that can be provided by automated systems; rather, managers should establish a proper balance between such measures and more qualitative ones that might also indicate important components of performance.

Control of Organizational Performance. While most of these examples of managerial control facilitate the attainment of goals, they are premised on prior actions that establish the very nature of those goals. Thus we also consider certain aspects of the manager's goal-setting and problem-finding activities as a related aspect of the control function. In particular, we include the efforts by the manager to identify problems and to set realistic goals as part of a broad domain of activity that we term managerial control of "organizational performance."

Problem identification is a pervasive feature of the manager's attempt to control performance in his/her organizational domain. When a department is blithely overspending its budget, when the traffic wardens are at the movies during the workday, the manager has a problem. Some analysts distinguish between problem identification of these two types. In the first case, the computer automatically identifies the problem on the basis of previously set criteria. In the latter case, the computer is merely a tool used by the manager during a purposive search for information that enables the manager to decide whether a problem exists. In either case, it is reasonable to conclude that computing has facilitated managerial control, through its manipulation of models, its restructuring of operational data, or its ad hoc search of available automated data.

At a fundamental level, managerial control is contingent upon the formulation of explicit, realistic goals. Computer-based data are one source of information that managers might utilize in the considerations that lead to the setting of such goals. In general, this remains one of the areas where management remains more an art than a science, and there are few instances where computing applications have directly determined what ought to be, as opposed to what is. Thus the role of computing has primarily been to increase the "realism" of the goals that are set.

One of the more widespread model-based systems which supports the development of realistic goals is the computerized "fiscal impacts" model. It employs sophisticated projection techniques as well as simulations to answer a variety of questions about the future financial condition of the government, given a particular pattern of land-use development. For example, incorporating certain assumptions about the relationships between different land uses and government revenues/expenditures, the system can use trend data on such factors as changes in the extent and value of residential and commercial property, of sales tax, of intergovernmental grants, and so on in order to estimate both probable future levels of revenue generation and also appropriate expansion or contraction in future expenditure (Dutton and Kraemer 1985).

One western city uses such fiscal impact models to evaluate the overall fiscal feasibility for the government of both its general plan for the city's future development over a twenty-year period and specific area plans from private developers covering shorter time periods. First, a series of environmental models are used to generate estimates of population, housing, and commercial and industrial activity on a year-to-year basis, in order to create a scenario about how the community is likely to grow and develop. The models can be used to generate multiple scenarios simply by changing assumptions and/or the values of parameters. Second, these estimates are entered into a fiscal impact model. The model incorporates factors representing empirically derived relationships between population, housing, and commercial and industrial activity and the expenditures required by government to provide some specified level of service on the one hand and the revenues (including intergovernmental grants) generated by these activities on the other hand. The model then operates on the estimated values, performing a year-by-year cash flow analysis of revenues and expenditures, and ultimately producing output reports that are essentially pro forma balance sheets of revenues and expenditures for the government if the assumed development scenario actually occurs.

The balance sheets are then examined to determine the overall fiscal impact for the government of the alternative scenarios (i.e., do revenues at least match required expenditures?) yearly and over the entire development period. If revenues do not match the required expenditures, the city officials can then simulate the effects of alternative changes in tax policy (e.g., increasing the property tax rate), in land use (e.g., including more activities that generate high revenue and/or excluding more activities that generate high expenditures), in the rate of development (e.g., implementing more rapidly those activities that generate high revenues). In this way, city officials can ask an array of "what if" questions, simulate what will happen to the government's financial conditions under different land use or fiscal policies, and thus enhance the information base for goal-setting and policy-making (see, for example: Dutton 1981; Dutton and Kraemer 1985; Kraemer 1981; Kraemer 1985).

ACTUAL USE OF COMPUTING FOR MANAGERIAL CONTROL

We have identified and described several types of computer-based systems which might aid a manager attempting to control the application of organizational resources, the activities of personnel, and the assessment of performance goals within his/her organizational domain. The obvious empirical question is whether use of such computer-based systems is widespread and whether managers attach differential value to the application of computing to these various efforts at control. The managers in our analysis were asked specifically whether computing had assisted their control function with respect to these domains of activity.

In general, we hypothesize that computing will serve the control function most effectively in the area of resource control. This is both because there are extensive applications of computing that serve resource control, particularly by means of operations-based decision support systems in the finance function, (Kraemer, Dutton and Northrop 1981, ch. 7) and also because most material resources are quantifiable and thus especially amenable to storage, analysis and control by automated systems.

The value of computing for the control of personnel is a more difficult area to predict, since the literature provides quite contradictory arguments about the extent to which current automated systems are effective in providing data with which to control personnel. The previous chapter did indicate that most of the local government personnel in our study do not feel that computing had substantially increased the level at which their work is supervised. The inference from those data is that managers are not likely to report that computing has notably increased their control of staff.

To the extent that the model-based DSS conception of computing corresponds to systems-in-use, managers should also report considerable utility from computing in the support of goal setting, since such models are developed explicitly to increase the realism of projections of future needs and resources. And, as we have noted, all three modes of computing use for managerial control might serve the problem-identification function.

Table 10.1 provides the responses of the managers to these issues regarding the impacts of computing on their control function. These data indicate the extent to which computing serves each domain of managerial control, although they do not distinguish whether this control is attained by one or another type of computer-based system.

As we expected, it is the most direct areas of resource control where the largest proportion of managers report that computing has had considerable value. More than half the managers indicate that

Table 10.1. The Utility of Computing for Managerial Control

	Utility of Computing to Managers Percent of Managers[a]					
	Very useful	*Useful*	*Somewhat useful*	*Not useful*	*No Com- puter-based Information*	*Mean Utility*
Domain of Control						
Resource						
Budgetary cycle	23	29	31	6	11	2.46[b]
Expenditure deci- sions	17	20	32	15	16	2.07[b]
Real costs of pro- grams and activ- ities	9	14	28	26	22	1.62[c]
Personnel						
Information on subordinate per- formance	2	10	25	22	41	1.08[b]
Control of staff	6	—	46	24	24	1.24[d]
Allocation of staff	4	10	26	26	33	1.25[b]
Performance						
Identifying prob- lems	3	10	35	18	35	1.29[b]
Setting realistic goals	1	11	33	25	29	1.31[c]

[a] Percent of 1,030 managers indicating this level of utility.
[b] Based on these scores: Very useful = 4; Useful = 3; Somewhat useful = 1; No information = 0.
[c] Based on these scores: Nearly all = 4; Many = 3; A few = 2; No = 1; No information = 0.
[d] Based on these scores: To a large extent − 3; Somewhat = 2; Not at all = 1; No information = 0.

computing has been useful or very useful in providing information during budget cycle and more than one-third indicate that computing has this level of utility on a broad range of expenditure decisions. Conversely, less than 1 in 6 managers report that computing is not useful in these areas, while between 11 and 16 percent of the managers do not receive any computer-based information to support these control functions. Computing has been far less useful in enabling managers to establish the "real costs" of programs—a substantially more subtle and difficult application of the technology.

Among the most striking data in the table are those indicating the limited value that computing has had regarding the manager's control of personnel. Overall, the value of computing for personnel control is mixed: about half of the managers report that it is at least somewhat useful for controlling staff and a slightly smaller proportion find computing somewhat useful in allocating staff or providing information on personnel performance; but about one-fourth of the managers find computing not useful, and about one-third of the managers have no relevant computer-based information with which to control staff.

Among the specific data in the table, it is interesting that only six percent of the managers have found computing to be "very useful" in controlling staff under their supervision, and a minuscule 2 percent indicate that computing has provided them with "very useful" information about the performance of their subordinates. And it is notable that a substantial proportion (between one-fourth and two-fifths) of the managers report that they simply do not have automated information available that supports their control of staff. Moreover, about one-fourth of the managers also respond that they do have some automated information that is relevant to personnel control, but that this information is not useful.

Slightly under half of the managers find computing at least somewhat useful in supporting operational control in the areas of problem identification and setting realistic goals. Between 18 and 25 percent of the managers find that computing is not useful for these two aspects of operational control, and about one-third of the managers report that there are no relevant computerized systems to support their control of operations in these areas. Thus, despite the claims that computing has been particularly applied to problem finding, the majority of managers in our study has not enjoyed this potential benefit.

In sum, the data in table 10.1 are generally consistent with our expectations. First, *the most widespread impacts of computing on managerial control concern the control of quantifiable resources,* particularly those resources measurable in monetary units. Second, the current effects of computing on managerial control of staff are surprisingly modest, since *one-half to two-thirds of the managers indicate either that computing is not useful or is not available to support staff control.* And third, only *about half the managers report that computing has aided their control functions in the planning/operations areas of problem identification and goal setting.*

DIFFERENTIAL EFFECTS OF COMPUTING ON MANAGERIAL CONTROL

It is evident that there is considerable variation among managers in the extent to which they have enjoyed increased control through the utilization of computing. One interesting question is whether aspects of the context of computing use seem to account for these differences. To simplify the analysis, the eight measures of managerial control discussed above were subjected to a factor analysis. As indicated in table 10.2, the variables cluster rather distinctly into two factors. The first factor corresponds to our notion of resource control above, and the second factor includes those measures that concern the control of staff and of performance objectives. Rather than using factor scores in the analyses that follow, we have developed more straightforward indices that sum and average all the managerial control variables that load heavily on one or the other factor. We term these indices "resource control" and "performance control."

The literature on computer-based systems generally argues that the context of computing use is of major importance in determining the impacts of computing on managerial control (Kraemer, Dutton, and Northrop 1980, 1981). This literature places particular emphasis on the value of a more sophisticated and extensive computer package, particularly for performance control. Both the extensiveness and the routinization of the computer package are often cited in discussions of those conditions that increase the manager's resource control. It

Table 10.2.　Managerial Control Factors

Aspect of Control	Performance Control	Resource Control
Expenditure decision utility	.22	.79
Budgetary cycle utility	.24	.74
Determining real costs	.27	.64
Allocation of staff	.77	.26
Setting realistic goals	.76	.34
Information on subordinate performance	.75	.16
Identifying problems	.75	.22
Control of staff	.65	.41
Percentage of variance explained	.81	.19
Eigenvalue	4.48	1.03

NOTE: N = the proportion of the 1030 managers in 40 municipalities who have computer-based information relevant to the aspect of control.

is also suggested that a manager with a more positive sociotechnical interface with computing is likely to derive greater benefits from the technology, including enhanced managerial control. The literature rarely addresses the question of whether different organizational environments facilitate control via computing, although it seems reasonable that computing would be especially useful for managerial control in organizational environments that are of greater complexity and scale and that are more professionalized.

In order to examine the effects of the context of computing use on the level of managerial control, we shall focus on those managers in the top one-fourth and the bottom one-fourth of the distribution of levels of control on each index. The central question is whether any aspects of the context of computing vary systematically between managers who enjoy high levels of resource control or performance control and managers who report only low levels of such control attributable to computing.

The analytic technique we have used to explore these issues concerning managerial control is discriminant analysis. The results of this analysis are displayed in tables 10.3 and 10.4. Several broad observations are apparent from an examination of the tables. First, it is evident from table 10.3 that *the context of use does distinguish between those experiencing high and low levels of managerial control from computing.* For each type of control, the discriminant function coefficient is highly significant and the selected variables are able to correctly classify between 64 and 69 percent of the relevant managers in terms of whether they experience high or low control effects from computing.

A second broad observation derived from table 10.4 is that *the context of computing use is associated more systematically with the level of resource control than with the level of performance control.* This is reflected in the higher proportion of managers correctly classified and especially in the considerably higher canonical correlation coefficient. Third, table 10.4 reveals that *for each type of managerial control, both user characteristics and the computer package are significant aspects of the context of computing use,* while the organizational environment is not included in either discriminant function.

In general, the same user characteristics are important in discriminating between high and low levels of both resource control and performance control. As we hypothesized, the dominant pattern is the clear linkage between greater managerial control and a more positive sociotechnical interface between managers and the computer package available to them. The manager's positive evaluation of the quality of computing services is very strongly associated with both types of managerial control, and greater control is also related in both instances to the manager's sense of greater competency with computing. We did not expect that the less professional managers would report somewhat greater resource control.

In contrast, the most crucial aspects of the computer package vary between performance control and resource control. The only aspect of the computer package that differentiates between high and low

Table 10.3. Capacity of Context of Use to Discriminate Between Levels of Managerial Control Attributed to Computing

	Performance Control	*Resource Control*
Canonical correlation coefficient	.285	.452
Percent cases correctly classified	64%	69%
Wilks' lambda	.918***	.795***

*** < .001

Table 10.4. Key Variables Discriminating Levels of Managerial Control Attributed to Computing

	Higher Performance Control	*Higher Resource Control*
Group Centroids	Higher = .263 Lower = −.333	Higher = .406 Lower = .628
Context of Use		
Organizational environment Computer package	Higher expenditure on computing (.47)[a]	Routinized computing (.71) Less sophisticated computing (−.57) Centralized computing (.37)
User characteristics	Positive orientation to computing staff (.75) Higher user competency with computing (.37)	Positive orientation to computing staff (.85) Higher user competency with computing (.20) Less user professionalism (−.17)

NOTE: N = 265/260 managers in high and low quartiles on each managerial control issue.
[a] Standardized discriminant function coefficient, with sign changed to accord with appropriate interpretation of data, given group centroids.

performance control is the level of expenditure on computing, with higher expenditure associated with higher control. Given the recurrent themes in the literature on managers and computing, it is surprising that greater performance control is not clearly associated with either a more sophisticated or even a more extensive computer package.

Greater resource control, however, is associated with a computer package that is more routinized and more centralized, but *less* sophisticated. These features of the computer package are consistent with a technological environment in which computing has been well integrated into standard operating procedures over a reasonable period, and has continued to emphasize the kinds of basic automated applications that have traditionally served financial control. It is also interesting that managers who enjoy greater resource control tend to use a computer package that has remained under the control of a single installation. While such centralized computing should facilitate greater control of resource use by central managers, our sample of department-level managers might have been expected to enjoy greater "local" resource control where the computer package has become more decentralized, thus distributing control of the finance-related automated systems to the department level. These data indicate, however, that managers report greater control of resources in those governments where computing (and presumably financial applications as well) remains relatively centralized. Perhaps this indicates that basic, routinized, automated financial applications effectively serve the control needs of both central managers and departmental managers.

CONCLUDING OBSERVATIONS

Given the very extensive claims made regarding the value of computing to managers, the data in this chapter indicate that, in public organizations at least, *the value of computing for managerial control is evident, but limited.* Only in the area of resource control do as many as half the managers in the analysis report that they are supported by automated applications that have considerable value. Fewer than 1 in 5 managers report that computing has substantial usefulness in his/her control of personnel, and an even smaller proportion attributes such utility to computing on our indicators related to managerial control of overall organizational performance. For personnel control and overall performance control, about 1 in 3 managers reports that there is no computer-based information that is relevant to such domains of control, and an additional 1 in 4 managers indicates that the available computer-based information simply is not useful for managerial control.

Our data do not facilitate a critical test of the extent to which the computing that does enhance managerial control is predominantly composed of model-based, operations-based, or data-based systems. An assessment of the areas where managerial control seems most facilitated by current systems-in-use suggests that the greatest benefits are being derived from operations-based systems, since relatively straightforward uses of operations-oriented data, particularly data generated in the finance function, seems most crucial in the areas of managerial control that are widely effective. At least, there are few indications that computing is widely credited with utility in those domains of control where model-based systems are likely to be important, such as staff allocation and goal setting.

It is quite clear in our analysis that *the context of computing use does have substantial importance in accounting for the utility of computing for managerial control.* Most importantly, those managers with a very favorable sociotechnical interface, both in terms of their orientation to the computing staff and also their personal computing competency, tend to report that computing has greater value for both resource control and performance control. Second, the nature of the computer package is also strongly linked with managerial control, particularly for resource control, where a solid, well-established and centralized package is available to managers who enjoy greater control. Third, differences in the organizational environment are not systematically associated with utility of computing to individual manager's control.

It should be noted that, as in earlier analyses, we cannot establish whether a "high" group or a "low" group of people is more powerfully influenced by the context of computing use. The previous paragraph focused on those who enjoy relatively high levels of managerial control due to computing, since that is our particular interest. But it is also possible that the strongest impacts of the context of use are among those managers who gain little or no utility from computing. In that case one would reverse the characterization, and observe that the contribution of computing to managerial control is lowest for managers who have a very negative sociotechnical interface and who operate with a computer package that is relatively new, is decentralized, and has emphasized more sophisticated applications.

If the managers in our analysis read the predominant promotional or professional literature on "computing for managers," they are likely to feel that they have somehow been left behind by the technological wave. In reality, it seems that only a few have thus far been swept away into a new world of computer-based managerial control. As one might expect, the greatest control benefits involve financial resources, the initial and in most cases the continuing core of automated applications in public organizations. But given the widespread availability of systems that routinely record operations-based data regarding personnel performance, it is surprising that so few managers have enjoyed increased control of their staff by means of computing. Despite images of strong, even Orwellian control of subordinates, the evidence in this and the previous chapter suggests that the actual current impacts of computing on superordinate-subordinate relations remain quite limited.

11. End-User Computing: An Overview of Findings

In this summary chapter we return to the issues and questions raised in the first chapter of the book and we re-examine them in light of the findings in the intervening chapters. In the final chapter which follows, we go beyond the findings and suggest the implications of the study for understanding the linkages between people and computers.

We have attempted to identify factors contributing to the relative "success" (or "failure") of computers and information systems in organizations. And we have taken a special perspective, which we term an "end-user" view of computing, to denote our particular interest in the impacts of computing on the people who actually use (or do not use) the computerized systems in their work environment. Basic to this end-user view are the assumptions that "success" has multiple dimensions and that the meaning and relevance of these dimensions might vary for different people, depending upon their role in the organization.

Consequently, we have focused on four areas of impacts and four role types that we believe are especially important for developing better understanding of the successful use of computers in service-sector organizations. The four areas of computing impacts that we believe are especially important are: (a) utilization, (b) job performance benefits, (c) work environment effects, and (d) computing problems. We distinguished four role-types because we thought that these different roles might be involved with computing in different ways and that the impacts of computing might vary considerably as a function of their distinctive roles. Thus, we examined computer impacts on four types of "information workers" in public organizations:

1. *Managers,* the top department-level administrators, primarily department heads and division heads.
2. *Staff professionals,* those who serve top managers in a mainly staff capacity, primarily planners, policy analysts, budget and management analysts, and accountants.
3. *Street-level bureaucrats,* those line personnel who directly provide public goods and services to citizen-clients, namely police detectives and patrol officers.
4. *Desk-top bureaucrats,* those administrative and clerical workers who provide general administrative assistance for internal government operations or in support of the provision of goods and services to clients, primarily departmental administrative assistants and bookkeepers, traffic ticket clerks, and records clerks.

In our study of these role-types we have been concerned with determining: (a) whether the impacts of computing, measured in terms of utilization, job performance benefits, work environment effects, and problems, vary across different people in organizations; (b) whether the nature and level of these computer impacts match conventional images and expectations in the literature; and (c) whether between-person variation in the level of computer impacts can be explained by factors in the context of people's use of computing. This third concern entailed assessment of whether there are critical factors in the context of computing use that might be systematically related to different levels of these impacts (i.e., relative success and failure) from computers and information systems. Accordingly, we conceptualized the context of computing use, and we developed multiple indicators for each of three general elements: (a) the organizational environment; (b) the computer package; and (c) the characteristics of the user. Thus, the classical formulation of our empirical analysis (figure 11.1) entails four dependent variables concerned with characteristic areas of the impact of computing on people in organizations, four end-user roles, and three sets of independent variables which characterize aspects of the context of computing use that might account for between-person differences in the level of these impacts.

SUCCESS AND FAILURE: THE END-USER VIEWPOINT

We had expected that end users in the organizations we studied, local governments, would report largely negative impacts from computer utilization, due to deskilling, loss of autonomy, increased pressures and so on. Yet judged on the basis of their impacts on end users' job performance, work environment, and problems with the technology, computers and information systems in local government must be considered relatively successful. In both the four-role and individual-role analyses, computing has generally had positive impacts on people who use the technology in their work. Moreover, the pattern of positive impacts is evident across all roles in our analysis, although the recipients of the greatest benefits vary on different computer impacts.

Figure 11.1. Conceptual Dimensions of the Analysis of People and Computers

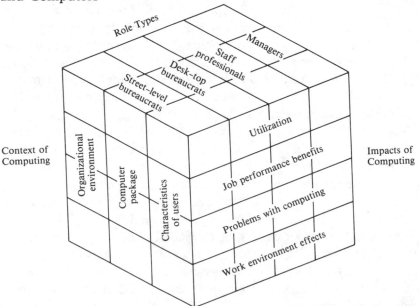

End users in all of our local government role-types attributed considerable job performance benefits to computing. In fact, the majority in *every* role reported positive effects on all three types of benefits (chapter 5). The largest proportions of end users reported positive effects of computing on improving service effectiveness, with information benefits and efficiency benefits ranking second and third.

End users also attributed few problems to computing. Users in all roles reported a low level of information problems, such as determining and maintaining accuracy of automated data or difficulties in altering data in computer systems. Most end users in all roles also reported moderate to low levels of operational problems, such as foul-ups in day-to-day operations, slow response to service requests, or unsatisfactory handling of job priorities. The frequency of such operational problems is low for one-fourth of the users, moderate for about half the users, and high for another one-fourth of our end users (chapter 7).

Users report that the effects of computing on the work environment tend to be either benign or marginal. Three-fourths of the end users indicate that computing has provided them with a greater sense of accomplishment in their work. Few report any impacts on the level of supervision and the majority report no change in their capacity to influence others. The only negative work environment effect reported by a plurality of end users is increased time pressure for staff professionals and desk-top bureaucrats—roles with pervasive data handling responsibilities. But decreases in time pressure due to computing are more common than increases among managers and street-level bureaucrats (chapter 9).

In short, local government computing can be regarded as a "success" from an end-user perspective, in the sense that *the majority of end users in our study report that computing has had positive effects on their job performance and work environment and they have experienced few problems with computing.*

VARIATIONS IN COMPUTER IMPACTS AMONG END USERS

Distribution of Benefits and Costs by Local Government Role-Types. While the computer's overall impacts on end users in local government organizations are positive, the distribution of benefits and costs is not equal across roles. Generally, *staff professionals* enjoy the greatest gains from computer use in terms of control over their work environment, even though many staff professionals use computing with less frequency than people in other roles. Staff professionals have both greater influence over others and lower supervision by others due to computing use than do managers, desk-top bureaucrats, and street-level bureaucrats (chapters 5 and 9).

Among staff professionals, those who fit the image of frequent, direct, hands-on use—the "total" users—gain more control in their work environment than the staff professionals who are instrumental or reactive users. Table 11.1 indicates that control is directly related to type of computer use among staff professionals. Nearly three-fifths of the total users experience high control in their work environment whereas two-fifths of the instrumental users and only one-fifth of the reactive users do so. Thus, staff professionals are the major gainers in control among the end users in our analysis, and among staff professionals it is the "total" users who enjoy the greatest benefits.

Managers, on the other hand, appear to be the biggest losers from computing, in the sense that they experience the smallest gains. Managers seldom use the technology in any mode, and most report few gains from their largely passive use of computing. Managers do report decreased time pressure and modest gains in control over resources due to computing. But they enjoy few gains in control over personnel and organizational performance as a result of computing, and they feel that their own performance is more closely

Table 11.1. Relationship Between Type of Computer Users Among Staff Professionals and Control in the Work Environment

Type of User	High Control[a]	Low Control	(N)
Total User	56%	44%	(86)
Instrumental User	40	60	(89)
Reactive User	22	78	(130)
Totals	100	100	(305)

[a] High Control means "high influence over others" and "low supervision by others;" Low Control means the opposite of these characteristics. In the construction of these variables, an "increase" in influence over others and "no change" or a "decrease" in supervision by others was considered an indicator of "high" control. For these data the chi-square is significant at < .001.

supervised. Finally, computer-based systems relevant to their functional needs in general, and to their needs for managerial control in particular, are either nonexistent or not particularly useful (chapter 10).

The *street-level bureaucrats* in our analysis are the most frequent users of computing in all three modes. The majority use computing daily in the indirect mode, and many of them make frequent direct use of computing. These end users experience a quite favorable array of computing benefits, and those who use more sophisticated computing and decentralized computing enjoy the biggest job performance gains from computer use. Computing reduces time pressure on the job for street-level bureaucrats, but they are also the role most likely to face increased supervision and they tend to have more problems with computing than those in other roles.

Desk-top bureaucrats tend to be the second most frequent users of computing (after street-level bureaucrats) in all three modes of use. They report increased time pressure in their work and less influence over others, but they also report less supervision of their work by others due to computing, and they attribute to computing a high sense of accomplishment with work and substantial information benefits. Given the pervasiveness of their information-processing tasks, they report surprisingly low levels of problems with computing. Thus, on balance, the street-level bureaucrats and the desk-top bureaucrats also seem to be beneficiaries of the use of computing in their work life. Despite notions that the routinization of computer use would "deskill" those in less discretionary jobs, those in the two "bureaucratic" roles we studied have a generally positive appraisal of the impacts of computing on their work.

Distribution of Benefits and Costs in Relation to Discretion and Pervasiveness of Data Handling. We had expected that the between-role differences in computing impacts would be clear, and that they would be related to the two dimensions used in our classification of organizational end users: *discretion in computer use* (based on autonomy in the organization's hierarchy); and *pervasiveness of data-handling* in work (chapter 2, figure 2.2). In general, we assumed that those in positions higher in the organizational hierarchy would have more discretion about computer utilization, and therefore we expected that staff professionals and managers would have higher proportions of low users or nonusers. However, since computing users in these positions could use the technology selectively, we expected to find higher proportions of the end users in these roles reporting job performance benefits and positive work environment effects. In contrast, we expected that those in roles with less discretion about computing use (desk-top and street-level bureaucrats) would report relatively higher levels of utilization, more substantial (and relatively negative) computing effects on their work environments, higher levels of problems with the technology, and more modest job performance benefits. Overall, despite some interesting between-role differences, *neither the autonomy nor the pervasiveness of an end-user role is a critical discriminating feature,* in the sense that neither is systematically associated with the differences.

Generally, our expectations about the relationship between *discretion* and utilization are supported by the findings but our expectations about discretion and both job performance benefits and problems with computing are not supported (table 11.2). As expected, there is a higher incidence of nonusers and low users among those role-types with greater discretion over computer use. For example, the "passive use > indirect use > direct use" pattern is strongest for staff professionals and managers (roles with greater discretion about use), whereas indirect use is highest for street-level bureaucrats and direct use is highest for desk-top bureaucrats (roles with less discretion about use). Computing does seem to facilitate gains in relative influence over others for those with greater discretion. But there are no other clear, systematic differences between role-types with greater and lesser organizational discretion over computer use in regard to the level of job performance benefits, work environment effects, or problems with computing.

We hypothesized that those roles with greater *pervasiveness of data handling* in their work would use computing more and as a result would experience greater performance benefits, work environment effects, and problems with computing. In fact, we found few effects of any kind that are systematically associated with the roles' pervasiveness of data handling (table 11.3). Only in the work environment effects are the roles differentially affected by computing, where two main effects stand out. Generally, as data handling is more

Table 11.2. Comparison of Findings with Expectations Regarding Computing's Differential Impacts on Role-Types with Higher or Lower Autonomy

	Expected Impacts/*Actual Impacts*	
Utilization:	Higher proportions of low users or nonusers *As expected, large majority are passive users*	
Job performance:	Among users, considerable benefits, especially information *As expected, but benefits not associated with autonomy*	
Work environment:	Substantial increases in control over others *As expected for influence, but supervision not associated with autonomy effects* Increases in control over job *Different effects not associated with autonomy*	
Problems:	Low level of problems with computing *As expected, but problems not associated with autonomy*	
Autonomy in the Organization's Hierarchy	HIGHER LOWER	Managers and Staff Professionals Desk-top and Street-level Bureaucrats
Utilization:	Most frequent direct and indirect use *As expected*	
Job performance:	Considerable efficiency and information benefits *As expected, especially high performance benefits*	
Work environment:	Reduction in control over others, control of job *Less influence over others, but other aspects not associated with autonomy*	
Problems:	High level of problems from computing *Low level of problems, not associated with autonomy*	

pervasive in a person's work, greater time pressure and less supervision by others are attributed to computing.

CONTEXTUAL FACTORS AFFECTING SUCCESS AND FAILURE

We hypothesized that the patterns of relationships between the context of use and the impacts of computing would be substantial. We have identified many cases where *the context of computing use does have a significant effect on the differential impacts of computing on people at work.* Our inferences, which have been developed in lan-

Table 11.3.   Comparison of Findings with Expectations Regarding Computing's Differential Impacts on Role Types Because of Pervasiveness of Data Handling in Work

Expected Impacts/*Actual Impacts*	
Higher Pervasiveness	Lower Pervasiveness
Staff professionals and desk-top bureaucrats	Managers and street-level bureaucrats

Utilization	
Greater overall use of computing	Less use of computing
Considerable differences in use, not associated with pervasiveness	

Job Performance	
More substantial benefits	Limited benefits
Substantial benefits, not associated with pervasiveness	

Work Environment	
Extensive effects, nature related to autonomy	Limited effects
More time pressure	*Less time pressure*
Less supervision by others	*More supervision by others*

Problems	
Higher levels of problems	Lower levels of problems
Low problems, not associated with pervasiveness	

guage that suggests the underlying causal patterns, are based on both our thorough statistical analyses and our many years of intensive field research in these and similar organizational settings. In general, a parsimonious set of variables representing the context of use sometimes explains (in a statistical sense) as much as 40 percent of the variance in the impacts of computing on people in a given role, and it often accounts for 10 to 25 percent of the variance.

We also expected that the patterns of relationships between the context of use and the impacts of computing would vary across roles in a relatively complex manner. Broadly, we anticipated that among those roles with greater discretion the characteristics of the user and the organizational environment would most importantly affect higher utilization, positive work environment effects, greater job performance benefits, and lower problems with computing. And among those roles with limited discretion we expected that the nature of the computer package would most affect utilization, job performance,

work environment and problems with computing. In short, we hypothesized that:

for those roles with:	These aspects of the context of use:	Will be most related to these impacts from computing:
+ Discretion	User characteristics and organizational environment	+ Job performance − Problems + Work effects + Utilization
− Discretion	Computer package	

Our findings generally support a more simplified observation—
namely, that *for roles with greater discretion the characteristics of
the user have the greatest effect on computer impacts and that for
roles with more limited discretion the nature of the computer package
has the greatest effect on computer impacts.* The characteristics of
the users, especially their sociotechnical interface, is the element in
the context of use that is most consistently related to computing
impacts across all role-types. However, the most accurate generalization is that *both the characteristics of the user and the computer
package tend to affect the impacts of computing on a given end user*
(table 11.4). The organizational environment seldom has systematic
effects on the impacts of computing on any role. Our findings
regarding each element in the context of computing use are characterized next.

User Characteristics. In most cases, the most powerful explanatory
variables are those measuring the characteristics of the individual
user, and especially those directly reflecting the quality of the sociotechnical interface between the end user and the computer package.
Generally, the end user who has greater competency regarding computing and who interacts with a computer staff that offers responsive
and efficient services enjoys the most positive effects from the technology. That is, a positive sociotechnical interface is consistently
associated with greater use, more substantial job performance benefits,
fewer problems, and greater control of the work environment for *all*
role types in our analysis. This pattern is particularly strong for
those in roles with greater organizational autonomy. The personal

Table 11.4. Findings About Role Types, Context of Use, and Computer Impacts

Role Type	Contextual Element	Computer Impacts			
		Utilization (greater)	Job performance benefits (greater)	Work environment effects (positive)	Computing problems (fewer)
Managers	Organizational environment	+Gov't complexity +Scale of service −Gov't professionalism			
	Computer package		Less computing expenditure Less sophisticated computing		Less computing expenditure
	User characteristics	+User orientation to computing staff +User computing competency	+User orientation to computing staff +User computing competency	+User orientation to computing staff +User computing competency[b]	+User orientation to computing staff +User computing competency
Staff professionals	Organizational environment	+Scale of service			+Government professionalism −Scale of service
	Computer package	+Routinization of computing +Extensiveness of computing			
	User characteristics	+User orientation to computing staff +User computing competency	+User orientation to computing staff +User computing competency	+User orientation to computing staff +User computing competency[c]	+User orientation to computing staff +User computing competency

Table 11.4. (continued)

Role Type	Contextual Element	Computer Impacts			
		Utilization (greater)	Job performance benefits (greater)	Work environment effects (positive)	Computing problems (fewer)
Street-level bureaucrats	Organizational environment				+Scale of service +Government professionalism
	Computer package	+Resource support for computing +Decentralized computing	Less extensive computing Decentralized computing		−Computing sophistication
	User characteristics	+User orientation to computing staff	+User orientation to computing staff	+User orientation to computing staff	+User orientation to computing staff
Desk-top bureaucrats	Organizational environment				+Scale of service
	Computer package	+Sophistication of computing +Resource support for computing			−Routinization of computing
	User characteristics				+User orientation to computing staff

a Generally, the computer package is not related to work environment effects, but there are selected instances where more developed computing (e.g., extensive, sophisticated, routinized) is strongly associated with negative work environment effects.

b The relationship is positive on positive work environment effects ("greater influence over others" and "greater sense of job accomplishment"), but not on negative work environment effects ("greater supervision by others" and "greater time pressure").

c The relationship is positive for "greater sense of accomplishment" only.

traits of the end user—age (and work experience) and user professionalism—are only occasionally significant aspects of the context
of use.

The Computer Package. In general, where the computer package is
more developed (in the sense of being more extensive, routinized,
resource intensive, sophisticated), there is higher utilization, greater
job performance benefits, and more favorable work environment
effects, but also greater problems with computing. In addition, centralized computing enhances managerial control, but decentralized
computing is associated with greater utilization and with greater
productivity benefits for street-level bureaucrats, especially for detectives (chapter 6), and for desk-top bureaucrats.

The Organizational Environment. The features of the organizational
environment are occasionally significant as part of an "alternative
explanations" framework regarding how the context of computing
use influences the impacts of computing on end users. The frequency
of computing problems is the impact most consistently linking the
individual with the environment. And utilization of computing by
managers is higher in larger, complex, and less professionalized
government environments. But in general, differences in the organizational environment are not crucial to an understanding of why
computing seems to have different impacts on different people.

While there are occasions where the characteristics of the user
dominate an explanation of differences between people in the impacts
of computing, it is generally the case that an analysis which incorporates *both* the characteristics of the user and the nature of the
computer package provides a more powerful and adequate explanation. Thus these two conceptual elements seem most appropriately
viewed as alternative (that is, complementary) explanations rather
than as competing explanations. It is the interplay between the user
and the computer package, both in the sense of the nature of the
sociotechnical interface and also in terms of the computer package
available to the user, that best explains how the context of computing
use importantly influences the impacts of computing on people at
work.

THE HUMAN–MACHINE INTERFACE: COMPUTER
SUPPORT FOR END USERS

Considered broadly and in the light of the special analysis chapters, these findings yield an intriguing point: many of the computing systems-in-use employed by the end users in our study are at odds with conventional images of the nature and role of computing support for "information workers." This point is demonstrated most convincingly in the case of detectives (chapter 6), and it seems to apply to our other role types as well (staff professionals in chapter 4 and managers in chapter 10).

We have called these prevalent systems-in-use *data-based systems* (see table 6.6) to differentiate them from more traditional concepts of decision support systems (the model-based system) and management information systems (the operations-based system). We have found that the conception of data-based systems seems to characterize the actual use of computing by end users more adequately than either of the two more traditional concepts. As a result, we have come to question whether current distinctions about computer-based systems give sufficient attention to key features emphasized in the data-based type. For example, Alter (1980) divides computer-based systems into two types as shown on the left in figure 11.2: EDP (which we call traditional MIS), and DSS (which we call traditional DSS). Alter further divides the decision support systems into seven types depending upon whether they are more data-based or more model-based.

It is our observation that data-based systems are widespread— they are found not only among DSS, but also in traditional EDP/ MIS as well. In earlier research (Dutton and Kraemer 1978), we described a form of "management-oriented computing" which was characterized by the generation, from the routine automated systems serving the operations of the government, of standard reports and, at times, special reports and analyses for managers. Alter also identifies such use of computing at the intersection of EDP and DSS. However, in contrast to Alter's characterization, we suggest that data-based systems seem to constitute a very large category of the systems-in-use by the end users of computing in our study of public organizations. Consequently, we draw the overlap between EDP/MIS and DSS substantially larger (figure 11.2 on the right).

In contrast to the traditional concepts of MIS and DSS, which are based upon the notion of "selective" use of information, the data-based system involves various forms of "prospecting" in order to find and link relevant data/information. Such prospecting typically involves direct, personal use of a computer terminal to search collections of information, which are a by-product of operational records or of specially generated data-bases that have been organized to aid information retrieval and analysis. Broadly, three kinds of use patterns might be involved:

1. Simple fact retrieval, involving the completely structured use of on-line data-bases to search for particular information.
2. More complex, less structured search with computer support tailored to perform the most frequently occurring searches.
3. Ad hoc, exploratory search with the aid of a generalized analysis system for search, summary, graphic representation, and calculation.

The computer package which supports such use provides interactive, easy access to the organized information and allows direct manipulation of the information by the user, who brings his/her knowledge and work experience to bear in using the information. The technology supporting the data-based system is moderately sophisticated, mainly involving computers with large storage capacity and on-line, remote access (sometimes interactive access) to the data-bases. Search of the data-bases is aided by preprogrammed keys on remote terminals, which facilitate routine fact-finding, by special software for frequently occurring searches, and by generalized data management and analysis software to support ad hoc retrieval and analysis.

Figure 11.2.   Conceptions of Data-Based Systems

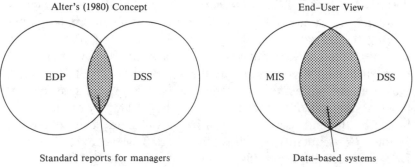

This human–machine interaction is important. Recent behavioral research indicates that decision making improves when users who are aided by computer terminals and easy-to-use retrieval software engage in active prospecting in an information-rich environment (Kunreuther and Schoemaker 1982). There is considerable reason to believe that the outcome of such human–machine interaction is no less a contribution to productive work than either mathematically optimal solutions to more narrowly defined problems or heuristic solutions to frequently encountered problems. The interaction between an end user who possesses rich, personal knowledge of a problem and its context, on the one hand, and a computerized system that instantly provides extensive, potentially relevant information, on the other hand, may represent a vast improvement over traditional management science methods.

There are several potential advantages of the type of human–machine interaction we have termed the data-based system. At minimum, there might be a reduced danger of solving, elegantly and optimally, the wrong problem, or of solving the right problem too late. Second, the easy accessibility to data and the direct relevance of the information to a decision at hand are critical determinants of whether the information system, and, ultimately, the information it generates, are actually used in decision making. And third, both the frequent, prospecting use of the system and also the benefits of use to the end user facilitate learning and routinize the process of use as part of the user's standard operating procedures for decision and action.

END-USER COMPUTING IN A CHANGING CONTEXT OF USE

One factor which makes the study of the impacts of computing both fascinating and frustrating is the magnitude and speed with which the context of computing use seems to change. This is most evident in the constant changes in the computer package, as new hardware and software developments emerge and are implemented. These changes then interact with the organizational environment and the end user, resulting in possible alterations in the structural relationships among these contextual elements and in possible changes in the patterns of computing impacts. Given these dynamics, it is reasonable for the reader to question the currency of our findings, based primarily upon data collected nearly ten years ago. Our continuous field research for more than fifteen years, as well as several other considerations, convince us that from the perspective of end-user computing, the changes in the nature and impacts of computing in organizational settings have been incremental and the findings reported in this book continue to be valid.

For end users themselves, the most notable changes that are occurring in the context of computing use concern their growing experience with computing and the increasing number of organizational end users whose mode of use is direct. In our analyses, the significance of differential levels of computing competence in accounting for the impacts of computing on end users has been assessed in every chapter. And many chapters have emphasized direct, interactive users, because they are the most interesting and, increasingly, the modal type of end user in most organizations. We have concluded that the impacts of computing on end users are contingent upon each of these factors—on both the levels of computing competence and the extent of direct use—and we infer from the available empirical research (discussed below) that the structural relationships between these factors and computing impacts remain similar.

It is the computer package itself in which the most substantial changes are manifest in the context of computing use. The most obvious change has been the developments in microcomputers and their associated software. It is inevitable that some readers will raise questions regarding whether changes in the computer package, and especially the advent of microcomputers, have invalidated our findings. Because most impacts of computing tend to become clear only over time, empirically sound answers to such questions will be possible in the years ahead, as microcomputers are diffused and routinized in the standard operating procedures of end users in organizations. But we recognize that it is important to address such reasonable questions, to the extent that it is possible, by examining the reported studies that do consider recent changes in computer technology, especially microcomputing technology.

It is important to begin such an appraisal by noting a general problem with the knowledge base regarding recent computing developments. We propose that one major value of our analysis is its specification of what *is*. The "leading edge" imagery of computing is so pervasive and so compelling that many observers have been persuaded that most systems-in-use in organizations are now characterized by high levels of utilization of very sophisticated technology. Such images have always been projected by those with commercial interests in promoting the technology and also by researchers and practitioners who desire to focus on interesting and exciting cases. (See, for example, virtually any issue of the computing trade publications, and also the "Mini-Symposium on Microcomputers in Local Government" [1984:57–87]).

However, even scholars who have done thoughtful research on high technology sometimes make knowledge claims about the nature of actual systems-in-use that seem to be influenced by this leading edge imagery rather than by valid and reliable empirical data. For example, in a recent book review essay on telecommunications technology in local government, Richard Bingham said of work from the URBIS Project:

Both of these books are well organized and well written. . . . They provide broad perspectives that might be applied to any new and complex technology. . . . In terms of computing technology itself, the books, although published in 1981 and 1983 are unfortunately dated. They are based on data collected . . . at a time when we were only in the beginning stages of the revolution in information processing. The widespread use of minis and micros by municipal government has essentially extended computing to all who wish to take advantage of it. Easy-to-understand software packages have made us all computer literates. Technological advances themselves have "democratized" computing. (1984:269–270)

The problem is that such assertions about minis and micros are not supported by the systematic, empirical research on computing— indeed they are at odds with the current facts. There are at least two recent studies in local governments that bear on these assertions. The first is an in-progress study of the evolution and future of computing in local governments (Kraemer, King, Dunkle, Lane, and George 1985). As part of that study, the investigators conducted a survey of 102 cities that historically have been among the more extensive and more experienced users of computing (i.e., over 50,000 in population and over ten years experience). The purpose of the survey was to find a single site with extensive use of microcomputers, where "extensive" was operationally defined as more than 100 microcomputers in use. Not one of the 102 cities in the survey had even 50 microcomputers in use. The median number of micros in use was 10 and the median number of micros planned for use in 1984–85 was also 10. These findings corroborate the data in another recent national survey which found that less than 15 percent of municipal governments currently own or lease even one microcomputer (Norris and Webb 1983). In short, the actual systems-in-use in public organizations and, even more obviously, the impacts of those computing systems, are not dominated by leading-edge technology and microcomputing.

These data should considerably temper popular assertions, since the actual systems-in-use and technology do not match the imagery:

1. There is no recent "revolution" in information processing; rather, a continuing evolution in the technology and its organizational impacts, has been occurring for nearly thirty years.
2. The use of minis and micros in local government is still limited. Most city and county governments in the United States still rely on one mainframe or minicomputer and use only one or a few microcomputers. Obviously, the larger governments typically have more than one mainframe and/or minicomputer and have several dozen microcomputers. But it seems hyperbolic and misleading to characterize such use of microcomputers as "widespread."
3. Computing has not been extended to all who wish to take advantage of it. The median number of city departments using microcomputers within these cities is 6.6. Departments that have traditionally been the most extensive users of mainframe- and mini-based computing are also the most extensive users of micros. Specifically, data processing, police, and finance are the departments which have the largest numbers of micros in use and which are the most extensive users of micros. Moreover, the major individual users of micros are staff professionals (data processing staff, budget and financial analysts, engineers, planners, manpower analysts, administrative analysts, and so forth)—not policymakers, managers, desk-top bureaucrats (with the exception of word-processing usage by secretarial/clerical staff) or street-level bureaucrats (Kraemer et al. 1985). Finally, control over procurement and distribution of microcomputers is largely in the hands of the data processing unit rather than the user departments, even when responsibilities are shared. Thus, it is hard to understand contentions that technological advances have "democratized" computing.

It is not our argument that widespread use of microcomputers will never occur in public organizations—a reasonable case can be made that this will happen. But we do suggest that their current use is limited and that their current deployment has not extended computing to all who wish to take advantage of it. The very modest empirical evidence also seems to support the hypothesis that microcomputing, like the computing advances that preceded it, will tend to reinforce the existing distribution of computing and other organizational resources, rather than dramatically altering that distribution.

It is possible that local governments are atypical of other organizations in the sense that they are far behind other organizational environments in the evolution of their computer packages. While we are aware of no conclusive empirical data regarding this possibility, there is one recent, systematic study which provides interesting evidence on this point. The very large survey of organizational end users in the private sector which, like our study, sampled end users randomly rather than purposively sampling microcomputer users, seems to support our observation that microcomputer use is less than pervasive in many organizational settings. Of the 4,448 organizational end users in the survey, only 8 percent primarily use microcomputers. Fully 92 percent of the users are primarily involved with mainframe computing systems (43 percent) and minicomputer networks (49 percent) in their work (Rushinek and Rushinek 1985). In short, despite the prevalent imagery of loading-edge technology innovations, the current computing context of most organizational end users does not seem one dominated by microcomputers.

Moreover, the few empirical studies of microcomputing impacts on organizational end users that have appeared in the literature seem quite consistent with the analyses in this book (Benson 1983; Culnan 1983; Rivard and Huff 1984; Rockart and Flannery 1984; Rushinek and Rushinek 1985). These studies can provide only preliminary comparison points with our analysis for several reasons. First, they tend to focus on only a few variables (mainly on management issues related to microcomputers) rather than on the full pattern of relationships between end users, the context of computing use, and the impacts of computing on individuals and organizations. And second, most tend to deal with relatively small samples of respondents from a few organizations within a particular regional setting. Table 11.5 indicates the samples and types of end users examined in these studies.

It is evident in the table that these studies are not fully comparable with our study or with each other. The samples of end users in our study and that by Rushinek and Rushinek are large, while the samples in the other studies are modest in size. We also share with Rushinek and Rushinek the decision to sample end users in many organizational roles, while most of the other studies mainly focus on managers and/or staff professionals. The studies also vary somewhat in such factors as the similarity of organizational settings and the mode of computing use. Culnan and Rockart and Flannery share our decision to use a "most similar systems" approach to selecting organizations for study, while the other studies examine end users in a diversity of organizations. Several studies examine only microcomputer user, but Benson and Rushinek and Rushinek look at all interactive users, regardless of their primary mode of use. Most studies also focus on individuals who are primarily nonprogramming end users, although all of Rivard and Huff's end users are programmers.

While none of these other studies examines a full range of dependent and independent variables relevant for analyzing the impacts of computing on organizational end users, we can extract some useful comparative data and observations that address significant issues shared with our research. Thus a synthesis of key findings in these studies is helpful in assessing the validity and currency of our analysis. Seven points seem especially noteworthy:

1. The organizational environment is not considered a significant factor in these studies of end-user computing. While Culnan (1983) found that organizational dynamism seems to result in greater use of commercial data-bases, there is no strong evidence in these studies that the organizational element in the context of computing use is significant in explaining the major dependent variables in end-user computing.

2. The user's personal traits, such as age and work experience, are seldom identified as important factors in accounting for between-individual variations in end-user computing. While Culnan (1983) did find some relationship between age and utilization (younger

Table 11.5. Comparison of End User Studies

Study Role-Types	Modes of Use Examined			Programmer	
	Passive	*Indirect*	*Direct*	*Yes*	*No*
Benson 1983 67 managers and 19 data processing professionals in 20 firms in St. Louis; (11 manufacturing, 2 insurance, 3 banking, and 1 each retail, mining, transportation, government)			X		X
Culnan 1983 184 professionals in a diversified natural resource firm		X	X		X
Danziger & Kraemer 1985 2,537 end users (managers, staff professionals, line personnel, office personnel) and 40 data processing managers in 40 city governments in U.S.	X	X	X		X
Rivard & Huff 1984 Unspecified number of data processing managers and professionals in 10 of 100 largest Canadian firms (3 manufacturing, 2 finance, 2 utility, and 1 each insurance, forestry, communications)			X	X	
Rockart & Flannery 1984 200 end users (staff professionals), 50 data processing managers in 22 organizations (20 manufacturing, 2 finance)			X	X	X
Rushinek and Rushinek 1985 4,491 end users (primarily managers, staff professionals, and office personnel) in many private sector organizations		X	X		X

NOTE: The three types of end users correspond directly with those categorized as "indirect," "intermediate," and "direct" by the Codasyl End User Facilities Committee (1979). See chapter 2, note 3 for the Codasyl definitions and ch. 3, opening pages, for our definitions.

people were higher users), modes of use were linked more to the task-related information needs of the role, not to personal traits.

3. Among role-types, middle managers, comparable to the managers and staff professionals in our study, were the largest group of end users. And personnel in staff agencies (e.g., finance and accounting, planning, personnel, marketing) were more frequent direct users of computing than were personnel in line agencies (Benson 1983; Rockart and Flannery 1984).

4. The analyses report a relatively high level of problems with microcomputer usage, mainly due to the lack of technical support for end users. These problems include lack of documentation, lack of data backup and security, lack of user support services, and lack of training (Benson 1983; Rivard and Huff 1984; Rockart and Flannery 1984).

5. The relations between data-processing staff and end users are critical to the success of end-user computing. In general, decentralization of computing, user support services, user education, and control of the computer package shared with users were supportive of end-user computing (Benson 1983; Rockart and Flannery 1984).

6. Direct use of computing resulted in greater user satisfaction with computing and in tangible benefits for organizational performance. However, the dominant type of hardware in the computer system does not seem crucial. In a large survey of end users, overall user satisfaction was not significantly related to whether the end user's computing was mainframe-, minicomputer- or microcomputer-based. Rather, software tailored to end users' needs was the key to higher satisfaction (Rushinek and Rushinek 1985). While most of the studies suggest that there have been productivity gains from the introduction of microcomputers, the evidence is anecdotal rather than systematic and does not compare the impacts of micros to the impacts of other types of hardware.

7. In the single study which explicitly examined the interactive use of computing on both mainframe computers and microcomputers, there was no appreciable difference in end users' patterns of computing usage. Although microcomputer users had almost twice the applications of mainframe users, they tended to undertake the same information processing tasks (for much of their work) and to use no more applications than direct, mainframe users (Benson 1983).

We believe that these findings are too preliminary and limited to serve as a general test of our analyses. It does seem that microcomputers have initially been made available primarily to those in roles higher in the organizational structure, resulting in a slightly different distribution of users than for mainframe-based use. However, this might be an artifact of the researchers' interests in microcomputer use among managers and staff professionals. The only notable difference between these findings and our own is that these end users of microcomputers seem to experience greater problems with the technology. This might be partially due to the newness of the technology and the inexperience of these end users with micros; but the studies emphasize, as we have, that reduction of problems with computing is contingent upon the responsiveness of data-processing specialists to the end users' felt needs.

Overall, there is no evidence in these studies that challenges our central analyses, either in terms of the relevance of any of the key explanatory variables or the validity of the structural relationships among those variables. Rather, each of these partial studies reinforces major findings in our own analysis of the impacts of computing on end users who are professional knowledge workers in organizations. Across an array of contexts of computing use, these studies seem consistent with our own emphases on the crucial importance of the sociotechnical interface and of a routinized and decentralized computer package, and on the value of increased direct use of computing in accounting for the differential impacts of actual systems-in-use on end users. Thus our final chapter explores the implications of our analyses for those concerned with successful end-user computing in current organizations.

12. PEOPLE AND COMPUTERS

From a policy perspective committed to improving the performance and work environment of information workers by means of computing, the findings summarized in the previous chapter are quite encouraging. There is clear evidence that the use of computer technology can enhance *both* the performance and the work environment of people in organizations, and that local governments, specifically, have been successful in utilizing the technology to accomplish these objectives. The kinds of benefits experienced by the workers in this study should be generalizable to the use of computing by other information workers in the public sector, and in the service sector more broadly. And the promise of even greater benefits from computing is a continuing challenge. Therefore, this final chapter considers the implications of our study for end users, computer specialists, and managers—and, more generally, for people in organizations.

PATHS TO SUCCESSFUL END-USER COMPUTING: USERS AND COMPUTER SPECIALISTS

Critical Success Factors from the End-User Perspecitve. Whereas much of the literature approaches critical success factors in computing from the perspective of the providers of computing services (Benson 1983; Bullen and Rockart 1981; Martin 1982; Orlicky 1969; Powers 1971), our study has approached issues of success from the perspective of the end users of computing in organizations.[1] Our analysis suggests five major conditions that seem to increase the contribution of computers and information systems to the work of end users:

1. If the computer package is more decentralized, so it is in the hands of the users;
2. If more developed computing capacity is available, especially that which permits human-machine interaction;
3. If the users have greater competency and experience with computing;
4. If the computer experts are more responsive to the felt needs of the users regarding the design and operation of the computer-based information systems;
5. If users routinely rather than selectively utilize computers and information systems.

As shown in table 12.1, characteristics of the technology importantly influence some impacts of computing.[2] Generally, as the computer package is more developed in terms of features such as extensiveness, routinization, and resource support, there are not only greater positive impacts on utilization, performance, and work environment, but also greater problems with computing. And as computing is more decentralized, its utilization and job performance benefits both increase.

But it is the characteristics of the users' relations with the technology and the technologists that most consistently appear as critical determinants of the level of benefits derived from computing. Thus, despite continuing images of the computer as a mechanistic and homogenizing technology, its impact is highly contingent upon the personal and interpersonal context within which computing is provided and used. In particular, both greater end-user experience and competence with computing and also more responsive computer experts (responsive to end users' needs to gain competence and experience, to receive assistance with computing problems, and to interface their own computing activities with the larger systems and data-bases of the organization) result in increased utilization, greater job performance benefits, more favorable work environment effects, and fewer problems with computing for end users. In addition,

Table 12.1. Summary of Findings About Role Types, Context of Use, and Computer Impacts

	Computer Impacts			
Role Type	Greater utilization	Higher job performance benefits	Favorable Work Environment effects	Fewer computing problems
Managers				
Organizational environment	Complex, large, less professionalized			
Computer package		Less developed computing	Centralized computing	Less developed computing
User characteristics	Positive STI	Positive STI	Positive STI	Positive STI
Staff Professionals				
Organizational environment	Large			Small, professionalized
Computer package	More developed computing	More developed computing	More developed computing	
User characteristics	Positive STI	Positive STI	Positive STI	Positive STI
Street-Level Bureaucrats				
Organizational environment				Large, professionalized
Computer package	More developed computing, Decentralized computing	More developed computing, Decentralized computing	More developed computing	Less developed computing
User characteristics	Positive STI	Positive STI	Positive STI	Positive STI
Desk-Top Bureaucrats				
Organizational environment				
Computer package	More developed computing	Less developed computing, Decentralized computing		Less developed computing
User characteristics				Positive STI

NOTE: STI means sociotechnical interface.

routine use of the computer systems tends to increase the end user's level of benefits and positive effects.

Implications for End Users. It is clear that the end user's own experience and sense of competency with computing is a critical factor in successful use. There is no substitute for hands-on involvement with the technology as a means to gain experience and competency and indicate to the particular end user whether such experience and competency with computing provide an adequate return on his/her investment. Computing is a costly activity for the end user to learn, to maintain competence in, and to use efficiently; but its benefits for job performance and work enhancement can be substantial.

Our analysis indicates that mainframe computing environments have thus far produced the greatest job performance benefits for street-level bureaucrats and desk-top bureaucrats, roles whose information processing tasks are most extensively automated and whose use has tended to be the most direct and frequent. However, these computing environments have also produced benefits for certain staff professionals—those who most closely approximate the image of the "total user" with hands-on, frequent use of computers and computer-based information. In fact, most staff professionals in our study are "passive users" of computerized data or reports based on such data. Interestingly, it is the user's professionalism, age, and previous positive computer experience that most distinguishes the staff professional who is a total user from the others. These findings and similar ones for managers suggest that for those in roles with greater discretion over computer use, the development of the individual's computing competence and the interaction with responsive computing specialists are of critical importance in generating higher utilization and greater benefits from computing systems-in-use.

Implications for Computer Specialists The recurring importance in our analyses of responsive expert assistance for end users supports the conclusion that the computer specialists have a crucial role to play within public and private organizations. This role is not necessarily diminished as more people use computing directly (interactively), whether through the mainframe environment, minicomputers, microcomputers, or combinations of these. Simply put, the computer specialists remain the key source of computing knowledge and skill in most medium- and large-scale organizations. Their expertise is particularly important with regard to the large transaction-processing systems and the organizational data bases which many end users need to access. The computer specialists can provide a broad organizational perspective that recognizes the need for "connectivity" (and the techniques of standardization to achieve it) among equipment, data bases and end users; in some instances, they also have the responsibility for achieving such connectivity.

End users, in contrast to these specialists, want computing capability tailored to meet their particular needs, and they usually expect it to be provided in a rapid and straightforward manner. They typically focus on some specific task(s) for which they believe computing is applicable and justifiable, and they desire technical assistance from a friendly (to their interests), helpful, accessible source. In fact, if the interests of both the organization and the end users are to be met, the computer specialists should be affiliated with a service unit that will: (a) provide technical training and consultation regarding both the computer unit's own facilities and any other computing capabilities that the end users might procure; (b) assist in the access to and use of relevant data-bases from the end users' own unit, and also from other organizational and external data-bases; and (c) provide training and help to insure that the end users' decisions regarding data and computing take into account the need for communication with others in the organization and that the equipment, software, data, and protocols are compatible with those used by others. *The most powerful conclusion of our study is that the impacts of computing on the end user are fundamentally contingent on the responsiveness of computing specialists to the user.*

Thus end-user computing represents a major "service" opportunity for the computer specialists. This observation is supported by the findings in recent studies by Benson (1983), Rockart and Flannery (1984), and Rivard and Huff (1984). But there is some question about whether the computer specialists will rise to the opportunity, because of the tendency of some computer units to operate more as "skill bureaucracies" than as "service organizations" (Danziger 1979). In a skill bureaucracy, the emphasis is less on a service orientation based on responsiveness to the needs and interests of clients than on a bureaucratic orientation based on internal interests, such as technical issues, peer-professional standards, and control and expansion of organizational domain. Two organizational arrangements through which this service role might be enhanced are the "information center" and the "computer store." Each establishes arrangements through which end users can obtain help from computer specialists in learning about, evaluating, procuring, using, and maintaining computing capability for their needs (Hammond 1982; Kuchia 1983; Mau 1982; Waltrip 1983; Youstra and Squire 1983). These conceptions of the role of computer specialists are currently gaining popularity and offer the prospect of substantially increasing the value of these specialists to the organization (Benson 1983).

MANAGERS AND END-USER COMPUTING

Our findings have two important sets of implications for managers, one set dealing with general issues regarding the management of the computer package and the other set dealing with the manager's own effective use of computing. The findings make clear that substantial benefits accrue to organizational end users, and at least some of these impact variables also suggest that there will be considerable benefits to the organizational units for which the manager has responsibility. Thus the manager must consider what kinds of arrangements in the computer package will be most likely to generate such benefits.

The Management of End-User Computing. In general, our findings suggest that the macro-level characteristics of the organization and its environment have only marginal direct effects on the impacts we have considered. The key elements in the context of computing use have been the nature of the computer package and the characteristics of the end user. In fact, most of the significant variables in our analysis are amenable to alteration by insightful intervention by managers.

Regarding *the computer package,* the most important features have been those that decentralize the technology, that place greater control of computing in the hands of end users, and that facilitate greater and more direct utilization of the technology by the end users. Various managerial directives and incentives can effect these changes in the organizational arrangements of the computer package. Managers must be aware that there are certain risks associated with substantial decentralization to end users, particularly in the areas of loss of central control both of hardware and also of data-bases and their uses. These risks are particularly high in those organizational units which introduce a substantial level of microcomputer use in stand-alone modes because managerial control of this technology can be particularly difficult. Yet microcomputers might also be the mode of computing which promises the greatest benefits to organizational end users, since it is the mode that most fully meets our conditions of success, given that the end user has substantial control over the hardware and the data-bases, and computing use is direct and likely to be extensive.

Ideally, managers will control the use of microcomputers, and all other computing activities, by means of general policies that insure sensible configurations of hardware, central control over the quality and manipulation of data-bases, central monitoring of the uses to which computing is put by end users, and "networking" approaches to all important computing activities, so that appropriate information is provided to unit, division and central managers and so that information is properly shared across relevant organizational sub-units.

Managers can also directly and indirectly influence the sociotechnical interface and the end users' involvement with computing. There is much to be gained from firm *managerial control of the computer specialists,* so that the specialists' activities are highly responsive to the needs of the end users for training and support, as well as for applications whose design and use are explicitly tailored to serve end users' activities. Among the strategies to facilitate this, managers can oblige the data processing department to assign specific staff to particular user groups/departments on a long term basis, so that rich working relationships can develop and so that computer specialists acquire greater sensitivity to the unique computing needs of particular end user groups. In addition, managers can require, at regular intervals, systematic end user evaluations of the quality of services they are receiving from the computer specialists in general and also evaluations of those individual staff who are directly responsible for serving them. Salary and status rewards for computer specialists might be attached to such evaluations.

Of equal importance are *managerial actions to enhance the computing competency of end users*. Organizational rewards, both material and symbolic, can be directed to those individuals who maximize their "desirable" utilization of computing, in terms of level of utilization, modes of use, efficiency of use, and user training and involvement. The nature of such "desirable" utilization must be defined by managers, given *their* conception of how computing can contribute most fully to organizational goals.

It is important to emphasize, however, that the computing competence of end users is probably not best achieved by a classic "top down" management approach. There is persuasive evidence, especially from European analyses of user involvement in computing systems design and use, that it is desirable to create conditions under which end users take an active and continuous role in the planning and shaping of the computer package which they are to utilize. This approach, called the "Scandanavian model" by some researchers (see, for example, Bjørn-Andersen 1983), emphasizes the individual, human values associated with end user computing in the workplace, rather than merely stressing computing developments which aim to maximize organizational efficiency and rationality.

Descriptions of this user-centered approach insist that computing in worklife should serve such objectives as quality of work, social responsibility, industrial democracy, self-actualization, individual influence and self-determination. To achieve such objectives, end users must have continuous, active, informed involvement in computing design and implementation processes, from the earliest stage. Moreover, end users must have *substantial* influence over all decisions in these processes, even to the point of "codetermination" (equality) with management (Bjørn-Andersen 1983; Bødker 1985; Briefs et al. 1983; Hedberg 1984).

While much lip service is now paid to a more user-centered orientation to computing, most managers are likely to find it extremely difficult to accept the actual implications of fully implementing this approach. In the short run such an approach is likely to be costly in both human and material resources, hence in classic cost-efficiency terms. While we believe that the extreme version of the "Scandanavian model" is infeasible and is too much at variance with crucial organizational goals relating to efficiency and control, our analyses of end users persuade us that there is a clear case for extensive and meaningful end user participation. Among other things, this would require partial acceptance among managers of such premises as a deemphasis on strict efficiency criteria in favor of quality-of-work concerns, the enhancement of the end users' technical expertise and influence over the computer package, and the reduction of top-down control of computing by managers and the computer elite.

We suggest that, in the medium and longer run, strategies for active end user participation can result in significant increases in the levels of computer competence among end users. (It is noteworthy, for example, that our actual measure of computer competence has been the level of the end user's participation in application design.) Substantial end user participation is also likely to generate benefits in the quality of the sociotechnical interface and in the nature of the computer package. Such changes in the context of computing use should mean that end users will employ computing more effectively and also that fundamental organization-as-a-whole goals, including maintenance, adaptability and even efficiency, will be better served.

The likely decentralization of computing within the organization, and particularly the implementation of microcomputers, require the development by managers of additional policies to insure the success of end user computing (Benson 1983; Rockart and Flannery 1984). Such policies would include:

1. Provide a top-down strategy for end-user computing which clearly reflects top managers' overall design for the acquisition and use of end-user computing and for the functional roles assigned to different modes of computing (e.g., interactive computing in the mainframe environment, stand-alone microcomputing, both).
2. Provide communication and other standards that microcomputers must meet for access to and appropriate interface with the mainframe environment.
3. Provide a list of approved or preferred vendors for both time sharing services and microcomputers, but allow procurement from other vendors on an exception basis.

4. Provide for quantity discounts on purchases of services, equipment, and software.
5. Provide for quick review, probably by the computing staff, of the strengths and shortcomings of end users' computing proposals and equipment purchases.
6. Provide for effective and responsive technical support and maintenance of end-user equipment, software, and data bases.

What is crucial, in our view, is that managers develop and implement a coherent plan regarding a complementary, and in some cases integrated, computer package and that they oblige computer specialists to serve managerial goals and end-user needs.

The Manager as End User. In addition to these implications for managers' roles in guiding end-user computing within the organization, an equally important implication of our study is the need for managers to examine their own roles as end users of computing. Our analysis of computing and managerial control (chapter 10) indicates that few managers enjoy direct and substantial benefits from the use of computing in their organizations. Yet the functioning of the computer package consumes an increasing share of organizational resources and of the manager's own time.

Among those in policy-and-analysis roles, it is the staff professionals, rather than the managers, who appear to be the biggest gainers from computer use. Despite modest levels of use by some staff professionals, they are the only group who have enjoyed both relative increases in their control over others and also relative decreases in the level of supervision of their work. We observed in chapter 9 that these beneficial effects of computing for staff professionals are in accord with the predictions by Downs (1967) and Lowi (1972) that an "information elite" would gain increased control from the expanding use of computers within the organization. This information elite parlays technical expertise in their functional domain with some sophistication in the use of the computer package to enhance their influence, and possibly even to dominate the policy process.

It is unclear whether this development should be of concern to managers. We argued in chapter 9 that one major reason why this information elite of staff professionals can gain increased control is because they can serve effectively in the "broker" role. As the role of computing expands within the organization, a manager could rely on the information elite to attend to the manager's requests in relation to the extensive capabilities of automated information systems and to intervene between the manager and the computer package, including the computer specialists, in order to insure that the manager is provided with computer-based services relevant to managerial functions.

As an alternative to staff professionals in a broker role, some argue for a "surrogate" relationship between managers and the computer elite, which includes the top computer specialists (managers, senior analysts, and programmers) in the computer unit, and skillful computer specialists in the user departments (Dutton and Kraemer, 1978). In their role as surrogates, computer specialists would use their knowledge and skills regarding computing to act as an extension of the manager's persona:

Greater management use of computing is likely to place increased demands on computing professionals . . . Satisfactory handling of these demands is likely to require that computing professionals (1) communicate effectively with top managers to advise them of available data and potential forms of reporting, as well as to help identify their information needs, and (2) develop the capacity to anticipate needs and how various data sources might be used effectively by managers. A co-requisite . . . is greater knowledge of the management function in organizations so that computing professionals can act as "surrogate managers" and anticipate top management's needs. (Dutton and Kraemer 1978:216)

To the extent that staff professionals and computer specialists remain responsive to the agenda of the managers they serve, both the broker role and the surrogate role can serve the manager's own computing needs and also extend the manager's influence and control over the organization's computer package. Our earlier research (Danziger, Dutton, Kling, and Kraemer, 1982; Dutton and Kraemer 1977; Kling 1978; Kraemer and Dutton 1984) concludes that those who dominate the organization can oblige their computing subordinates to serve their agenda. We have termed this phenomenon "reinforcement politics," and the conception holds that although various groups might have substantial influence over the provision of the computer package, it is the needs and interests of the dominant coalition within the organization that are primarily served by those who provide computing services.

Because top central managers might be only one element in (or might even be excluded from) the dominant coalition, the reinforcement politics perspective suggests the managers' goals from computing will be only partially met. And even if these managers do have dominant control of the organization, there are important shortcomings with a manager's reliance on brokers or surrogates to fulfill his/her goals from computing. Minimally, there is bound to be some goal displacement and suboptimization of goals, from the manager's perspective. More broadly, the manager who relies on brokers or surrogates for computing has accepted a dependency relationship, with its associated uncertainties and instabilities. As a fundamental level, if the behavior of staff professionals and computing specialists is dominated, in classic "bureaucratic" style, by their own interests and agenda, their centrality as an information and computer elite could become a problem or a threat to the manager's control and/or the manager's achievement of goals.

Our analysis is particularly germane to the manager's role as an end user of computing. We suggest that the manager will be better served in the future if the staff professionals can be redirected into a "mentor" role and computer specialists into a "consultant" role (figure 12.1). As a *mentor,* the staff professional would provide the manager with the same computing arrangements as his/her own, teach the manager the quick and easy ways to use those arrangements, screen packaged applications for the manager's use, work with the computer specialists to develop any special applications that might be useful for the manager, and frequently interact with the manager over the use and effectiveness of the manager's evolving computing activities.

As *consultants,* the computer specialists would advise the manager on the computing resources that can be used to meet his/her computing needs (e.g., word processing, spreadsheet analysis, data-base management) and on the organization's data resources that can be used to meet his/her information needs. The difference between this consultant role and the general role of the computer specialists is that the consultant focuses explicitly on the manager's personal needs rather than the needs of the organization and its divisions. Rockart and Flannery (1984) suggest that this consultant role should be applied to all levels of management.

The broker and surrogate roles described earlier are largely outgrowths of centralized, mainframe computing. If functioning properly, these roles insure that the operational systems of the organization are built with a view toward management uses and needs and they further insure that these uses are exploited by means of the generation of special report and analyses which increase the information benefits that computing can provide to the array of functions performed by the manager.

In contrast, the mentor role for the staff professionals and the consultant role for computer experts are outgrowths of the development of more decentralized and accessible computing and of the increasing value to the manager of taking a more active role in exploiting his/her information environment. This viewpoint is even more compelling with the evolution to personal computers, which bring powerful capabilities to the manager's desk top. It is now feasible and, we believe, desirable, for the manager to use computing directly.

Figure 12.1.   Role Models in Support of Manager's Use of Computing

	Type of Professional	
	Staff professional	Computer specialist
Centralized, main-frame based	BROKER •gets manager the information he/she requests	SURROGATE •anticipates manager's needs and develops data systems in support thereof
Decentralized, microcomputer–based	MENTOR •helps manager to become direct user of computing	CONSULTANT •advises manager on his/her personal computing resources and options

Type of Computing Environment

The mentor role for the staff professional derives from the fact that many of the applications for managers are the same as, or similar to, those already used by staff professionals. This comparability of applications, in conjunction with the staff professional's technical expertise and role as an aide to the manager, gives the staff professional the appropriate knowledge and insights to serve effectively as mentor on the information processing needs and activities of the manager.

The argument for the mentor role is also reinforced by our analysis of data-based computing systems. Our characterization of these data-based systems is one that is fully consistent with a realistic view of the manager's basic computing needs, the kinds of systems that can meet those needs, and the manager's own capacities to use computing in the direct mode. With some assistance from a mentor, the manager can increasingly do routine prospecting-oriented computing, facilitated by straightforward software and relevant data. Despite the differences in function, managers can enjoy arrays of benefits for decision and action that are comparable to those characteristic of the use of data-based systems by detectives.

The case for the consultant role for the computer specialists is also a derivative of more decentralized and accessible computing and of the fact that in many instances the staff professionals themselves will not possess the knowledge, skills, or computing experience required to understand fully the evolving computer package. Thus both they and the managers will benefit from the broader perspective and technical knowledge of computer specialists who are responsive to their computing needs.

Given the complexity of the information environment and the computer package in the manager's organizational setting, it is clear that the manager will continue to need effective assistance from staff professionals and computer experts in the roles of broker and suggorate, respectively. But we suggest that in the near future the most significant benefits to the manager from the computer package will accrue to those managers who actively utilize data-based systems, with the continuing support of mentors from among staff professionals and consultants from among the computer experts.

PEOPLE AND COMPUTERS

Overall, the research in this book suggests that the impacts of computers on people in organizations can be quite favorable. We find that, somewhat contrary to our expectations, most end users of computing in local government, whether in top managerial positions or "lowly" clerical positions, have enjoyed considerable net benefits from the application of computing to their work. Substantial majorities of end users report that computing has increased their job satisfaction, has improved the quality of information relevant to their work, has enabled them to perform their tasks more effectively, has not generated major problems in use, and so on.

There can be little doubt that many people in our analysis have a generally positive assessment of the role of computing in their work life. However, it is also clear that computing is not the wondrous tool reported in the promotional literature. Virtually no end users find that computing is problem-free and a substantial proportion report at least occasional problems or disbenefits in the use of the technology. And on some activities where computing might generate substantial benefits, the majority report that computing has simply had no effect at all.

Our focus on the individual person as the unit of analysis has resulted in a compelling empirical case that computing has quite differential impacts across individuals, across roles, and across domains of work. The nature and the level of computing impacts on people vary, and many of the differences are systematically associated with aspects of the individual's context of computing use.

On the basis of our analyses, we have stressed that computer technology is not a homogenizing force which requires all users to adapt to its relentless imperatives and which affects all users in the same manner. Rather, the technology-in-use combines with the traits of the individual user to create a dynamic context within which the impacts of computing are shaped. In our view, these findings, and particularly the critical importance of the sociotechnical interface in accounting for the impacts of computing, support the basic conclusion that the context of computing use can be manipulated so that it is more likely to serve the interests and needs of end users.

In this final chapter, we have identified some of the strategies which might enhance the impacts of computing on end users. We view this as a fundamental goal, although we recognize that subtle adjustments might be necessary to insure that computing impacts favorable for end users will also contribute to crucial organizational objectives. Nothing in our analysis persuades us that computing will necessarily be a positive force in people's work environments. But if people in organizations understand the dynamic forces in the context, they can enjoy relatively greater net benefits from computing. Thus we conclude this book as we began it, with an emphasis on people rather than on computers and technological determinism, because we believe that human betterment is best advanced when computing is shaped by people to serve the people who are its end users.

Appendix: Research Methodology and Data

DATA-COLLECTION APPROACHES

The research methods utilized in the URBIS Project provide many types of data which facilitate the study of computing in organizations from many perspectives. Since most empirical measures are subject to one or another form of bias, it is usually desirable to employ "multiple operationism"—the use of alternative measures that attempt to tap the same phenomenon (Webb et al. 1966). In analyzing the impacts of the computer package on end users in American local governments, we have used: (a) numerous exploratory case studies; (b) an extensive, multipart survey instrument in virtually the entire population of larger cities and counties; and (c) intensive field research in a relatively large number of sites, including structured case coding, discursive case reports, and a lengthy survey instrument. This appendix briefly characterizes the research strategy of the URBIS Project. Fuller elaboration can be found in Danziger, Dutton, Kling, and Kraemer (1982). Kraemer et al. (1976), and Kraemer, Dutton, and Northrop (1980).

Phase I: Census Survey. The primary intent of the Census Survey was to provide base-line data on computing arrangements and on the policies relating to the computer package in American local governments. This survey provided a data base with which to analyze the characteristic patterns of use and diffusion of current computer technology and also to select appropriate sites for more extensive study in the later phase of the research.

A three-part survey of cities and counties was designed. Each part entailed a separate mail questionnaire, with telephone follow-up. The three surveys were sent in early 1975 to all cities with greater than 50,000 population and all counties with greater than 100,000 population—403 municipalities and 310 counties in all. One gathered information on the personal views of the government's chief executive toward computer technology in local government. The second collected extensive information from each computer installation serving the government, measuring such characteristics of the computer package as types of equipment, levels and types of personnel and budget, and the kinds of policies governing the use of the computer package. The third questionnaire, which also was completed by each computer installation, was an inventory of the current and near-future automated applications provided to the local government by that installation.

Phase II: Field Studies. The central purpose of the second major phase of the project was to perform an empirical evaluation of the impacts of automated information systems on local governments and on the people who might use computing in these governments. The data upon which the tables in this book are based were collected during Phase II. In this section, we describe how the sites for Phase II were selected, and how we identified the activities and people for our intensive analysis of the impacts of computing on people.

Sampling design. The design for sampling cities was most critical for the analyses in a companion book, *The Management of Information Systems* (Kraemer, Dutton and Northrop 1981), and has had no major effect upon the analyses or conclusions in the present book. However, the design did determine the cities from which some of the data and insights in this book have been derived. Consequently, it seems appropriate to explain the sampling strategy briefly, although it is fully stated in that book.

For Phase II, we needed a sample that was small enough to allow intensive field research in each site and large enough to enable us to make generalizations. We decided to study only municipal governments so that the organizational units would be comparable. Our interest in alternative computing policy configurations, many of which were relatively rare, meant that we could not use conventional probability sampling, as it would not provide a sample of sites with the array of policy mixes from which the optimal computer policies for America's "future cities" could be identified (Kraemer et al. 1976).

Our solution was a variation of a disproportionate stratified sampling technique. Six key computer package characteristics were identified: (a) total number of automated applications; (b) degree of centralization of the package; (c) charging policy for computing services; (d) sophistication of hardware; (e) level of integration of data in the system, (f) extent of user involvement in application adoption, design, evaluation, and programming. Each of the six variables was dichotomized on the basis of Phase I data for city governments, with all scores below the third quartile treated as low scores and all scores above the third quartile as high. This produced a partitioned sample with $2^6 = 64$ strata. All cities were located in their proper stratum, a balanced set of 40 strata was then randomly selected, and a specific city was selected randomly from each stratum. These 42 cities are listed in table A.1. While the municipal governments that we studied in Phase II were somewhat more "developed" with regard to computing than were other municipalities circa 1975, with the continued expansion and evolution of the computer package in most governments, "high" development of 1975 would be more "typical" today.

Information-processing tasks. People tend to speak generally about the impacts of computers and computer-based information systems. However, we felt that an assessment should focus on the specific tasks computers perform. For this reason, primarily, Phase II used the "information processing task" (IPT) as a focal analytic unit for selecting respondents, gathering data, and assessing policy outcomes.

Table A.1.   Cities Visited in Phase II Study

City	Population	City	Population
Albany, N.Y.	115,876	Milwaukee, Wisc.	717,124
Atlanta, Ga.	497,024	Montgomery, Ala.	183,471
Baltimore, Md.	905,759	New Orleans, La.	593,471
Brockton, Mass.	89,040	New Rochelle, N.Y.	75,385
Burbank, Calif.	88,580	Newton Mass.	91,073
Chesapeake, Va.	89,580	Oshkosh, Wisc.	53,155
Cleveland, Ohio	751,046	Paterson, N.J.	144,830
Costa Mesa, Calif.	72,729	Philadelphia, Pa.	1,948,609
Evansville, Ind.	138,690	Portsmouth, Va.	110,963
Fort Lauderdale, Fla.	139,543	Quincy, Mass.	87,966
Florissant, Mo.	66,006	Riverside, Calif.	139,269
Grand Rapids, Mich.	197,534	Sacramento, Calif.	254,362
Hampton, Va.	120,779	San Francisco, Calif.	715,674
Kansas City, Mo.	507,242	San Jose, Calif.	446,504
Lancaster, Pa.	57,589	Seattle, Wash.	530,890
Las Vegas, Nev.	125,641	Spokane, Wash.	170,516
Lincoln, Neb.	149,518	St. Louis, Mo.	622,236
Little Rock, Ark.	132,482	Stockton, Calif.	107,459
Long Beach, Calif.	358,673	Tampa, Fla.	277,736
Louisville, Ky.	361,453	Tulsa, Okla.	331,800
Miami Beach, Fla.	86,974	Warren, Mich.	179,234

NOTE: 1970 Census populations.

Information processing task is a term used to signify an activity which has a specific objective, explicitly involves information processing, and *could* be automated (Kraemer et al. 1976). IPTs were sampled on the basis of two criteria. First, we wished to generalize about the impacts of computing on different activities and different people. Consequently, we sampled IPTs from each of six generic types: record keeping, calculating/printing, record searching, record restructuring, sophisticated analytics, and process control (see Danziger 1977). Second, since we could investigate only a few IPTs, we wanted to generalize to people beyond any single functional area of government services. Hence, we chose seven IPTs within four functional areas. Table A.2 indicates the general characteristics of each IPT type and the specific IPT(s) studied.

Data collection. Each city selected for Phase II was visited by one to three of six investigators, including the authors. We spent an average of three person-weeks in each of at least eight sites as part

Table A.2.   Types of Information-Processing Tasks and Associated Applications

Type	Characteristics	Applications Chosen
1. Record keeping	Activities that primarily involve the *entry, updating and storage of data,* with a secondary need for access; the computer facilitates manageable storage and easy updating for nearly unlimited amounts of information.	Traffic ticket processing
2. Calculating/ printing	Activities that primarily involve *storing, calculating and printing of stored data* to produce specific operational outputs; utilizes the computer's capabilities as a high-speed data processor.	Budget control (reporting)
3. Record sharing	Activities where *access to and search of data files* is of primary importance; by defining parameters, relevant cases can be retrieved from a file with speed and comprehensiveness; on-line capability of computer is particularly useful.	Detective investigative support Police officer support
4. Record restructuring	Activities that involve *reorganization reaggregation and/or analysis of data;* the computer is used to link data from diverse sources or to summarize large volumes of data as management and planning information.	Policy analysis
5. Sophisticated analytics	Activities that utilize *sophisticated, visual, mathematical, simulation or other analytical methods to examine data;* the special capabilities of computers make possible the manipulation of data about complex, interdependent phenomena.	Patrol manpower allocation
6. Process control	Activities that approximate a cybernetic system; *data about the state of a system is continually monitored and fed back to a human or automatic controller* which steers the system towards a performance standard; the computer's capabilities for real-time monitoring and direction of activities are utilized.	Budget control (monitoring)

of the fieldwork. This field research resulted in three kinds of systematic data, as well as extensive "informal" information.

First, 50 to 100 self-administered questionnaires were completed by the end users of computer services in each site. Respondents were selected on the basis of their roles in city government and their relationships to the seven IPTs. Table A.3 shows each kind of respondent, the number of questionnaires distributed to respondents of each role, and the percentage of returned questionnaires. We obtained a high response rate for most roles, the average being 82 percent, due to investigators' collecting most questionnaires while in the city and to thorough follow-up by mail and phone. These lengthy questionnaires measured end users' perceptions of the impacts, problems, and benefits associated with computing, as well as the users' own characteristics. The analysis of these questionnaires is the key data source throughout this study because it provides comparative assessments of the impacts of computing within relatively well defined roles in each city. For many analyses, we focus only on those people who *are* end users of computing. Thus these analyses select only those who make some use of computing and have some involvement with those who provide computing services. The numbers of respondents in each chapter are reported in the appropriate tables.

The methods used for respondent selection were specifically tailored to each information-processing task. The general strategy was to identify those roles most important to each information-processing task and to sample among people within those roles. Certain roles, such as mayor, manager, and head of the budget-reporting unit, defined specific respondents. In these cases, each specific respondent was contacted. Other roles, such as council member, detective, or traffic ticket clerk, defined larger groups of potential respondents. In these cases we generated a list of all people in the relevant role. A random sample of people on the list was selected and these people served as the respondents to our questionnaire. About 65 questions were completed by all respondents, and there were an additional 35 questions directed explicitly to those in selected roles, such as managers and detectives.

Second, about 40 personal, semistructured interviews were conducted in each city with elected officials and municipal personnel involved with the seven IPTs. These probing questions to multiple

Table A.3. Survey Respondents and Response Rates

Kind of Respondent	Number of Questionnaires Distributed	Number Returned	Response Rate
User department and division heads	544	477	88%
CAO, mayor, council	197	141	72
Budget reporting and monitoring heads	70	59	84
Traffic ticket directors	42	33	79
Police manpower allocation supervisor	40	39	98
Detective supervisors	90	80	89
Total managers	983	829	84%
Staff of mayor, council or manager/CAO	149	106	71%
Urban data bank custodians[a]	102	89	87
Budget analysts	82	69	84
Accountants	86	75	87
Police manpower allocation analysts	57	47	82
Police computing specialists	6	6	100
Total staff professionals	482	392	81%
Detectives	527	419	80%
Patrol Officers	541	443	82
Total Street-level Bureaucrats	1,068	862	81%
User department administrative assistants	158	117	74%
User departments accountants	96	80	83
Traffic ticket supervisors	69	53	77
Traffic ticket clerks	172	143	83
Police records division clerks	67	61	91
Total Desk-Top Bureaucrats	562	454	81%
All Respondents	3,095	2,537	82%

[a] Includes planning staff and specially identified data bank custodians.

respondents, along with department records and our own judgment, provided us with fuller understanding regarding the personal, inter-personal, and intraorganizational dynamics surrounding the impacts of computing.

The third source of systematic data came from one additional questionnaire that was completed by the data-processing manager(s) and staff of each computer installation. These installations included independent computing departments, subunits of the finance de-partment, police units, utility and planning department installations, joint city and county installations, and so forth.

Finally, a source of relatively systematic data was the lengthy case study reports which were written up by the field researcher after each site visit. These detailed case reports followed a specific format to increase their comparability, and they inform many of the dis-cussions in the book.

"Exploratory" Case Studies. Throughout the research project, ad-ditional city and county governments were subjected to detailed field study. These case studies served different purposes at different stages of the research. In total, more than fifty additional local governments were field research sites at one time or another during the URBIS research. Some of the sites were selected within the context of a comparative case study project during 1975, other sites were studied because of particularly interesting configurations of automated ap-plications or computer policies, and still others were chosen because they were especially useful sites in which to develop and refine research instruments. The written case reports, transcribed interviews with city and county government personnel, and other written doc-uments from these exploratory case studies provide further grounding for the discussions and analyses in this book.

ANALYTIC METHODS

Units and Levels of Analysis. Our primary objective in *People and Computers* is to measure and explain the nature and magnitude of the impacts of computing on the individual end users who work in the local governments in our analysis. Thus individuals are the "object units of analysis"—that is, the units whose behavior is to be explained (see Eulau 1969). Many of our variables are actually measured at the individual level. This includes all of the variables measuring the impacts of computing (e.g., measures of utilization, benefits, problems, and work effects). The user characteristic variables, such as age and computing competence, are also measured at the individual level. However, the other variables in the context of computing use are at higher levels of analysis than the individual. Thus we treat these as contextual variables at the individual level, matching the appropriate features of the computer package and the organizational environment to the specific end user who is the object unit of analysis. Using this conceptual approach, we can generalize about the effects of the specific context of computing use experienced by each individual in our analysis.

Variable Value Distributions. The impacts of computing on end users are initially presented by means of descriptive statistics. The data are normally partitioned into four groups, corresponding to the four role-types: managers, staff professionals, street-level bureaucrats, and the desk-top bureaucrats. In most cases, the tabular data include: frequency distributions, using the responses in the original questionnaire; means, based on scores associated with each response; and coefficients of variation, a statistic which indicates the magnitude of the spread of values around the mean, standardized across variables, by using the ratio of the standard deviation on the mean.

Assessing Between-Role Differences. To assess whether there are significant differences between roles in the distribution of values on a given variable, both chi-square and Kendall's tau are employed. Chi-square establishes whether there is a statistically significant difference in the distribution of cases in a bivariate analysis, taking into account the marginal distributions on each variable. It is a conservative measure, since it can be used where both variables are nominal. In fact, where one variable distinguishes two roles (and is thus dichotomous, allowing treatment as an ordinal variable) and the other variable measures a computing impact (and is thus arguably ordinal), Kendall's tau also might be an appropriate measure of covariation. We have normally taken the conservative approach, identifying those cases where chi-square is significant, although we sometimes provide the tau and its significance in parentheses.

Assessing Elements of the Context of Computing Use. In the "competing explanations" framework, the set of variables measuring the organizational environment, the computer package, and the user characteristics are each treated as an independent set of explanators. A multiple regression analysis, using the relevant set of variables, establishes the total variance in the dependent variable that can be accounted for (as measured by the R^2 statistic) by the independent variables. The statistical significance of the regression equation is reported as the F statistic.

In the "alternative explanations" framework, all three elements of the context of computing use are viewed as part of an interdependent explanation of the dependent variable. In our conceptual framework (in chapter 2), we assume that the organizational environment is a basic setting within which the computer package and the user exist. Thus the organizational environment is a contextual element that must be considered prior to the other elements, and it might affect the other contextual elements as well as the dependent variable. The computer package and the user characteristics might be independent of one another or they might interact in some manner, but neither can be considered a prior condition of the other. Thus our approach is to use a combination of regression techniques in order to establish the linkages between the elements of the context of use and the dependent variable. Specifically, the variables representing the organizational environment are first entered into a multiple regression (as a set), and then the variables representing the computer package and the user's characteristics are entered in a stepwise fashion until the probability of F-to-enter for the next variable is $>.05$. The data display indicates the percentage of the total R^2 that is attributable to the selected variables from each contextual element. The total explained variance and the significance of the regression equation (as measured by the F value) are also displayed.

Assessing Key Variables in the Context of Computing Use. The final step in the regression analyses described above also specifies the variables in the context of computing use that have significant explanatory power regarding the between-individual differences in the level of a given impact of computing. In the tables, we list these variables, as well as indicating their standardized betas and statistical significance (by means of the T statistic). This set of data provides a useful means of establishing the relative explanatory power, as well as the direction of effects, of the key variables in the context of use.

In several of the special study chapters, we also use discriminant analysis as a method of identifying the most powerful explanatory variables. Discriminant analysis selects those variables in the context of computing use that best distinguish between the specified groups (for example, those with high computing problems and those with low computing problems). In these analyses, we list the explanatory variables which are significant, and the standardized discriminant function coefficient for each variable. To indicate the overall discriminating power of the set of explanatory variables, we also indicate the Wilks' lambda and the percent of all actual cases that they "correctly classify" into the specified groups. In the tables, the signs of the discriminating variables are changed so that they are consistent with their accurate interpretation, given the values of the group centroids. Although both "Wilks" and "direct" methods of discriminant analysis (in SPSS) are employed, results are based on the former, more stringent approach.

Response-Response Bias. As in other research based in part on survey analyses of individual respondents, it is important to note that there might be response-response bias between the dependent variables and those independent variables measured at the individual level of analysis. It is impossible to dismiss this problem unless either the two sets of variables are totally uncorrelated or the analyst eliminates any analyses where there are both dependent and independent variables derived from responses of the people in the analysis.

Since our research is fundamentally interested in the assessments of computing by end users and since the orientations of these end users toward the computer package (that is, their STI) are a crucial aspect of the explanatory variables in our conceptual framework, it would be infeasible to eliminate all instances where there are dependent and independent variables based on user responses. In the analyses in this book there are clear examples where the most powerful explanatory variables are, in fact, responses by users regarding their assessment of the behavior of those technical staff who provide computing service.

While we cannot disprove that there is a response-response bias in these findings, there are important considerations that seem to support the validity of the analysis. Most significant is the fact that the statistical associations between orientations to computing staff and the various computing impact measures vary quite substantially between individuals, across impact measures, and across roles. There are few instances where the correlation between this independent variable and any dependent variable is extraordinarily strong. Indeed, there are many instances where a powerful response-response bias might be anticipated, and yet the actual correlation is quite modest or even nonexistent (see, for example, the analysis of benefits and problems configurations in chapter 8).

Moreover, our extensive fieldwork convinces us that, at the individual level, the sociotechnical interface can be extremely important in accounting for the impacts that an individual end user experiences in the use of the computer package. It was common in field interviews to find quite striking differences in the impacts of computing on people in the same role within a city, despite the fact that those people shared virtually all aspects of the organizational environment and the computer package. In fact, people in the same role within a department would often present remarkably different perceptions not only of how computing affected their individual work, but also of such "shared" factors as the attitudes of the departmental leadership toward the use of computers and the kinds of automated information that was available and relevant.

For these reasons, it is not unexpected that individual-level characteristics best account for differences in some impacts of computing. Overall, the quantitative analyses that constitute the heart of this book, on the conditions associated with greater benefits and costs from computing experienced by end users working in public organizations, are fully consistent with our more subjective understandings from extensive field research.

DEPENDENT VARIABLES IN THE STUDY: IMPACTS OF
COMPUTING

Our essential interest is to understand the impacts of computing on
end users in organizations. In our effort to generate comparable
variable measures across more than 3,000 end users in 40 public
organizations, the most feasible strategy was to focus on those variables that were based on self-responses. These data were collected
on the user's questionnaire described earlier in the appendix.

Clearly, self-assessments are only one method of tapping the individual-level impacts of computing on people in organizations. Other
interesting measures could be the product of actual observation of
individuals by a researcher or could be the by-product of operational
data recording individuals' actions. The greatest caution must be
applied in interpreting those cross-sectional measures where end users
report on the changes effected by computing, especially on job performance. The end users are reporting, at one point in time, their
assessments of the impacts of computing on themselves and on the
organization. A longitudinal design would provide the most conclusive data for making such causal inferences.

However, on the basis of our very extensive field research, including
interviews and observations, we are convinced that the users' own
responses on these questionnaires are reasonably valid and reliable
indicators of the impacts that the use of computing has on their
work. We also suggest that most of these impact variables are based
on questions that are quite explicit and are well grounded in the
domain of work that is being explored. The reader should consider
whether our causal language, which we believe provides a reasonable
and accurate portrayal of the patterns that exist, is appropriate for
these data.

The list that follows explicates each of the impact variables in
our analysis, including the relevant question(s) and alternative responses. Where the impact variable is an index, further information
is provided to explain its construction.

Direct Use: Please indicate how often you personally use a computer terminal
to get information from a computerized file: Never; At least once a year;
Several times a year; A few times a month; A few times a week; Daily.

Indirect Use: Please indicate how often you request others (by phone, radio
or in person) to get information from a computerized file: Never; At least

once a year; Several times a year; A few times a month; A few times a week; Daily.

Passive Use: Please indicate how often you receive reports that are based on computer data: Never; At least once a year; Several times a year; A few times a month; A few times a week; Daily.

Total User: This category selects those end users who: Personally use a computer at least once a year; Request others to provide information from a computer at least several times a year; Receive computer-based reports at least a few times a month.

Instrumental User: This category selects those end users who: Never personally use a computer; Request others to provide information from a computer at least a few times a month; Receive computer-based reports at least once a year.

Reactive User: This category selects those end users who: Never personally use a computer; Request others to provide information from a computer at least several times a year; Receive computer-based reports at least once a year.

Resource Efficiency: This measures the extent to which respondents perceive cost and staff reduction benefits due to the use of computing. The scale is the average response to three items:

—Where they have been applied, computers have reduced the number of people necessary to perform tasks in my department;
—Computers allow departments to handle a greater volume of service without corresponding increases in cost;
—Where they have been applied, computers have reduced the cost of department operations.

The response categories provided were: 0=Disagree; 1=Somewhat disagree; 2=Somewhat agree; 3=Agree. Scale scores were summated and averaged, and could therefore range from 0 (low resource efficiency) to 3 (high resource efficiency).

Service Effectiveness: Please circle the one code which best describes your agreement or disagreement with the following statement about computing:

Computers have failed to increase the effectiveness of my department in serving the public: Disagree; Somewhat disagree; Somewhat agree; Agree, don't know. (Direction reversed in the analyses to reflect a favorable assessment. Note that there might be some semantic distinction between the negative and positive forms.)

Information Benefits: This measures the extent to which respondents perceive information retrieval benefits from the use of computing. The scale is the average response to four items:

—The computer makes new information available to me which was not previously available.
—The computer provides me with more up-to-date information than that available in manual files.
—Computers have made it easier for me to get the information I need.
—Computers save me time in looking for information.

The response categories provided were: 0=Almost never true; 1=Sometimes true; 2=Frequently true; 3=Nearly always true. Scale scores were summated and averaged, and could therefore range from 0 (no/low benefits) to 3 (high benefits).

Computing Assists on Arrests: For how many of your last 10 arrests did the use of computerized information assist in the arrest? Number of computer-assisted arrests reported by detective.

Computing Assists on Clearances: For how many of your last 10 cleared cases (either by arrest or investigation of people in custody) did the use of computerized information assist in the clearance? Number of computer-assisted clearances reported by detective.

Computing Links to People in Custody: Consider the last 5 people which you had a role in linking to uncleared cases. For how many of these 5 did the use of computerized information assist in making this link? Number of computer-assisted links reported by detective.

Computing Increases Workable Cases: How many of your last 10 actively investigated cases would have been "unworkable" without the use of computer files? Number of cases made "workable" according to detective. (For purposes of uniformity, "unworkable" refers to a case which has no leads significant enough to continue active investigation.)

Information Problems with Computing: This measures the extent to which the respondents attribute negative features to the use of automated files for information retrieval purposes. The scale is the average response to two items:

—Information is difficult to change or correct once it has been put on a computerized file.
—Computerized data are less accurate than data in manual records and files.

The response categories provided were: 0=Almost never true; 1=Sometimes true; 2=Frequently true; 3=Nearly always true. Scale scores were summated and averaged, and could therefore range from 0 (no/low problems) to 3 (high problems).

Operational Problems with Computing: The scale measures the extent to which users experience operational problems in utilizing computer services in their local governments. It is an average over three items related to computer operation problems:

—Foul-ups in day-to-day computer operations.
—Slow response of data processing to requests for information.
—Difficulty in getting priority in using the computer.

The scale values for the individual items were: 0=Not a problem; 1=At times a problem; 2=Often a problem; 3=Very often a problem. The three items were summated and averaged. Scale scores were computed under the condition that at least two of the three items had valid (non-missing) responses. Scores on could range from 0 (no problems) to 3 (very often problems). Cronbach's alpha equals .70 for the total scale.

Time Pressure at Work: Has computing increased or decreased time pressures in your job? Decreased; Not affected; Increased; Don't know.

Sense of Accomplishment at Work: Has computing raised or lowered your sense of accomplishment in your work? Lowered; Not affected; Raised; Don't know.

Supervision of Work: As a result of computing, is your work more or less closely supervised? Less closely supervised; No difference; More closely supervised; Don't know.

Influence over Others at Work: Has computing given you more or less influence over the actions of others? Less influence; No change; More influence; Don't know.

Utility of Computer-Based Information During Budget Cycle: How useful to you has computer-based information been during the annual budget cycle? No computer-based information; Not at all useful; Somewhat useful; Useful; Very useful.

Utility of Computer-Based Information for Day-to-Day Expenditure Decisions: How useful to you has computer-based information been for day-to-day expenditure decisions? No computer-based information; Not at all useful; Somewhat useful; Useful; Very useful; Does not apply to my position.

Utility of Computer-Based Information Regarding Real Costs of Programs: Does computer-based information provide you with the real costs of programs and activities? No computer-based information; No it does not; Yes, for a *few* programs and activities; Yes, for *many* programs and activities; Yes, for *nearly all* programs and activities.

Utility of Computer-Based Information for Control of Staff: How much has computer-based information increased your ability to control staff and units under your responsibility? No computer-based information; Not at all; Somewhat; To a large extent.

Utility of Computer-Based Information for Manpower Allocation: How useful to you has computer-based information been in allocating manpower? No computer-based information; Not at all useful; Somewhat useful; Useful; Very useful.

Utility of Computer-Based Information for Problem-Identification: How useful to you has computer-based information been in identifying problems, abuses, or inefficiencies in the unit(s) you supervise? No computer-based information; Not at all useful; Somewhat useful; Useful; Very useful.

Utility of Computer-Based Information for Setting Realistic Goals: Has computer-based information aided you in setting realistic goals for units or individuals you supervise? No computer-based information; Not at all; Yes, in a *few* cases; Yes, in *many* cases; Yes, in *nearly all* cases.

Performance Control: This measures the extent to which automation has provided benefits to managers in control of staff and operational performance. The scale is the average response to five items:

—How much has computer-based information increased your ability to control staff and units under your responsibility? 0=Not at all; 1.5=Somewhat; 3=To a large extent.
—Has computer-based information aided you in setting realistic goals for units or individuals you supervise? 0=Not at all; 1=Yes, few cases; 2=Yes, many cases; 3=Nearly all.
—How useful to you has computer-based information been in allocating manpower? 0=Not at all; 1=Somewhat; 2=Useful; 3=Very useful.
—Has the computer provided you with information about the performance of your subordinates? 0=No cases; 1=Few cases; 2=Many cases; 3=Nearly all cases.
—How useful to you has computer-based information been in identifying problems, abuses, or inefficiencies in the unit(s) you supervise? 0=Not at all; 1=Somewhat; 2=Useful; 3=Very useful.

Scale scores were summated and averaged, and could range from 0 (low benefits) to 3 (high benefits). The scale was computed for all respondents who had valid answers to at least half (3) of the items.

Resource Control: This measures the extent to which automation has been useful to managers in control of financial resources. The scale is the average response to four items:

—How useful to you has the computer-based information been during the annual budget cycle?

—How useful to you has computer-based information been for day-to-day expenditure decisions?

—How useful to you has computer-based information been for salary questions and negotiations?

—Does computer-based information provide you with the real costs of programs and activities?

The response categories for the first three items were: 0=Not at all useful; 1=Somewhat useful; 2=Useful; 3=Very useful; response categories for the fourth item were: 0=No, it does not; 1=Yes, for a few programs; 2=Yes, for many programs; 3=Yes, for nearly all programs. The scale was summated and averaged, applying a missing value to the response choice of "no computer-based information."

INDEPENDENT VARIABLES IN THE STUDY: THE CONTEXT OF COMPUTING USE

Our conceptual framework in chapter 2 identified the elements of the context of computing use that might have substantial effects on the impacts of computing on end users. We noted in that chapter that there is a delicate trade-off between a set of explanatory (that is, independent) variables that is sufficiently comprehensive and one that is comprehensible and manageable.

Our approach has been to use a variety of techniques in order to reduce a large number of potentially important explanatory variables to a much smaller set that, as much as possible, represents that larger set. To achieve this goal, we used a series of variable reduction techniques. First, we generated a quite long list of relevant indicators of the three elements of the context of computing use. Second, we grouped these variables into the appropriate contextual element.

Third, where appropriate, we developed indices to combine related measures. Fourth, we examined the resulting variables in each set for cases of exceptionally high multicollinearity. In those cases where the multicollinearity was greater than .70, a decision was made to delete one of the measures. Fifth, we attempted to identify the sets of explanatory variables that seemed to share an underlying dimension, by the use of factor analysis (see table 2.4). The final product of this variable reduction process was a set of twelve explanatory variables that tap major dimensions of the context of computing use. The explication below characterizes the last three aspects of this process.

Organizational Environment

Number of Departments in Government: This is the total number of departments that are present in the city, as identified from an extensive list of possible departments.

Size of Legislative Body: This is the total number of members on the local legislative body (council, commission).

Government Employees per Citizen: This variable measures the level of government operations, utilizing the total number of government employees, normalized by size of population. Total number of employees in the government for 1970 was obtained from city data books.

Land Area Served: This is the land area serviced by the local government (in square miles for 1970). The data was obtained from city data books.

Population Served: This is the total population of the city in 1975, and was obtained from U.S. Census reports.

Partisanship in Local Politics Index: This index measures the degree to which partisan politics plays a role in the local government. It is constructed using weighted values of assessments from our field research, of a variable measuring the degree to which Republican and Democratic officials form opposing groups, and of a variable measuring the influence of the Democratic party and of the Republican party in community politics. Scores could range from 0 to 5 for each variable and the final index values could range from 0 to 10.

Reform Government Structures Index: This index measures the degree to which the local government has adopted certain characteristics of the reform movement. It is a summated index of four characteristics: (a) the presence of a council-manager or commission system; (b) the percentage of council seats in local elections that are elected "at-large"; (c) the use of a non-partisan ballot; (d) the reliance on merit appointments for government jobs.

These multiple categoried variables (all obtained from field research analysis) were recorded to vary between 0 (no reform) and 1 (reform) and summated to produce an index ranging from 0 (no reform) to 4 (reform).

Professional Practices of Government Departments Index: This index measures the degree to which professional management practices are used in the city government. Three indicators of these management practices (obtained from field research) were used:

—"Do departments and agencies within your local government establish written objectives for the programs and services they provide?" 0=No; 2=Yes, for some programs; 4=Yes, for nearly all programs.

—"Do city departments have measures of performance in meeting the objectives of city programs?" 0=No; 1=Yes, for a few programs; 2=Yes, for about half of the programs; 3=Yes, for most of the programs; 4=Yes, for all of the programs.

—"Have city departments and agencies implemented cost accounting procedures for estimating costs of major programs or activities?" 0=No; 1=Yes, in a few cases, 2=Yes, in some cases; 3=Yes, in many cases; 4=Yes, general procedure.

These three variables were summated and scores could range from 0 (no professional management practices) to 12 (extensive professional management practices).

Central Management Control Index: This index measures the degree of executive management power within the city. It consists of three measures:

—Has a team management strategy (management decision making by a small group of top managers) been tried or implemented in this city? 0=No; .5=Yes, tried but not maintained; 1= Yes, implemented.

—How much authority does the mayor have to reorganize departments and agencies? 0=Legislature has the primary authority to reorganize; .5=Commission form; .75=Mayor (executive) can reorganize only with legislative approval; 1=Mayor (executive) has primary authority to reorganize; 1=council-manager form.

—Is the mayor or the council responsible for initial preparation of the annual budget? 0=No, the council is primarily responsible for preparation; .5=commission form; 1=yes, mayor (executive) has primary authority to reorganize; 1=council-manager form.

This index is a summation of the three measures, and can range from 0 (no executive management power) to 3 (high executive management power).

Computer Package

Total Applications: This index provides the total number of computerized applications within the relevant computer installation(s). The score is the summation of the total number of applications circled by the EDP manager from an inventory of computer applications listed in the Phase II Application questionnaire.

Level of Applications Development Index: Applications within the Phase II Application questionnaire for each computer installation were classified as one of six application types: record keeping, record searching, record restructuring, process control, calculating/printing, or sophisticated analysis.

This variable indicates the breadth of application types: how many different kinds these six types of applications are in a given installation. This variable ranges from 0 (no applications) to 6 (has all application types).

Total On-line Applications: This index indicates the total number of applications within the computer installation that are on-line. It is the summation of all applications in the Phase II Application questionnaire that were circled by the EDP manager as available and on-line in the installation.

Number of Technical Skills Among Staff: This index determines how many different types of sophisticated analyses are done in the relevant computer installation, according to the responses to six specific questions on the Phase II Applications questionnaire. The more technically sophisticated an installation, the higher its index value. The index's values range from 0 to 100.

Computing Expenditure per Capita: This variable indicates the number of dollars allocated to EDP, per person within the city. It is calculated by dividing the total EDP budget by the total population of the city.

Computing Budget as a Percentage of Government Budget: This variable measures the percent of the government operating expenditures for that year that were allocated to EDP. This is a city-level measure. In cities in which there are multiple installations, the budgets were summed across the installations.

Number of Computing Installations in Government: This index measures the degree to which there are a variety of computing facilities located within a city. The measure was constructed using the responses by EDP managers to a Phase II Installation question: "How many of each of the following kinds of computer installations provide data-processing services to your city departments?" The total number included: (a) subunit of the Finance Department; (b) subunit of another department; (c) independent data processing department under the chief executive; (d) public regional installation; (e) facilities management organization; (f) service bureau. Except for service bureau which was given a score of "1" no matter how many service bureaus were used, the exact numbers of units providing computing given by the EDP manager were used. These values were summated with a low score indicating one or only a few installations (centralized) and a high score indicting multiple installations (decentralized).

Sophistication of Operating System Hardware: This is a measure of an installation's hardware sophistication, as determined by assessment of its computing mainframe hardware and operating systems. For each machine in an installation, each mainframe and its operating system are given "sophistication scores," which are combined, at the relevant installation level.

Total Core Capacity: This variable indicates the combined total core capacity in kilobytes for all central processing units within the computer installation(s).

User of Computer Policy Board: This variable indicates whether the installation uses a policy board. Installations were scored based on the response of the EDP manager to the following Phase II Installation questionnaire item: "Does your government have a user board or committee which recommends policies that affect the design and development of applications?" The response categories are 1=no and 2=yes.

Year Computing Began in Government: This variable indicates the first year that the government utilized computing services on a regularized (non-ad hoc) basis.

Independent Computing Department: This variable indicates whether the organizational location of the EDP installation is an independent EDP department or is a subunit of another department.

Charges for Computing Services: This variable indicates whether user departments pay full costs for computing services from their operating budget for actual use, pay a fixed rate charge, or receive "free" computing.

User Characteristics

Member of Computer Application Design Group: Have you worked as a member of a group designing a computer application in your department? There are no computer applications in my department; Never; On *some* computer applications; On *almost all* computer applications.

Computer Courses Taken: Have you participated in any courses, conferences or seminars providing a general background regarding what computers can do and how they do it? No; Yes.

Believes Does Not Understand Computing: I lack a good understanding of what computers can do. Disagree; Somewhat disagree; Somewhat agree; Agree; No opinion.

Interested in Computing: How interested are you in computers and data processing? Not interested; Somewhat interested; Interested; Very interested.

Year of Birth: In what year were you born? Year of birth.

Years in Type of Job: For how many years have you worked in the kind of job you now have? Years in present kind of job.

Years Involved with Computing: For how many years have you been directly involved in using computers or computer-generated information? Number of years.

Member of Work-Related Organization: Are you currently a member of a regional, state, or national organization or association for your profession or occupation, other than a union? No; Yes, but never attend meetings; Yes, and attend meetings.

Recent Courses Related to Work: When did you last take a professional course related to your work? Never; More than five years ago; Three to five years ago; One to two years ago; Within the last year.

Highest Educational Level: What is the highest educational level you have completed? Some high school; High school degree; Some college; College degree; Some graduate or professional school; Graduate or professional degree beyond bachelors.

Evaluation of Data Processing Unit Service: The scale measures the individual end user's overall view of the sociotechnical interface, in terms of the responsiveness of the technical computing staff to the end user's needs. It is the average score based on the responses of the end user to two questionnaire items:

—Data processing personnel are more intrigued with what the computer can do than with solving the problems of my department.
—Data processing staff confuse our conversations with their technical language.

The response choices are: 0=Disagree; 1=Somewhat disagree; 2=Somewhat agree; 3=Agree. Scale scores can range from 0 to 3 with a high score indicating negative views regarding the responsiveness of data processing personnel.

Notes

1. Assessing the Impacts of Computing on People in Organizations

1. In the local government sector, which is the locus of the empirical fieldwork of our research, virtually all cities and counties use computing. Computing expenditures by these governments amount to several million dollars a day. The average government has about three dozen applications operational and an equal number of applications in development or planned.

2. The label "management information systems" or "MIS" covers many different kinds of computerized systems, depending upon the particular definition an author chooses to use. For example: "The system which monitors and retrieves data from the environment, which captures data from transactions and operations within the firm, and which filters, organizes, and selects data and presents them as information to managers is called the management information system" (Murdick 1980:11).

Contrary to what one might expect because of the term "management" in the label, the term MIS generally does not refer to systems designed to serve the top managers of an organization, although it was originally intended to do so and to distinguish such systems from routine data processing or business data processing or transaction-oriented data processing in organizations. However, the MIS label has been appropriated in common usage, especially by data processing professionals, to refer to the bulk of, if not all of, what they do—routine data processing or business data processing or transactions-oriented data processing.

The label DSS (decision support systems) has now come to signify those systems oriented toward managers and originally intended to be covered by the MIS label. For example, Steven Alter uses the label "EDP" instead of MIS and makes the distinction as follows:

"The main difference between DSS and EDP systems is in their basic purposes. EDP systems are designed to expedite and/or automate transaction processing, record keeping, and business reporting; DSSs are designed to aid in decision making and decision implementation. Note, however, that as Fig. 1 indicates EDP systems and DSSs are by no means mutually exclusive. In fact, decision-oriented reporting systems often grow out of standard EDP systems that were initially developed to improve efficiency in transaction processing and/or record keeping. Instead of belaboring the degree of overlap or nonoverlap between DDSs and EDP systems, we will simply concentrate on systems designed primarily to help people make decisions" (Alter 1980:1-2).

We use the MIS label to refer to the transaction-oriented, computerized systems that are part of the routine operational activities of an organization. The labels of "EDP" (electronic data processing) or "DP" (data processing) are also frequently used to refer to these computerized systems, as the discussion by Alter indicates. These systems, which we label MIS, constitute the bulk of the computerized systems in most organizations today.

Alter's Figure 1.1. Electronic Data-Processing Systems versus Decision Support Systems (Alter 1980)

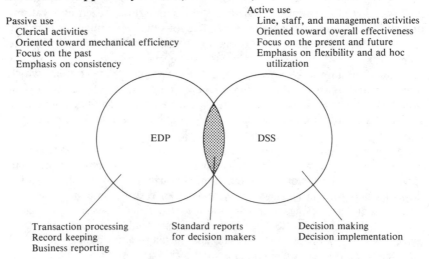

Passive use
  Clerical activities
  Oriented toward mechanical efficiency
  Focus on the past
  Emphasis on consistency

Active use
  Line, staff, and management activities
  Oriented toward overall effectiveness
  Focus on the present and future
  Emphasis on flexibility and ad hoc
    utilization

EDP   DSS

Transaction processing   Standard reports   Decision making
Record keeping   for decision makers   Decision implementation
Business reporting

2. Studying End-User Computing

1. Although we often try to use "he/she" style pronouns, we sometimes use the male gender for reasons of literary simplicity, and we mean it to signify both male and female members of organizations. Clearly, both men and women fill managerial, staff, and bureaucratic positions in organizations.

2. Figure 2.1 does not include an arrow to indicate the possible interactive effects between the computer package and the user characteristics. We do assume that such effects are possible. For example, aspects of the computer package, such as its routinization and its sophistication, might have a systematic effect on the nature of the sociotechnical interface experienced by users of that computer package. Or the computing competency of end users might affect the sophistication of the applications in the computer package. Our analytic approach for assessing elements of the context of computing use as alternative explanations does allow for such effects between the computer package and the user characteristics. Because both contextual elements are entered into the regression analysis at the same stage, any interactive effects between these independent variables will be incorporated into the regression equation. We do not attempt to specify these interactive effects, which are secondary to our key research questions.

3. Our classification of end users fits nicely with that provided by the Codasyl End-User Facilities Committee (1979) which breaks down end users into three categories:

(a) Indirect end users who use computers through other people, e.g., managers who receive routine reports that have been prepared from computerized data.
(b) Intermediate users who specify information requirements for reports they ultimately receive, e.g., middle managers and staff professionals who request special analyses and reports.
(c) Direct users who actually use terminals for their own needs.

We believe that Codasyl classification and our own are especially useful when considering the full range of end users in organizations.

While most end users are in the first two categories, the number of direct users is increasing due to the advent of time-sharing, interactive systems, and microcomputers. Thus, there is growing interest in the "direct" end user category and several authors have developed classifications for these end users.

Martin (1982) and McLean (1974) break down the "direct" user category into three additional classes:

(a) Data-processing professionals who write code for others.
(b) Data-processing amateurs who are non-data-processing professionals and who write code for their own use.

(c) non-data-processing trained users who use code written by others in the course of their work, but know nothing about programming.

Rockart and Flannery (1984) break down "direct" users into six types based upon differences in computer skills, method of computer use, application focus, education and training requirements, and support needed. The six types and their key characteristics are:

(a) Nonprogramming end users who access computer data through software provided by others.
(b) Command-level users who have a need to access data on their own terms, perform simple inquiries, and generate their own reports.
(c) End-user programmers who use both command and procedural languages directly for their own information needs.
(d) Functional support personnel who are sophisticated programmers supporting other end users within their particular functional areas.
(e) End-user computing support personnel who are similar to functional support personnel but located in a central data processing organization or information center.
(f) Data-processing programmers who are similar to the traditional COBOL programmers except that they program in end-user languages.

4. It is important to note that police detectives and patrol officers constitute the only groups among the street-level bureaucrats role in our analysis. The currrent level of computerized information activities for these personnel is probably more extensive than that found among other street-level bureaucrats because of the high level of automation in the police function. But their information uses are representative of those undertaken by other street-level bureaucrats such as welfare workers and health workers, in that much of their work is case-oriented and therefore involves similar (and extensive) information processing, concerned with information retrieval, case tracking, and record searching. This argument is developed more fully in chapter 6.

4. Staff Professionals and Computers: Types of Utilization by End Users

1. There are several other studies consistent with our own in this regard: Guthrie 1972; Sartore 1976. In later chapters, we examine the impacts of computing on staff professionals and we *do* find substantial computing impacts on the staff professionals, relative to other end users, particularly on work environment effects (see chapter 9). If anything, these later chapters suggest that computing has expanded the role of those staff professionals who make greater use of the technology.

2. Greater elaboration of the use of computers in budget monitoring, police manpower allocation, and policy analysis with urban databanks, plus

data on the actual use and impact of computers by staff professionals in these tasks, is provided in chapters 6–8 of Kraemer, Dutton, and Northrop (1981).

3. Our analysis uses both Wilks and direct methods of discriminant analysis. The Wilks method is similar to step-wise regression—it first selects the variable with the strongest capacity to discriminate between (based on the largest distance between) the paired styles of staff professional users, and then enters in the next strongest variable, and the next, and so on. In contrast, the direct method brings in all the variables at one time and examines them as a set. The Wilks method is a more stringent test of relationships than the direct method. Our analytic results using these two methods are very similar, and therefore, we use them interchangeably in the discussion of findings which follows.

4. The specific standardized canonical coefficients upon which table 4.4 is derived as shown below in table 4.8.

5. Performance Benefits from Computing

1. The respondents are obviously well-suited to judge the benefits of computing on their own work. Conclusive findings about such benefits will ultimately be based on multiple measurement techniques, including various "objective" and unobtrusive measures. The end users' assessments seem one valid and interesting indicator of benefits at the individual level of analysis.

6. Police Detectives and Computers: Productivity Impacts

1. The existing empirical studies of computing in police agencies primarily treat the department as the unit of analysis. Both Colton (1978) and Laudon (1974) suggest that automated police intelligence networks, while they might have other organizational effects, also increase the data upon which detectives and patrol officers can draw in determining action regarding a specific individual or case. Kraemer, Dutton, and Northrop (1981:113–121) conclude that computers somewhat improve the department-level performance of detectives, relative to performance in departments without automation, on such characteristics as workable cases, cleared cases, and time savings in information use. It is not clear from these studies whether the department-level measures are representative of most individuals in a department or whether the aggregated measures mask significant individual-level differences in the impacts of computer technology on detectives. Thus, we attempt to add to this modest empirical base, by analyzing with greater precision and

specificity the impacts of computing upon the productivity of individual personnel.

2. Valid empirical measures of productivity are a difficult challenge in the social sciences, and this is particularly true for something as complex as the role of a particular mode of information over a period of time. Despite some promising exploratory work on quite simple effects of computing, precise measures remain a desirable goal of research. The measures in this analysis seem defensible and interesting ones, although they are obviously imperfect, since all data are self-reported and some ask the respondent to make an appraisal of an effect over time. However, the measures do seem reasonable, and the measures of arrest, clearance, and workable cases have quite strong objective grounding.

3. Kraemer, Dutton, and Northrop 1981:108, 128–130; The 14 major police investigation files that are automated are: criminal histories (includes aliases); field interrogation reports; fingerprints; intelligence compilations; known offenders; modus operandi; owner of motor vehicle; owner of registered firearms; pawn tickets; persons passing bad checks; photograph index; stolen property; stolen vehicles; traffic/parking violations; etc.

4. As noted in chapter 1 and note 1 of that chapter, these ideal types are simplifications designed to focus on key distinctions rather than to describe all varieties of computerized systems.

7. Problems with Computing

1. There are, of course, other problems with computing that an analyst could measure at the organizational level, including such operational problems as cost overruns in the development of new automated systems and such behavioral problems as inter-unit conflicts caused by the use of automated information.

2. These operational problems are relevant to those whose computing is predominantly provided by means of shared hardware or is provided by intermediaries. Few local government personnel currently have operational control of a stand-alone microcomputer.

3. Staff professionals seem to have a higher frequency of operational problems than managers and street-level bureaucrats, but a lower frequency of information problems than desk-top bureaucrats. And street-level bureaucrats differ significantly from managers, having more frequent operational problems.

4. The table also indicates that operational problems are reported with greater frequency by those in less professionalized governments.

12. People and Computers

1. A recent case study of Shank, Boynton, and Zmud (1985) involved the use of critical success factor analysis in MIS planning. Although different from our analysis, this case study is interesting because it involved the views of both the providers and the end users of computing services and it might signal an evolving change in professional practice.

2. Although end users attribute greater efficiency benefits to less developed computer packages, our overall findings on information benefits and effectiveness benefits and, in particular, our focussed studies on performance benefits for detectives and staff professionals indicate that such benefits do generally increase as the computer package is more developed, at least in the sense of being more routinized, more extensive, and more interactive.

References

Ackoff, R. L. 1967. "Management Misinformation Systems." *Management Science* 14(4):B147–B156.

Alter, S. L. 1980. *Decision Support Systems: Issues and Challenges.* New York: Pergamon Press.

Anochie, O. M. and H. J. Smolin. 1978a. *Cooperative Approaches to Local Government Data Processing.* ICMA, MIS Special Report #2, May. Washington, D.C.: ICMA.

Anochie, O. M. and H. J. Smolin. 1978b. *Directory of Data Processing in Small Local Governments.* ICMA, MIS Special Report. Washington, D.C.: ICMA.

Attewell, P. and J. B. Rule. 1984. "Computing in Organizations: What We Know and What We Don't Know." *Communications of the ACM* 27(12):1184–1192.

Bennett, J. L. 1983. *Building Decision Support Systems.* Reading, Mass.: Addison-Wesley.

Benson, D. H. 1983. "A Field Study of End User Computing: Findings and Issues." *MIS Quarterly* 6(4):35–45.

Bingham, R. 1984. "The Wired City." *Urban Affairs Quarterly* 20(2):265–72.

Bjørn-Andersen, Niels. 1983. "En Skandinavisk Model for det Automatiserede Kontor", paper delivered at Danish Data Processing Conference, Ebeltoft, Denmark.

Blau, P. and R. A. Schoenherr. 1971. *The Structure of Organizations.* New York: Basic Books.

Blumenthal, S. C. 1969. *Management Information Systems: A Framework for Planning and Analysis.* Englewood Cliffs, N.J.: Prentice-Hall.

Bostrom, R. P. and J. S. Heinen. 1977. "MIS Problems and Failures: A Socio-Technical Perspective, Part I: The Causes." *MIS Quarterly* 1(3):17–32.

Bødker, Susanne. 1985. "UTOPIA and the Design of User Interfaces", pp. 109–124 in Proceedings, Conference on the Development and Use of Computer-based Systems and Tools". Aarhus University, August 19–23, 1985.

Braverman, H. 1974. *Labor and Monopoly Capital.* New York: Monthly Review Press.

Brewer, G. D. 1973. *Politicians, Bureaucrats, and the Consultant.* New York: Basic Books.

Briefs, Ulrich, Claudio Ciborra and Leslie Schneider, eds. 1983. *Systems Design For, With and By Users.* New York: North Holland Publishing Co.

Bullen, C. and J. F. Rockart. 1981. "A Primer on Critical Success Factors." Cambridge, Mass.: Center for Information Systems Research, MIT.

Business Week. 1983. "Special Report on Middle Managers," April 25: 50–86.

Carlson, E. D., B. F. Grace, and J. A. Sutton. 1977. "Case Studies of End User Requirements for Interactive Problem Solving Systems." *MIS Quarterly* 1(1):51–63.

Child, J. 1984. "Managerial Strategies, New Technology, and the Labor Process," In D. Knights, D. Collinson, and H. Willmott, eds., *Job Redesign: Organization and Control of the Labour Process.* London: Heinemann.

Child, J., R. J. Loveridge, J. Harvey, and A. Spencer. 1985. "The Quality of Employment in Services." In Tom Forester, ed., *The Information Technology Revolution,* pp. 419–438. Cambridge: MIT Press.

Child, J. and R. Mansfield. 1972. "Technology, Size, and Organizational Structure." *Sociology* 7:71–91.

Codasyl End User Facilities Committee. 1979. "Codasyl End User Facilities Committee Status Report." In *Information and Management Two,* pp. 137–163. New York: North Holland.

Colton, K. 1978. *Police Computer Systems.* Lexington, Mass.: Lexington Books.

Cooley, M. 1981. *Architect or Bee?* Slough: Langley Technical Services.

Crompton, R. and G. Jones. 1984. *White-Collar Proletariat: Deskilling and Gender in Clerical Work.* London: Macmillan.

Culnan, M. J. 1983. "Chauffeured versus End User Access to Commercial Databases: The Effects of Task and Individual Differences." *MIS Querterly* 7(1):55–67.

Danziger, J. N. 1977a. "Computers and the Frustrated Chief Executive." *Management Information Systems Quarterly* 1(2):43–53.

Danziger, J. N. 1977b. "Computers, Local Government, and the Litany to the EDP." *Public Administration Review* 37(1):28–37.

Danziger, J. N. 1979. "The 'Skill Bureaucracy' and Intraorganizational Control: The Case of the Data-Processing Unit." *Sociology of Work and Occupations* 21(3):206–218.

Danziger, J. N. 1985. "Social Science and the Social Impacts of Computers: Reflections on Concepts and Empirical Research." *Social Science Quarterly* 66(1):3–21.

Danziger, J. N., W. H. Dutton, R. Kling, and K. L. Kraemer, 1982. *Computers and Politics: High Technology in American Local Governments.* New York: Columbia University Press.

Deardon, J. 1966. "Myth of Real-Time Management Information." *Harvard Business Review* 44(3):123–132.

Dee, N. and J. C. Liebman. 1976. "A Model for Selection of Urban Recreation Facilities." In S. Bernstein, ed., *Computers and Public Administration,* pp. 334–343. London: Pergamon Press.

DeKadt, M. 1979. "Insurance: A Clerical Work Factory." In A. Zimbalist, ed., *Case Studies in the Labor Process,* pp. 242–256. New York: Monthly Review Press.

Delehanty, G. E. 1966. "Office Automation and the Occupation Structure: A Case Study of Five Insurance Companies." *Industrial Management Review* 1(2):99–108.

Delehanty, G. E. 1967. "Computers and the Organization Structure in Life Insurance Firms: The External and Internal Economic Environment." In C. A. Myers, ed., *The Impact of Computers on Management,* pp. 61–98. Cambridge: MIT Press.

Dery, D. 1981. *Computers in Welfare.* Beverly Hills, Calif.: Sage Publications.

Dickson, G. W., J. K. Simmons, and J. C. Anderson. 1969. "Behavioral Reactions to the Introduction of a Management Information System: Some Empirical Observations." Minneapolis: Management Information Systems Research Center, College of Business Administration, University of Minnesota.

Dickson, G. W. and J. K. Simmons. 1970. "The Behavioral Side of MIS." *Business Horizons* 13(4):59–71.

Downs, A. 1967. "A Realistic Look at the Payoffs from Urban Data Systems." *Public Administration Review* 27(3):204–210.

Dutton, W. H. 1981. "The Rejection of an Innovation: The Political Environment of a Computer-Based Model." *Systems, Objectives, Solutions* 1(4):179–201.

Dutton, W. H. and K. L. Kraemer. 1977. "Technology and Urban Management: The Power Payoffs of Computing." *Administration and Society* 9(3):304–340.

Dutton, W. H. and K. L. Kraemer. 1978. "Management Utilization of Computing in American Local Governments." *Communications of the ACM,* 21(3):206–218.

Dutton, W. H. and K. L. Kraemer. 1985. *Modeling as Negotiating.* Norwood, N.J.: Ablex.

Eason, K. D., L. Damodaran, and T. F. M. Stewart. 1975. "Interface Problems in Man-Computer Interaction." In E. Mumford and H. Sackman, eds., *Human Choice and Computers,* pp. 91–105. New York: American Elsevier.

Edwards, G. 1978. "Organizational Impacts of Office Automation." *Telecommunications Policy* 2(2):128–136.

Ein-Dor, P. and E. Segev. 1982. "Organizational Context and MIS Structure: Some Empirical Evidence." *MIS Quarterly* 6(3):55–67.

Eulau, H. 1969. *Micro-Macro Political Analysis.* Chicago: Aldine.

Federico, P. A., K. E. Brun, and D. B. McCalla. 1980. *Management Information Systems and Organizational Behavior.* New York: Praeger.

Gasser, L. 1983. "The Social Dynamics of Routine Computer Use in Complex Organizations." Ph.D. dissertation, University of California, Irvine.

GAO (General Accounting Office). 1978. Developing State Automated Information Systems to Support Federal Assistance Programs: Problems and Opportunities. Washington, D.C.: GPO.

GAO (General Accounting Office). 1981. Solving Social Security's Computer Problems: Comprehensive Corrective Action Plan and Better Management Needed. Washington, D.C.: GPO.

Gifford, D. and A. Spector. 1984. "The TWA Reservation System." *Communications of the ACM* 27(2):650–665.

Gilchrist, G. and A. Shenkin. 1982. "The Impact of Scanners on Employment in Supermarkets." *Communications of the ACM* 25(7):441–451.

Giuliano, V. 1982. "The Mechanization of Office Work." *Scientific American* 247(3):148–165.

Glenn, E. and R. Feldberg. 1979. "Proletarianizing of Clerical Work: Technology and Organizational Control in the Office." In A. Zimbalist, ed., *Case Studies in the Labor Process,* pp. 51–72. New York: Monthly Review Press.

Gorry, G. and M. S. Morton. 1971. "A Framework for Management Information Systems." *Sloan Management Review* 13(1):55–70.

Guthrie, A. 1972. "A Survey of Canadian Middle Managers' Attitudes Towards Management Information Systems." Ph.D. dissertation, Carleton University, Ottawa, Canada.

Guthrie, A. 1974. "Attitudes of the User-Managers Towards Management Information Systems." *Management Informatics* 3(5):221–232.

Hackman, R. and G. Oldham. 1975. "Development of the Job Diagnostic Survey." *Journal of Applied Psychology* 60(2):159–170.

Hammond, L. W. 1982. "Management Considerations for an Information Center." *IBM Systems Journal* 21(2):131–161.

Hedberg, B. and E. Mumford. 1975. "The Design of Computer Systems: Man's Vision of Man as an Integral Part of the System Design Process." In E. Mumford and H. Sackman, eds., *Human Choice and Computers,* pp. 31–59. New York: American Elsevier.

Hedberg, B., E. Mumford, and N. Anderson. 1977. *Computer Systems, Work Design, and Job Satisfaction.* New York: Pergamon Press.

Hedberg, Bo. 1980. "Using Computerized Information Systems to Design Better Organizations and Jobs", pp. 19–33 in N. Bjørn-Andersen ed., *The Human Side of Information Processing.* New York: North Holland Publishing Co.

Hoos, I. R. 1960. "When the Computer Takes Over the Office." *Harvard Business Review* 38(4):102–112.

House, W. C., ed. 1983. *Decision Support Systems: A Data-Based, Model-Oriented, User-Developed Discipline.* New York: Petrocelli Books.

ICMA. 1978. *Low Cost Information Processing Technologies for Small Local Governments.* Washington, D.C.: ICMA.

ICMA. 1982. *Local Government Police Management.* Washington, D.C.: ICMA.

ICMA. 1983. *Microcomputers in Local Government.* Washington, D.C.: ICMA.

Immel, A. R. 1985. "The Automated Office: Myth versus Reality." In Tom Forester, ed., *The Information Technology Revolution,* pp. 312–321. Cambridge, Mass.: MIT Press.

Inbar, M. 1981. *Routine Decision-Making: The Future of Bureaucracy.* Beverly Hills, Calif.: Sage.

Jenkins, W. I. 1978. *Policy Analysis: A Political and Organizational Perspective.* London: Martin Robinson.

Keen, P. G. W. 1980. "Decision Support Systems: A Research Perspective." In G. Fick and R. Sprague, eds., *Decision Support Systems,* pp. 23–44. New York: Pergamon Press.

Keen, P. G. W. and E. M. Gerson. 1977. "The Politics of Software System Design, or What Do You Do When the Systems Analysis Doesn't Work?" San Francisco: Pragmatica Systems.

Keen, P. G. W. and M. S. Morton. 1978. *Decision Support Systems: An Organizational Perspective.* Reading, Mass.: Addison-Wesley.

King, J. L. 1984. "Successful Implementation of Large-Scale Decision Support Systems in National Economic Policy Making." *Systems, Objectives, Solutions,* 3:183–205.

King, J. L. and K. L. Kraemer. 1985. *The Dynamics of Computing.* New York: Columbia University Press.

Kling, R. 1978. "The Impacts of Computing on the Work of Managers, Data Analysts and Clerks." Irvine, Calif.: Public Policy Research Organization.

Kling, R. 1979. "Social Analyses of Computing: Theoretical Perspectives in Recent Empirical Research." *Computing Surveys* 12(1):61–110.

Kling, R. 1983. "Value Conflicts in Instructional Computing: Technology and Social Choice in American Schools." Irvine, Calif.: Public Policy Research Organization.

Kling, R. and W. Scacchi. 1979. "Recurrent Dilemmas of Computer Use in Complex Organizations." *AFIPS Conference Proceedings* 48:107–115.

Kling, R., W. Sacchi, and P. Crabtree. 1978. "The Social Dynamics of Instrumental Computer Use." *SIGSOC Bulletin* (Summer), 10:9–21.

Kraemer, K. L. 1981. "The Politics of Model Implementation." *Systems, Objectives, Solutions* 1(14):161–178.

Kraemer, K. L. 1985. "Modeling as Negotiating: The Political Dynamics of Computer Models." In R. F. Coulam and R. A. Smith, eds., *Advances in Information Processing in Organizations,* 2:275–307. Greenwich, Conn.: JAI Press.

Kraemer, K. L., J. N. Danziger, W. H. Dutton, A. Mood, and R. Kling. 1976. "A Future Cities Survey Research Design for Policy Analysis." *Socio-Economic Planning Sciences* 10(11):199–211.

Kraemer, K. L., S. Dickhoven, S. Fallows Tierney, and J. L. King. 1986. *Computer Models in Federal Policy Making.* New York: Columbia University Press.

Kraemer, K. L. and W. H. Dutton. 1984. "The Interests Served by Technological Reform: The Case of Computing." In R. Miewald and M. Steinman, eds., *Problems in Administrative Reform,* pp. 101–122. Chicago, Ill.: Nelson-Hall.

Kraemer, K. L., W. H. Dutton, and A. Northrop. 1980. "Management Control, the Automated Budget, and Information Handling." *Information Privacy* 2(1):7–15.

Kraemer, K. L., W. H. Dutton, and A. Northrop. 1981. *The Management of Information Systems.* New York; Columbia University Press.

Kraemer, K. L., J. L. King, D. E. Dunkle, J. P. Lane, and J. F. George. 1985. "Microcomputers in Large U.S. Cities." Irvine, Calif.: Public Policy Research Organization.

Kuchia, R. J. 1983. "Designing an Information Center for a New Headquarters." In G. P. Huber, ed., *DSS-83 Transactions,* pp. 116–120. Third International Conference on Decision Support Systems, June 27–29. Boston. Austin, Texas: The Institute for Advancement of Decision Support Systems.

Kunreuther, H. C. and P. J. H. Schoemaker. 1982. "Decision Analysis for Complex Systems: Integrating Descriptive and Perscriptive Components." In. G. R. Ungson and D. M. Braunstein, eds., *Decision Making: An Interdisciplinary Inquiry,* pp. 263–278. Boston: Kent.

Laudon, K. 1974. *Computers and Bureaucratic Reform.* New York: Wiley Interscience.

Lawrence, P. R. and J. Lorsch. 1967. *Organization and Environment.* Cambridge: Harvard University Press.

Leavitt, H. J. and T. L. Whisler. 1958. "Management in the 1980s." *Harvard Business Review* 36(6):41–48.

Leduc, N. 1979. "Communicating Through Computers." *Telecommunications Policy,* 3:235–244.

Lee, D., Jr. 1973. 'Requiem for Large Scale Models." *Journal of the American Institute of Planners* 39(3):163–178.

Limaye, D. and D. Blumberg. 1976. "PROMUS: An Urban Planning and Management System." In S. Bernstein, ed., *Computers in Public Administration,* pp. 167–189. London: Pergamon Press.

Long, R. 1984. "Microelectronics and the Quality of Working Life in the Office: A Canadian Perspective." In M. Warner, Ed., *Microprocessors, Manpower, and Society,* pp. 273–293. Aldershot, England: Gower.

Loveridge, R. J., P. A. Clark, J. Tann, and J. Child. 1981. "Work Organization in Britain: A Comparative Longitudinal Investigation into the Problems of Innovation in Technology and Work Organization." Birmingham, England: Management Centre, University of Aston.

Lowi, T. 1972. "Government and Politics; Blurring of Sector Lines." *Information Technology: Some Critical Implications,* pp. 131–81. New York: The Conference Board.

Lucas, H. C. 1973. *Computer Based Information Systems in Organizations.* Palo Alto, Calif.: Science Research Associates.

Lucas, H. C. 1975. *Why Information Systems Fail.* New York: Columbia University Press.

McLean, E. R. 1974. "End Users as Application Developers." *Proceedings of the Guide/Share Applications Development Symposium: MIS Quarterly* 3(4):37–46.

Malvey, M. 1981. *Simple Systems, Complex Environments: Hospital Finance Information Systems.* Beverly Hills, Calif.: Sage.

Mann, F. C. and L. K. Williams. 1958. "Organizational Impact of White Collar Automation." In *Annual Proceedings of Industrial Relations Research Associates,* pp. 59–68.

Marenko, C. 1966. "The Effects of Rationalization of Clerical Work on the Attitudes and Behavior of Employees." In S. Stieber, ed., *Employment Problems of Automation and Advanced Technology,* pp. 412–429. New York: St. Martin's Press.

Markus, M. L. 1979. "Understanding Information Systems Use in Organizations: A Theoretical Approach." Ph.D. dissertation. Case Western Reserve, Cleveland, Ohio.

Martin, E. W. 1982. "Critical Success Factors of Chief MIS/DP Executives." *MIS Quarterly* 6(2):1–9.

Mason, R. 1977. "A Theory of the Productivity of Systems Which Produce and Distribute Information." Los Angeles, Calif.: UCLA Graduate School of Management.

Mau, S. 1982. "The Information Center." *Access* 82:153–161.

Meindl, J. 1985. "Micros in Medicine." In T. Forester, ed., *The Information Technology Revolution,* pp. 359–371. Cambridge: MIT Press.

Menzies, H. 1981. *Women and the Chip: Case Studies of the Effects of Informatics on Employment in Canada*. Montreal: Institute for Public Policy.

"Mini-Symposium on Microcomputers in Local Government." 1984. *Public Administration Review* 44(1):57–78.

Mumford, E. 1972. *Job Satisfaction*. London: Longmans.

Mumford, E. and O. Banks. 1967. *The Computer and the Clerk*. London: Routledge & Kegan Paul.

Mumford, E., D. Mercer, S. Mills, and M. Weir. 1972. "The Human Problems of Computer Introduction." *Management Decision* 10(1):6–17.

Murdick, R. G. 1980. *MIS: Concepts and Design*. Englewood Cliffs, N.J.: Prentice Hall.

Neumann, F. 1950. "Approaches to the Study of Political Power." *Political Science Quarterly* 65(2):162–188.

Norris, D. F. 1984. "Computers and Small Local Governments: Users and Uses." *Public Administration Review* 44(1):70–78.

Norris, D. F. and V. Webb. 1983. "Microcomputers, Baseline Data Report." Washington, D.C.: International City Management Association, July.

Olson, M. H. 1983. "Remote Office Work: Changing Work Patterns in Space and Time." *Communications of the ACM* 26:182–187.

Orlicky, J. 1969. *The Successful Computer System*. New York: McGraw-Hill.

Pack, H. and J. Pack. 1977. "Resurrection of the Urban Development Model." *Policy Analysis* 3(3):407–427.

Pendleton, J. C. 1971. "Integrated Information Systems. In *AFIPS Conference Proceedings* (Fall 1971), pp. 491–500. Joint Computer Conference, Montvale, N.J.: American Federation of Information Processing Societies Press.

Pettigrew, A. 1975. "Towards a Political Theory of Organizational Intervention." *Human Relations* 28(3):191–208.

Pettigrew, A. and E. Mumford. 1975. *Implementing Strategic Decisions*. New York: Longman.

Pfeffer, J. 1981. *Power in Organizations*. Marshfield, Mass.: Pitman.

Pounds, W. F. 1969. "The Process of Problem Finding." *Industrial Management Review* 11(1):1–19.

Powers, R. F. 1971. "An Empirical Investigation of Selected Hypotheses Related to the Success of Management Information Systems Projects." Ph.D. dissertation, University of Minnesota. Ann Arbor, Mich.: University Microfilms.

Pugh, D. S., D. J. Hickson, C. R. Hinings, and C. Turner. 1969. "The Context of Organization Structures." *Administrative Science Quarterly* 14(1):91–114.

Rivard, S. and S. L. Huff, 1984. "User Developed Applications: Evaluation of Success from the DP Department Perspective." *MIS Quarterly* 8(1):39–50.

Rockart, J. F., and L. S. Flannery. 1983. "The Management of End User Computing." *Communications of the ACM* 26(10):776–784.

Rushinek, A. and S. Rushinek. 1985. "The Effects of Sources of Applications Programs on User Satisfaction: An Empirical Study of Micro, Mini, and Mainframe Computers." Paper presented at the ACM Conference on End User Computing, Management Information Systems Research Center, University of Minnesota, May 2–3.

Sartore, A. B. 1976. "Implementing a Management Information System." Ph.D. dissertation, University of California, Irvine.

Sartore, A. B. and K. L. Kraemer. 1977. "Research on Impacts of Computers on Local Government Personnel and Organization." In K. L. Kraemer and J. L. King, eds., *Computers and Local Government*, Vol. 2: *A Review of Research*, pp. 129–189. New York: Praeger.

Shank, M. E., A. C. Boynton, and R. W. Zmud. 1985. "Critical Success Factor Analysis as a Methodology for MIS Planning." *MIS Quarterly* 9(2):121–129.

Simon, H. A. 1960. *The New Science of Management Decision.* New York: Harper and Row.

Slocum, J. W., Jr., 1982. "Decision Making: An Interdisciplinary Focus." In G. R. Ungson and D. L. Braunstein, eds., *Decision Making: An Interdisciplinary Approach,* pp. 288–292. Boston: Kent.

Sollenberger, H. 1968. *Major Changes Caused by the Implementation of a Management Information System.* New York: National Association of Accountants.

Spector, A. ad D. Gifford. 1984. "The Space Shuttle Primary Computer System." *Communications of the ACM* 27(9):872–900.

Tomeski, E. 1972. "Effects of Computerization in Public Personnel Administration." D.P.A. dissertation, New York University.

Waltrip, R. 1983. *The HOBO System.* Sacramento, Calif.: County Data Processing Department.

Weimer, D. L. 1980. *Improving Prosecution.* Westport, Conn.: Greenwich Press.

Werneke, D. 1985. "Women, The Vulnerable Group." In T. Forester, ed., *The Information Technology Revolution,* pp. 400–416. Cambridge: MIT Press.

Whisler, T. L. 1967. "The Impact of Information Technology on Organizational Control." In C. A. Meyers, ed., *The Impact of Computers on Management,* pp. 16–49. Cambridge: MIT Press.

Whisler, T. L. 1970. *The Impact of Computers on Organizations.* New York: Praeger.

Wilkins, R. 1981. "Microelectronics and Employment in Public Administration: Three Ontario Municipalities." Montreal: Institute for Research on Public Policy.

Youstra, R. and E. Squire. 1983. *Information Center Implementation Guide.* IBM Technical Bulletin, April. New York: IBM Corporation.

Index